A CULTURAL
HISTORY OF ANIMALS

VOLUME 4

A CULTURAL HISTORY OF ANIMALS

GENERAL EDITORS: LINDA KALOF AND BRIGITTE RESL

Volume 1
A CULTURAL HISTORY OF ANIMALS IN ANTIQUITY
Edited by LINDA KALOF

Volume 2
A CULTURAL HISTORY OF ANIMALS IN THE MEDIEVAL AGE
Edited by BRIGITTE RESL

Volume 3
A CULTURAL HISTORY OF ANIMALS IN THE RENAISSANCE
Edited by BRUCE BOEHRER

Volume 4
A CULTURAL HISTORY OF ANIMALS IN THE AGE OF ENLIGHTENMENT
Edited by MATTHEW SENIOR

Volume 5
A CULTURAL HISTORY OF ANIMALS IN THE AGE OF EMPIRE
Edited by KATHLEEN KETE

Volume 6
A CULTURAL HISTORY OF ANIMALS IN THE MODERN AGE
Edited by RANDY MALAMUD

A CULTURAL HISTORY OF ANIMALS

IN THE AGE OF ENLIGHTENMENT

Edited by Matthew Senior

BERG

Oxford • New York

English edition
First published in 2007 by
Berg

Editorial offices:
First Floor, Angel Court, 81 St Clements Street, Oxford OX4 1AW, UK
175 Fifth Avenue, New York, NY 10010, USA

Paperback edition published in 2011

Berg is the imprint of Oxford International Publishers Ltd.

Library of Congress Cataloging-in-Publication Data

A cultural history of animals / edited by Linda Kalof and Brigitte Resl.
     p. cm.
  Includes bibliographical references and index.
  ISBN-13: 978-1-84520-496-9 (cloth)
  ISBN-10: 1-84520-496-4 (cloth)
  1. Animals and civilization. 2. Human-animal relationships—History. I. Kalof,
Linda. II. Pohl-Resl, Brigitte.

  QL85C85   2007
  590—dc22   2007031782

British Library Cataloguing-in-Publication Data

A catalogue record for this book is available from the British Library.

ISBN 978 1 84520 372 6 (volume 4, cloth)
     978 1 84788 820 4 (volume 4, paper)
     978 1 84520 496 9 (set, cloth)
     978 1 84788 823 5 (set, paper)

Typeset by Apex Publishing, LLC, Madison, WI

Printed in the United Kingdom by the MPG Books Group

www.bergpublishers.com

CONTENTS

ILLUSTRATIONS

INTRODUCTION

CHAPTER 1

CHAPTER 4

CHAPTER 5

CHAPTER 6

CHAPTER 7

SERIES PREFACE

A Cultural History of Animals is a six-volume series reviewing the changing roles of animals in society and culture throughout history. Each volume follows the same basic structure, and begins with an outline account of the main characteristics of the roles of animals in the period under consideration. Following from that, specialists closely examine major aspects of the subject under seven key headings: symbolism, hunting, domestication, entertainment, science, philosophy, and art. The reader, therefore, has the choice between synchronic and diachronic approaches: A single volume can be read to obtain a thorough knowledge of the subject in a given period from a variety of perspectives, or one of the seven main aspects can be followed through time by reading the relevant chapters of all six volumes, thus providing a thematic understanding of changes and developments over the long term.

The six volumes divide the topic as follows:

Volume 1: A Cultural History of Animals in Antiquity (2500 BCE–1000 CE)

Volume 2: A Cultural History of Animals in the Medieval Age (1000–1400)

Volume 3: A Cultural History of Animals in the Renaissance (1400–1600)

Volume 4: A Cultural History of Animals in the Age of Enlightenment (1600–1800)

Volume 5: A Cultural History of Animals in the Age of Empire (1800–1920)

Volume 6: A Cultural History of Animals in the Modern Age (1920–2000)

General Editors, Linda Kalof and Brigitte Resl

The Animal Witness

MATTHEW SENIOR

Ah! I will no longer be obliged to seek among animals the gaze of kindness that is forever denied me among humans.[1]

—Jean-Jacques Rousseau

But cannot this cat also be, deep within her eyes, my primary mirror?[2]

—Jacques Derrida

An Experiment on a Bird in the Air Pump (1768) by Joseph Wright of Derby is highly suggestive of the role and fate of animals during the Enlightenment.[3] Light, emanating from a candle at the center of the composition, illuminates the severe, almost dyspeptic face of a scientist conducting a demonstration on a bird in an air pump before a small group of onlookers. (See Figure 0.1.) The scene takes place presumably in Wright's native Derbyshire, where public demonstrations of scientific experiments were popular in the 1760s. Juxtaposed against the scientist's face, a small white cockatoo lies helplessly on the bottom of the vacuum chamber, its wings outspread in distress, peering out at the virtual observer of the experiment and the painting. The single black eye of the cockatoo is exactly parallel to that of the demonstrator, as though the artist wanted observers of this painting to confront both the eye of reason—that of the grey-haired scientist who figures admirably the "adulthood of reason" Kant identified as the spirit of *Aufklärung*—and the eye of the suffering bird. All of the other gazes in the painting are structured in opposition to the vision of the scientist and the bird, most notably the voluntary blindness of the young woman in the lower right of the painting who refuses to watch the experiment.[4]

FIGURE 0.1: *An Experiment on a Bird in the Air Pump,* by Joseph Wright of Derby, 1768, Oil on canvas, 183 × 244 cm. London, National Gallery.

Wright of Derby modified certain details of the experiment for dramatic effect. James Ferguson, the Scottish astronomer whose lectures were the inspiration for the painting, noted in his journals that real animals were rarely used to demonstrate the air pump.

> If a fowl, a cat, rat, mouse or bird be put under the receiver, and the air be exhausted, the animal is at first oppressed as with a great weight, then grows convulsed, and at last expires in all the agonies of a most bitter and cruel death. But as this experiment is too shocking to every spectator who has the least degree of humanity, we substitute a machine called the "lung-glass" in place of the animal; which, by a bladder within it, shows how the lungs of animals are contracted into a small compass when the air is taken out of them.[5]

Were a real bird to be used for the experiment, it would have been a common species, such as a sparrow, not a prized white cockatoo, which figures in the painting because its white plumage catches the light of the candle so effectively. Seeing the rare bird about to be suffocated in a glass globe does illustrate the reality of cruel animal experimentation, however, and does reveal a common method used by wildlife painters and collectors to kill their specimens without damaging their feathers.[6]

ENLIGHTENMENT AND BLINDNESS

The theme of vision as cognition figures prominently in the work of the major thinkers of the Enlightenment. For Descartes, the mind should only assent to ideas that are clear and distinct: "I call *clear* that truth which is present and manifest to an attentive mind, just as we say that we see objects clearly when, being present, they stand out, and our eyes are disposed to see them; and *distinct* that truth that is so precise and different from all of the others that it appears manifestly to anyone who *sees* it as he should."[7] For Locke, who argued against Cartesian innate ideas and sought to prove that all knowledge comes from the senses, the visual metaphor for consciousness is equally prominent: "The mind is at no pains of proving or examining, but perceives the truth, as the eye doth light, only by being directed towards it. Thus the mind perceives that white is not black, that a circle is not a triangle, that three are more than two, and equal to one and two."[8]

And yet Enlightenment thinkers also offered a severe critique of human vision as well. Descartes, along with other anatomists, discovered that the human eye worked like a *camera obscura*, thus disproving a long-held view that objects themselves emitted images.[9] Descartes also declared that what the human mind sees is as dissimilar to the object it represents as language is to its referents. At the beginning of *Le Monde,* a treatise largely devoted to optical phenomena, Descartes declares: "It is well known that words, which have no resemblance to the things they signify, do allow us to conceive of these things, and often without our even thinking about the sounds of the words ... And if words, which signify nothing, except according to the conventions of men, are sufficient to make us conceive of things with which they have no resemblance, why wouldn't nature have established another sign which makes us have the sensation of light, even though this sign has nothing in itself that resembles this sensation?"[10] Vision is a central metaphor for reason during the Enlightenment, but exacting observation and measurement reveals that human vision is subject to error.

Some of the distortions of vision are hinted at in Wright's painting. Close inspection reveals that the large beaker of fluid containing a human skull, at the base of the air pump, has a glass rod protruding from it. The rod appears to bend sharply to the right, an illusion created by the refraction of light in the water. Descartes, again, studied refraction inside and outside of the human eye and devised algebraic and geometrical formulae that described this phenomenon.[11] Another indication of the limitations of vision is the object of the experiment itself: the invisible oxygen that is pumped in and out of the chamber. Deeper human truths are also not clearly revealed by the light of the candle. The older man in the foreground who chooses not to watch the bird, but rather stares at the human skull in the beaker, is interpreted by art critics as pondering his own mortality.[12]

The young woman who covers her eyes has an emotional response to the sight of animal suffering, as though the cold dispassionate gaze of reason would prevent her from seeing with her heart and making a deeper, prerational connection to the bird. This is the other pole of Enlightenment thought, the gradual move away from Cartesian reason toward sensation and *sentiment*. Jacques-Henri Bernardin de Saint-Pierre (1737–1814) declared this other source of truth in a deliberate parody of Descartes: "*Je sens donc j'existe*" ("I sense, therefore I am").[13] Rousseau argued that the question of whether animals had souls was one that reason could not resolve. Pure reason is "deaf" to the inner call of sentiment: "They [Cartesians] are deaf to the interior voice that cries out to them in a tone difficult to ignore: *A machine does not think*, neither movement nor structure can produce thought."[14]

REPRESENTATION

Another canonical painting from the period 1600–1800, Diego Velázquez's *Las Meninas* (1656), also poses the question of the limits of human vision and the animal witness. (See Figure 0.2.) In this composition, dubbed the "theology of painting," the Spanish Infanta and her retinue (the *meninas*) are rendered in exquisite detail as they look outward toward the real subjects of the painting, King Philip IV of Spain and his queen, Mariana of Austria, while Velázquez himself can be seen working at his easel, as he pauses for a moment to observe his subjects. According to Michel Foucault, this work can be understood as "the representation of classical representation itself and the definition of the space it opens."[15] Although the painting is highly realistic and self-referential, as we see the "little angel" in exquisite detail and contemplate the self-aware gaze of Velázquez, who has painted a mirror image of himself, Foucault claims that this masterpiece is marked by a "profound invisibility."[16]

As was the case with Wright's painting, there are degrees of obscurity, distortion, and blindness in this depiction of the Spanish court. The true subjects of the painting (the royal couple) stand outside the limits of the canvas; they are only visible as faint reflections in a mirror suspended on the back wall of the gallery and directly visible to the viewer of the painting. True to the Cartesian ordering of reality, the self of the painter is much more clear and distinct than the objects he contemplates. The most important and programmatic blindness in the painting that Foucault dwells on is the inability of the painting to capture the artist in the act of painting. We cannot see the actual surface Velázquez is working on, nor can we see him in the act of painting. We can see the finished result, and we see the center of the truth of the artwork—the artist's own awareness of himself—but we cannot see a human being *making* the order of representation. The elusive point that Foucault attempts to establish is that, during the age that stretches from Descartes to Kant, when the human

FIGURE 0.2: *Las Meninas or The Family of Philip IV*, by Diego Rodríguez de Silva y Velázquez, ca. 1656, Oil on canvas, 316 × 276 cm. Madrid, Museo del Prado. Photo: Scala/Art Resource, New York.

mind arrived at a truth, whether that truth came from self-contemplation or perception, there is something about the link between representations and their referents, or about the general convention governing representations and reality, that can neither be questioned nor captured by representation itself, hence the "profound invisibility" of *Las Meninas*.

The other blindness or "essential void" that Foucault sees in the Spanish masterpiece is easier to grasp: "the necessary disappearance of that which founds it—the person it resembles and the person for whom it is made."[17] The presence of the king is fleeting, disappearing; the painting clearly points to itself as unable to capture the image of the king and queen, except as a faint reflection in a mirror, which is neither seen by Velázquez nor part of his painting process. Having stated this failure, however, the painting can present itself as a "pure representation." Looking at this stunning painting, one could come to the conclusion that human beings in such art (even though it is a realistic and mimetic art) are in a state of grace (as pure representations) that they never attain in life. Painting is the standard for real life, not the other way around.

The role of animals in Foucault's account of this highly cerebral, self-referential tableau is to serve as pure objects. "The dog, stretched out on the floor, is the only element in the painting that neither sees nor moves, because its only purpose, with its rough outline and the light playing on its satin coat, is to be seen as an object."[18] *Las Meninas* represents a kind of anthropology in which humans see and make representations, while dogs and other animals are simply objects. Their blank unreflective stares are the mirrors of minds incapable of self-awareness. Human vision, in all of its intensity, gazes out of the painting and ponders the distinction between representation and reality. In the painting, the dog looks tiredly at the floor, seemingly uninterested in the drama of representation going on about it. It does not exchange glances with human subjects nor does it encounter its own gaze and its own subjectivity, as the painter Velázquez does.

REPRESENTATION AND NATURAL HISTORY

The reduction of animals to the status of pure objects and the triumph of mechanism in biology were accompanied by a revolution in natural history. Within the episteme of representation, as seen in *Las Meninas*, where painting and all other human signs are clearly designated as artificial and bearing no resemblance at all to the objects they represent, but rather acquire their meaning by referring to themselves, as "pure representations," within this paradigm, paradoxically, animals and plants emerge as ideal objects for language to test its truths on. Later in *Les Mots et les choses* Michel Foucault describes the emergence of new methods in botany and zoology as exemplars of a new kind of writing based on representation:

The Classical Age gives an entirely different meaning to history: for the first time, things themselves become the object of an exacting gaze which is transcribed into smooth, neutral, faithful words. That is why, in this "purification," the first form of history to be constituted was natural history. Because to construct itself it can simply apply words, without intermediary, to things themselves. The documents of this new kind of history are not other words, texts or archives, but rather the clear spaces where things are juxtaposed—herbariums, collections, gardens. The locus of this history is an atemporal rectangle, where, stripped of all commentary, of all accompanying language, beings present themselves side by side with their visible surfaces contrasted according to common traits, and, as a result, already virtually analyzed, and bearing only their names (*por-teurs de leur seul nom*).[19]

ECCE ANIMOT

Until recently, I found Foucault's description of the dog and its marginalized role in classical representation to be convincing.[20] It aligns so well with the exclusion of animals from the realms of reason and language in Descartes. However, approaching this painting from the vantage point of the animal witness, it is possible that the dog bears the burden of making the painting more than a "pure representation." The dog, after all, is closer to the King and Queen than any of the human subjects. Its eyes are closed, and it appears to have just been roused from sleep by a court dwarf who treads playfully on its back. In some sense the dog recognizes the King in a way that none of the humans do. Its warmth and proximity make up for the failure of Velázquez to capture the King and Queen as anything other than distant shadows. One of the early objections to Descartes' theory that animals have no rational powers had been the observation that animals have an uncanny ability to recognize individuals. A dog *would* be able to tell a man from an automaton and distinguish its owner among many men, an observation celebrated in literature, two examples being the recognition of Odysseus by his dog in the *Odyssey* and a similar scene in the legend of Tristan and Isolde.

Jacques Derrida's essay, "The Animal that therefore I am (More to Follow)" is attentive to the dialectical tension between human and animal vision and thought that we have found in *Las Meninas*.[21] Although not specifically engaging the work of Foucault, as he did in an earlier essay challenging Foucault's exclusion of madness from the heart of classical reason, Derrida's invocation of animal vision in this essay provides the elements for a rereading of the dog in Velázquez's masterpiece and the agency of the animal in general during the Enlightenment.

Derrida's essay takes root in routine private encounters with his cat in his Paris apartment. The animal greets the philosopher each morning, follows him to the shower, looks impassively at his naked body, including a matter-of-fact glance at his genitals. The cat asks to be fed and eventually wants to be let out. Derrida experiences a range of emotions and thoughts that are remarkably diverse and nuanced, without parallel, really, in the history of philosophy. A vague sense of shame makes him want to cover his nakedness; he feels observed by a "seer," a "visionary," or perhaps "an extra-lucid blind person." The cat is "entirely other" (*tout autre*), "unreadable," undecidably "good" or "bad," "innocent" or "cruel."[22] The most important aspect of exchanging glances with the cat is the shift from seeing the animal to "being seen and seeing oneself seen naked" (*se voir vu nu*) by it.[23] Derrida refers to a passage in Levinas to make the distinction: if one looks into the eyes of the other in order to *see oneself seen*, then one will not even notice the color of his or her eyes.[24]

This initial phenomenology of the animal gaze insists on the enigmatic and entirely other perspective of the animal and suggests that the animal *regard*, when taken seriously, troubles and confuses many of the binary oppositions and associations of humanism: good versus evil, sight versus blindness, innocence or cruelty, nakedness and shame. Derrida then chooses to focus on the question of nakedness and shame before the animal. In both the Greek and Judeo-Christian creation myths, man in the state of nature is essentially naked and lacking. Prometheus stole fire from the gods and gave technology to man to make up for human nakedness and vulnerability vis-à-vis other animals. In Genesis, man is happily and unselfconsciously naked before the Fall and is allowed to name and dominate the animals. Having listened to the serpent, however, Adam sins and must cover his nakedness while the animal remains free of this injunction. Derrida notes that although both the Greek philosophical tradition and the Biblical tradition insist, in their founding myths, that the human is essentially a lacking animal, the tables are turned and animals are declared to be lacking reason and language.

Clearly Derrida wants to go beyond this impasse, stating that it is not a question of whether the animal speaks a language but whether the animal *responds*. To explore what kind of meaningful communication might occur between humans and animals, Derrida embarks on an imaginary reconstruction of Eden before the Fall. Close reading of the Biblical text reveals that God let Adam name the animals, not knowing what he would do, but wanting to see (*pour voir*) what the result would be. Adam's calling or naming of the animals and their *response* to this calling and naming serves as a model for a different, premetaphysical rapport with animals. Derrida feels a kind of vertiginous identity with both God, who was hidden and watched this scene, and Adam, who stood naked before the animals, looked into their eyes without shame, called them by name, and saw a response to this naming in their eyes. This is the prelapsarian fantasy that Derrida conjures up in his Paris apartment.

In the second half of the essay, the most important thinker of poststructuralist philosophy passes in review the figure of the animal in his major texts and shows how useful animals have been in rethinking many absolute, "indivisible" borders in philosophy and how the animal is essential to a new kind of autobiographical writing, "zoo-auto-bio-bibliography."[25] The key to this new perspective is the coining of a neologism—*animot*—to replace the older philosophical language that made a massive distinction between "Man" and all of the other animals, unified under the collective plural "the animal."[26] *Animot* is a homonym of the plural in French for animals (*animaux*). This hybrid word offers a perspective on animals that goes beyond and confuses previously existing philosophical and biological classifications: "neither a species, nor a genus, nor an individual. It is an irreducible living multiplicity of mortals."[27] In the ideal visual exchange with the cat, then, the animal would not see Derrida (nor would he see the cat) as a species, a genus, or an individual, but rather as part of "an irreducible living multiplicity of mortals"—one creature among many, a creature not cut off by an indivisible line from all of others, but rather part of the collective whole of all living things, yet also possessing a difference, an elusive identity that it is the work of philosophy to investigate.

Derrida's language might sound like highly theoretical postmodern obscurantism, but the "irreducible living multiplicity of mortals" seems a very real, empirical characterization of animal life such as appears in the recent film *March of the Penguins*. The remarkable creatures in this film display an amazing collectiveness and social solidarity (no doubt longed for by human cinema audiences) and an equally uncanny sense of individuality, which allows them to recognize their mates and offspring in a huge flock of what seem to humans to be identical birds.

Two final remarks about the concept of *animot* in Derrida: the word includes *mot*, meaning "word" in French, as an attempt to restore a kind of language to animals, or at least think of the absence of language in animals as "other than a lack."[28] Elsewhere in the essay, Derrida suggests that poetry, as opposed to philosophy, can find language that expresses the shared linguistic abilities of humans and animals. The other major point regarding *animot* concerns Derrida's presentation of himself, in autobiographical fashion, under the banner of the neologism he has created: "*Ecce Animot*."[29] This is a deliberate reference to Nietzsche's *Ecce Homo*, and before that, to the words of Pontius Pilate in the Bible, offering the scourged Christ for visual inspection to a hostile crowd. The image of the suffering human savior, visually eliciting compassion and identity on the part of the onlooker, became a motif in Western art. *Ecce Animot* refers to all of these meanings and broadens them to include a plea for seeing the animal, being seen by the animal, and seeing the human as an animal. This wide-ranging exploration and valorization of animal vision makes possible a dialectical reading of Foucault's comments on *Las Meninas* and an analysis of many other visual encounters between humans and animal during the period 1600–1800.

VORACIOUS VISION

The idea that animals are naïve, instinctive judges of the visible, but sometimes superior to humans in their visual acuity, is a theme found in many sources from the Renaissance onward. One of the stories revived from antiquity concerned Zeuxis, a Greek painter who won a competition for the best artist in Athens by drawing a painting of grapes so convincing that birds flew up and pecked at the painted fruit.[30] Zeuxis lost the contest ultimately, however, when his rival Parrhasius sketched in a curtain around the picture of the grapes and succeeded in fooling Zeuxis, who asked that the curtain be drawn back to fully reveal his painting. The Greeks considered deceiving a human to be a much greater accomplishment than fooling gullible birds.

The idea of deluded animal vision is depicted in Jean de La Fontaine's fable, "The Dog Who Dropped His Food for a Reflection" (*Le Chien qui lâche sa proye pour l'ombre*). A dog, seen in Jean-Baptiste Oudry's illustration for this fable, stares at his reflection in a river while carrying a piece of meat in his mouth. (See Figure 0.3.) Since animals lack self-awareness, according to

LE CHIEN QUI LÂCHE SA PROYE POUR L'OMBRE . Fable CXX .

FIGURE 0.3: *Le Chien qui lâche sa proye pour l'ombre* (The Dog Who Dropped His Food for a Reflection), Engraving by Jean Ouvrier after drawing by Jean-Baptiste Oudry, redrawn by Charles Nicolas Cochin, in Jean de La Fontaine, *Fables choisies mises en vers*, Paris, 1755–1759. Melbourne, The State Library of Victoria, Rare Books Collection.

classical reason, the dog does not recognize his own image in the water and opens his mouth to try to seize the meat of the imaginary dog he sees reflected in the water. "This Dog, seeing his food represented in the water, / Dropped it in favor of the reflection and almost drowned. / The river became agitated; / With great difficulty he made it back to the banks / With neither the reflection nor the food."[31]

Another familiar story on this theme from seventeenth-century France is Charles Perrault's fairy tale, *Le Petit Chaperon Rouge* (Little Red Riding Hood). In this tale, though, gullible, voracious vision is exercised at the expense of humans and their overly rational vision of the world. At the end of the tale, the Wolf first gains entry to the Grandmother's house by mimicking the voice of Little Red Riding Hood. When the young heroine of the tale arrives at the house, the Wolf displays his mastery of language by repeating a phrase he has learned from the Grandmother: "Turn the bolt and the latch will fall."[32] Something about the Cartesian inevitability of locks opening because latches fall is reassuring to Little Red Riding Hood, who walks into the house of her doom. The Wolf's use of language is a comic refutation of Descartes' claim that animals lack a true understanding of language because they are only capable of repeating words, without understanding their meanings.[33] It may be true that the Wolf is simply repeating what he has heard, but it is a deadly tactic against presumptuous, overly rational humans.

After climbing into bed with the Wolf, the naïve Petit Chaperon Rouge is completely unaware of the voracious speech and vision of the beast. The final words she hears are the Wolf's progression from seeing to devouring. "All the better to see you with … All the better to eat you with!" The French language has the expression *dévorer des yeux* to describe this kind of voracious vision. What is being enacted in all of these stories of gullible yet voracious animals is the restoration of immediacy to the human being. The animal, who is ignorant of the impasse of dualism, devours the human subject, seizes the person, body and soul, thereby overcoming the rational blindness of *Las Meninas* and other classical representations.

The total misunderstanding of animal vision is a theme in Werner Herzog's *Grizzly Man*, a filmed autobiography of the life of Timothy Treadwell, an amateur naturalist who lived in close proximity to Alaskan grizzly bears. As Herzog points out in the film, Treadwell misread the gaze of the bears as one of recognition, when, in fact, tragically, the animals saw in the naturalist only a source of food. Derrida's strictures about the absolute otherness of animal vision and the absolute otherness of animals in general could be a bitter moral to this story, although the psychological mechanism of the film might function very much like *Little Red Riding Hood* as a return to childhood fears and fantasies of being devoured that violently restore the immediacy of the self in a world paralyzed by representation. It is telling in this regard that Treadwell's constant flirtations with animal devouring were captured on film, as though he were taunting the bears to violate the camera and restore an animal immediacy to vision.

Of course it must also be said that Treadwell succeeded in making a kind of nature film and an autobiography that is unique and moving. His footage of wild foxes and bears has no equivalent for its authenticity and raw beauty. I have been told by a colleague who has taught *Grizzly Man* to undergraduate students in a film course that they identify very positively with Treadwell and view Herzog's presence in the film as intrusive and censoring, as though Treadwell's life represented a kind of wish fulfillment that should not be tampered with, an extreme case of *Ecce Animot* that provides cinema audiences with a powerful vehicle for recovering a sense of their own animality.

THE EVIDENCE OF THINGS UNSEEN

Caravaggio's *The Conversion of Saint Paul* is another instance where an animal gaze serves as a pathway leading beyond human blindness. (See Figure 0.4.) The horse in this painting was "taken directly from Dürer's 1505 *Large Horse*," according to Walter Friedlaender.[34] It is a large realistic piebald whose hooves seem capable of inflicting serious injury on the prostrate Saul if the animal does not raise its foot to avoid stepping on its fallen master. Friedlaender further observes that the animal has an important role to play in the scene of conversion: "Caravaggio's horse has, if I may say so, a heart and takes a subjective and subdued part in the succession of events which Caravaggio has concentrated into his painting."[35]

In the Epistle to the Hebrews, faith is described by the apostle Paul himself as "the evidence of things unseen."[36] In Caravaggio's painting, the blindness of the proud Roman soldier Saul and the gaze of the animal are used to convey another order of reality that humans do not ordinarily see. Derrida experienced a kind of return to Eden in the uninhibited, shame-free way his cat looked at him. Here, after the Fall, which theologians sometimes referred to as the "happy fall," the gaze of the animal is similarly redemptive.

As in the stories of voracious devouring, the gaze of the horse is accompanied by a violent physical restoration of the human akin to devouring. Faith here has the appearance of an equestrian accident followed by a concussion, perhaps. One is reminded of a similar animal accident in Rousseau. In the Ninth Promenade of the *Reveries of the Solitary Walker*, Rousseau gives a riveting account of how he was struck by a huge dog and knocked unconscious. When the aging philosopher recovers consciousness, blood is streaming from his face, but he feels no pain. Jean-Jacques is in a strangely euphoric state: "The first sensation was a delicious one. My only awareness of myself was through this feeling. I was born in that instant to life."[37]

FIGURE 0.4: *The Conversion of St. Paul,* by Michelangelo Merisi da Caravaggio, 1601, Oil on canvas, 230 × 175 cm. Rome, Santa Maria del Popolo. Photo: Scala/Art Resource, New York.

CONFINEMENT: THE SALPÊTRIÈRE
AND THE MENAGERIE

Another major paradigm of Enlightenment thought and power, involving humans and animals, is revealed in various practices of confinement, restraint,
and surveillance. One of the early defining gestures of the absolute monarchy under Louis XIV was the mass confinement of the mentally ill and the
indigent, beginning with the construction of the Hôpital Général, a group of
work camps for imposing labor and moral correction on those segments of the
population who were not productive members of society. Within these "*cités
de la moralité pure*" ("cities of pure morality"), the mentally ill were singled
out for *exhibition* as well. The mode of this exhibition resembled that of the
Ménagerie, another invention of classical reason. "[The mad] who are chained
to the walls of their cells are not really men who have lost their reason, but
rather beasts given over to a natural rage ... This model of animality is typical
of asylums and gives them their aspect of cages and menageries."[38]

The parallel between the Ménagerie and the Hôpital Général proceeds from
a desire to reduce unreasonable humans to the level of animals and to display both humans and animals as pure visual objects. The similarity between
the two structures also stems from the fact that the same royal architect,
Louis Le Vau (1612–1670), designed the plans for both the Salpêtrière (1657)
and the Versailles Ménagerie (1662). Both constructions featured an octagonal
plan, designed to separate humans or animals into groups and to confer maxi-
mum visibility from a central point of view.

The Salpêtrière is a model for a more primitive kind of power that physically restrains its subjects, while the Ménagerie anticipates Jeremy Bentham's
Panopticon, a more subtle form of power designed to control the free, self-
governing individual who applies his or her own discipline based on the fear of
being observed and judged. Both architectural innovations have their theatrical, visual aspect, based on looking at animals and looking at humans as animals. Both structures are also capable of dialectical reversals in which animals
return the human gaze.

UNREASON

The history of the Salpêtrière as a place of human confinement begins in April
1656, with a royal edict calling for the arrest and confinement of indigents,
prostitutes, and the mentally ill.

Paris was inundated at this time with an infinite number of vagabonds and
beggars who were leading openly licentious lives. To curb this libertine
behavior and, at the same time, to help these souls, the King issued written

orders during the month of April, setting aside five different houses and calling them collectively the Hôpital Général. He ordered that the poor of all ages and both sexes should be confined there, that the infirm and the old should receive all manner of assistance, that those unable to work should be employed on various tasks, and that all should be instructed in the duties of piety.[39]

Following the royal decree, the first arrests took place, yielding about 800 women and a number of children for the Salpêtrière. Later, the institution's population grew to 4,000. Le Vau was put in charge of plans to expand the Salpêtrière in 1656. The inmates were segregated according to the crimes they had committed and their capacity to work. The infamous *"basses loges,"* where the seriously mentally ill were locked up and constrained like animals, were added later, sometime before 1754.

Le Vau's most important architectural innovation at the Salpêtrière was a new chapel. Maximilien Vessier, the author of a history of the Salpêtrière, describes its structural uniqueness: "Four naves and four angled chapels, for a total of eight separate entryways and a single altar in the middle. Eight independent doors, which allow the different categories of detainees to participate in the religious services, cordoned off with their group, but also united with the assembly, and, [following the service], to return to the asylum without ever encountering the other pensioners."[40] The octagonal radial plan of the edifice, with lines of sight converging at a central point, is identical to Le Vau's plans for the Ménagerie. Both structures impose a visual order on a kind of disorder, one applied to the natural world and the other to a disordered human world of criminality and madness.

Today, one might wonder why the poor, the disabled, prostitutes, criminals, and the insane were grouped together. One common denominator was idleness. Foucault calls the Salpêtrière a "city of pure morality" because to be incapable of work was considered a moral failing, a sin. In addition to the shared trait of idleness, the other common denominator of all inmates of the Salpêtrière was unreason (*déraison*). The disparate mass of individuals confined to the hospital was understood to be a group in revolt against reason.

Within the category of *déraison*, there was a further distinction between this general trait shared by all of the inmates and those who suffered from true madness (*folie*). This was the extreme, often incurable, form of unreason. Foucault draws an analogy with original sin: "What original sin can be considered in relation to diverse kinds of sin, that is what *folie* is in relation to other kinds of unreason: the principle, the original movement, the greatest guilt in its instantaneous contact with the greatest innocence, the ultimate model, continually repeated, of what must be forgotten in shame."[41] There was a separate vocabulary and special treatment for the mad. According to contemporary police registers, there were the insane (*des insensées*), demented people (*des hommes en démence,*), the deranged (*des gens à l'esprit aliéné*), and the truly mad (*des personnes devenues tout à fait folles*).[42] Some of the *insensées* were confined with other inmates, unless they were deemed "*furieuse*"—violent or totally incapable of work. The *furieuses* were kept in the *basses loges*.

A visitor to the Salpêtrière at the end of the eighteenth century describes the state of the *furieuses*. "Mad women given to episodes of fury are chained up like dogs to the doors of their cells (*loges*), and separated from their guards and visitors by a long passageway covered with iron bars; the women's food is passed to them across these bars, as well as their straw, which they sleep on; rakes are used to clean away some of the filth surrounding them."[43] A human being who had lost his or her rationality was treated like an animal. Foucault comments: "Those who are chained to the walls of the cells are not really men who have lost their reason, but rather beasts fallen prey to a natural rage, as if, at its extreme point, madness, separated from the less serious *moral* unreason with which it was confined, broke through and joined ranks with the immediate violence of animality. This model of animality is evident in the asylums and gives them a feeling of cages and menageries."[44] In its purest form, madness, in the case of the *furieuses*, was distinguished from the other forms of *déraison* with which it was confined. It was identified with pure animal violence and liberty. It was this pure animal liberty that was most feared and constrained by classical reason.

According to many accounts, the mad, like animals, were indifferent to extreme conditions. Pinel reports that a man at Bicêtre did not like to wear a wool shirt in the coldest months of winter and took great pleasure in applying snow and ice to his bare chest and letting it melt, "*avec une sorte de délectation*" ("with a sort of extreme pleasure").[45] Treating the mad like animals was actually considered to be the only way to cure them. A Scottish farmer named Gregory became famous for curing mania using tactics similar to those used in animal domestication. According to Pinel, "His method consists in making the alienated do the roughest farm chores and in using some of them as beasts of burden or lackeys; at the slightest sign of revolt, they are reduced to obedience with a volley of blows."[46] In this model the insane are not ill; on the contrary, they are physically stronger and healthier than ordinary men and women.

In general, one of the key purposes of confinement was to hide scandalous behavior and avoid the effects of contamination, but viewing the insane chained up in their cells was an exception to the rule. It was considered an edifying moral spectacle to observe the mentally ill in La Salpêtrière.[47] The meaning of this display was not to exalt and celebrate madness, as had been the case during the Renaissance, but to show it as entirely objectified and tamed. According to Foucault: "During the classical period madness is on display, but from the other side of the bars; if it is shown, it is from a distance, beneath the gaze of a reason that no longer has any relationship with it and cannot be compromised by any resemblance to it."[48]

There is one final nuance about *la folie* during the classical age and its association with animality. The spectacle of the totally mad, animal-like human being provoked a religious response. The mentally ill person was a reminder of the underlying bestiality of all humans, a state which anyone could revert to without the grace of God. Many religious orders, such as the Lazarists, were dedicated to the treatment of the mentally ill. Saint Vincent De Paul, the founder of the Lazarists, had a brother who became mentally ill and was committed to the Bicêtre hospital. De Paul reacted as follows: "We must honor Our Lord in that condition He found Himself in when they sought to bind Him because he had become mad, *quoniam in furorem versus est,* in order to sanctify that state in those whom divine providence has kept there."[49] From a religious perspective, the insane person, although behaving like an animal, and in need of being treated like an animal according to seventeenth-century understandings of madness, was still a human being, distinct from the other animals in nature. Christ assumed this aspect of the human condition and allowed himself to be taken for mad, thereby sanctifying this condition and inspiring Christians to imitate him. The Christian redemption and recuperation of the insane person as still human makes an ultimate distinction between confined humans and animals during the Classical Age and shows the theological underpinning of ultimate differences between humans and animals.

LA MÉNAGERIE

Le Vau's other innovation in the architecture of confinement, similarly based on equivalences between humans and animals, was the Versailles Menagerie. We see the same radial design, the same structure for confining, segregating, and classifying animals according to visible differences. The Menagerie was the first zoo to both organize the spectacle of animals from a single vantage point and to separate the animals according to species. But there are differences between the Menagerie and the Salpêtrière. Versailles was an enchanted space where the monarch had tamed all of nature and where the principal role of animals was to amuse the king and his guests.[50]

Another subtle difference concerns the visibility of the spectator. In the Salpêtrière, the priest celebrating Mass is visible to all, just as the spectator watching the scene of animal-like madness is visible to the afflicted inmate, who performs for the spectator. In the Menagerie, however, the point of view of the king and his guests is elevated and hidden. Foucault speculated that Le Vau's Menagerie might have been the source for the Panopticon. "Bentham does not say whether he was inspired, in his project, by Le Vau's Menagerie at Versailles … But one finds in the program of the Panopticon a similar concern with individualizing observation, with characterization and classification, with the analytical arrangement of space. The Panopticon is a royal menagerie; the animal is replaced by man, individual distribution by specific grouping, and the king by the machinery of a furtive power."[51]

Figure 0.5 is an engraving based on a painting by Pieter Boel (1622–1674), an animal painter who studied animals at the Menagerie and drew sketches of them that served as the basis for tapestries in the Gobelins manufactory.[52] Boel's painting displays the dialectic of human and animal vision that takes place in the Menagerie. On the one hand, the painting has a kind of Panopticon feel to it because no human spectators are visible in the raised pavilion. Animals or humans walking in the courtyards below are subject to the power of unseen observing eyes. Humans are probably more susceptible to being manipulated in this fashion, although certain animals could probably learn to fear a human spectator hidden behind blinds in a tower. Boel's painting does show how animals react to being seen by a visible human spectator. The painter has abandoned the panoptical place within the tower and joined the birds in their compound, offering himself and viewers of this painting to the *regard* of the birds. The artist derives several advantages from this: The wild birds react to the encroaching human presence and freeze in a posture designed to make them less visible to predators. If the painter moves one step closer, the

1. *Canes musquées.* 2. *Damoiselles.* 3. *Oyseaux Royals.* 4. *Oyes de Canada.* 5. *Poulles de Turquie.* 6. *des Outardes.*

FIGURE 0.5: *Demoiselle Cranes and Other Birds*, Versailles Ménagerie, Engraving by Gérard Scotin after painting by Pieter Boel, ca. 1670. Paris, Bibliothèque nationale de France, département des Estampes et de la Photographie.

animals will flee. The immobility of the animals and their wary stares create a powerful naturalistic effect. The stillness of the birds also provides the painter with a natural pose for his subjects. This image captures the power of surveillance to shape the behavior of animals, and by extension, humans; and it also establishes a relationship between seeing and wild animal freedom. There is something analogous to Derrida's lesson about the natural shamelessness of animals that can be gleaned from this image. To be seen by an animal that will not tolerate being approached is perhaps as revealing and redeeming as sharing a gaze with a cat that is indifferent to human nakedness.

The painting poses questions that Foucault does not address in his discussions of the Menagerie, just as he did not speculate on the subjectivity of the dog in *Las Meninas*. This is the question of the dialectical transformation of the Panopticon into a "zoopticon." What do we look like to animals? What is the effect of being seen by a multitude of animals? What is the mutual mirroring going on between a group of exotic birds and courtiers at Versailles?

Despite my emphasis on the freedom of the birds and the possibility of flight, Boel's portrait can also be viewed as a study of restrained, controlled, and civilized animality.[53] These are not the wild, "impossible animals" that Foucault refers to in regard to Renaissance animality—the wild creatures seen in the paintings of Bosch and Breughel. The birds are carefully displayed and named and behave in a dignified, civil manner. The most prominent bird is the *Oyseau Royal* (a black crowned crane). Next to it is a Demoiselle, still called a demoiselle crane. The birds seem to form a social order with the *Oyseau Royal* at the center of the composition. The exotic fowl could be viewed as refined courtiers who have transcended their animality and live according to the laws of civility. They represent animality tamed and civilized, even in animals themselves. This is the reverse of the Salpêtrière, where the insane become animals. Here, by the miracle of the King's organizing powers, animals behave like humans.

LIBERATION

A concluding parallel between the Salpêtrière and the Menagerie concerns the fact that both were liberated during the Revolution. It is well known that Pinel opened the *loges* and let the inmates out, hoping to begin an era when madness would be considered an illness, not a crime. The animals at Versailles were also considered victims of royal despotism by the revolutionaries. On August 10, 1792, a committee of Jacobins arrived at Versailles, demanding, "in the name of the People and Nature [that the King] return to liberty creatures that leave the hands of the Creator free and have been unjustifiably detained by the vanity and pomp of tyrants."[54] Both of these gestures, the opening of the *loges* by Pinel and the dismantling of the Menagerie by the Jacobins, mark the end of an era, the end of absolutism and confinement, the revolutionaries thought. But all of these structures of confinement persisted under different guises: The Menagerie became the Panopticon; the liberated animals of Versailles were transferred to the Jardin des Plantes; the *furieuses* were reclassified as *hystériques* and put on display until the time of Charcot.

THE ZOOPTICON

An artist from Minnesota, Doug Argue, has captured some of the enduring meaning of the exchange of human and animal gazes that occurs in the Menagerie. (See Figure 0.6.) Mary Abbe gives an evocative description of this immense (12 ft. × 23 ft.) fresco that took two years to complete:

> Rows and rows of white leghorn chickens, their flesh delicately tinted by red and green underpainting, peer from cages stacked 35 high along either side of a wooden walkway that seems to recede into infinity. Ceiling fans hover like tiny helicopters. The birds—their red combs cocked and feathers ruffled—scrutinize viewers with the benign indifference of 1,000 individualized sphinxes.[55]

In published comments about the painting, Argue credits his reading of a Kafka story, "Investigation of a Dog," with providing him the originating idea for the painting. In this story a dog poses the question: "Whence does the earth procure

FIGURE 0.6: Untitled, by Doug Argue, 1993, Oil on canvas, 366 × 701 cm. Private Collection.

that food that it gives us?"[56] This led Argue to ask himself: "Who am I? Where do I get my food?" Thus the primordial link between food and identity (and not nakedness and identity, as in Derrida) is the subject of this painting.

Another theme that Argue has discussed in relation to the painting (which he calls "infinite chickens") is his desire to "create infinity, in a single individual work, in a painting that was both flat and infinite in space."[57] For some reason, an endless number of chickens are necessary for the human to conceive of infinity. On this level, this is another case where a human visual and imaginative deficiency is overcome by means of animals. The idea of infinity, like the other limit-experiences we have discussed (representation, madness, faith, seduction, esthetic beauty) can only be approximated by appeal to an animal witness.

This painting also tells us a great deal about animals in the present. The cruel confinement of poultry is a reality in western Minnesota, which is notorious for chicken and turkey megafarms. The sameness of all of the white birds is reminiscent of *The March of the Penguins,* and of Derrida's "irreducible living multiplicity of mortals," but this is a dystopian vision of the flock or the herd; the sameness here would seem to refer inevitably to cloning and genetic engineering. (See Figure 0.7.) The variety of fowl seen in Boel's Menagerie scene has been replaced by an Escher-like, dizzying vortex of sameness that hints at the human need to control nature and conquer time itself with this eternal perpetuation of the same species, while driving out true biological diversity on the planet.

FIGURE 0.7: Untitled, by Doug Argue, Detail. Private Collection.

Harried and persecuted by his fellow citizens, Rousseau had sought relief in the company of animals and in the contemplation of plants. The animal gaze that mirrors human vision in "infinite chickens" does not inspire the same pre-Romantic feelings about nature. This is an animal gaze that was not meant to be seen, a zoopticon that shows one extreme of Enlightenment rationality and its instrumentalization of life. Argue's painting restores visibility to an animal gaze that is normally hidden. It is a disturbing *Ecce Animot* that forces us to confront our own status as animals and think what we must look like in the eyes of these infinite chickens waiting for slaughter in their wire cages. These animals allow us to ponder the extent of our own surveillance and control. Perhaps we wouldn't ever see our position in the world as the hidden masters of these animal Treblinkas nor ever understand, without Argue's painting, that what we do to animals we do to ourselves.[58]

CHAPTER ONE

The Souls of Men and Beasts, 1630–1764

MATTHEW SENIOR

The modern English word *soul* has ancient roots in Anglo-Saxon culture and carries with it beliefs about the afterlife in pre-Christian Europe. The *Oxford English Dictionary* cites a passage from *Beowulf*, composed sometime between 750 and 800, as the first example of the word *soul* in Old English. The hero of the saga is described at the moment of his death: "His soul [*sawol*] fled from his breast to its destined place among the steadfast ones."[1] Following Beowulf's death in mortal combat against a dragon, his soul leaves his body and journeys to Valhalla to join the souls of other fallen warriors. Earlier in the narrative, when Beowulf struggles against the monster Grendel, his men come to his aid, "seeking to cut straight to the *sawol*" of the hero's demonic adversary.[2] The soul is thus the source of life for Beowulf and the monster—it literally leaves his chest upon death—and it is also the center of consciousness that survives after death.

In Norse mythology, as in many aboriginal cultures, animals have souls that may live on in the afterlife. Valhalla is alive with examples of such beliefs: Odin sits on a throne attended by wolves, while two ravens named Hugin (thought) and Munin (memory) go forth into the world each day to gather information and whisper it into the ruler of Valhalla's ears upon their return. A rooster named Gullinkambi awakens the warriors each morning to a glorious day of hacking each other to pieces in battle, followed by miraculous healing of their wounds and feasting on "the flesh of the divine boar Saehrimnir, a marvelous beast, daily slain by the cook Andhrimnir, and boiled in a great caldron."[3] This is the folkloric background to the word *soul* in English, a world where, according to Jan Bremmer, "domestic animals, especially the horse and the ox, were believed to possess a surviving soul."[4]

One encounters a similarly physical and animal soul in Homer. Prior to the outbreak of the Trojan War, the Greeks seek to avoid war with their enemies by declaring a truce and sacrificing animals to the gods. The deaths of the animals are described in terms similar to those that will be used to describe human deaths in the *Iliad*: "Agamemnon dragged his ruthless dagger across the lambs' throats and let them fall to the ground, dying, gasping away their life breath (*thymos*), cut short by the sharp bronze."[5] When the first Greek soldier dies in battle, Homer describes the death as a similar loss of animal soul. "Agenor stabbed with a bronze spear and loosed his limbs; Elephenor's life spirit (*thymos*) left him, and over his dead body now the savage work went on."[6]

This very animal sense of the word *soul*, referring to a life shared by humans and animals, a life whose physicality also had deep spiritual implications, survived in English and other European languages until the radical changes in philosophy, science, and religion that occurred during the Enlightenment. The primitive concept of the soul, as seen in Homer and Beowulf, was enriched and refined by Greek philosophy and additions from Judaism and Christianity. But until Descartes, the soul remained inextricably rooted in the animal body. It was a vital principle that accounted for movement, sensation, nutrition, reproduction, and varying degrees of memory and rationality in humans and animals. In 1637, with the first public revelation of the *bête-machine* hypothesis in the *Discourse on Method*, Descartes tore asunder the common psychic and physical ground shared by humans and animals in the concept of the soul and touched off a long controversy about the nature of animal and human souls. By the latter half of the eighteenth century, the metaphysical idea of the soul itself was subject to doubt and mockery. In the *Philosophical Dictionary* (1764), Voltaire wrote: "We call soul that which animates. We don't know much else because of the limits of our intelligence. Three fourths of the human race doesn't go any further than this, and doesn't worry about the 'thinking being'; the other fourth is still looking; nobody has, nor ever will, find the answer."[7] This chapter will examine the origins of the concept of the soul in Western philosophy and religion and analyze how the animal soul was crucial to the definition of human nature.

HOMER: ONE OR MANY SOULS

In Homer there are several types of soul: *psychē, thymos, noos,* and *menos*.[8] With the exception of a pig slaughtered in the *Odyssey*, only humans are described as possessing a *psychē*, a soul that leaves the body at death and travels

to the Underworld. In early Greek texts, *psychē* is not the center of consciousness and wakefulness, but rather a version of the subject that emerges during
sleep, fainting, or trances, and survives as a diminished shadow of the person
in Hades.[9] There are frequent depictions in Homer of the *psychē* leaving the
body at the moment of death, as well as an insistence that this form of the soul
is an incomplete version of the self, lacking in speech, memory, and physicality.
When Odysseus enters the Underworld, he cannot speak to the soul of his
mother, Anticleia, until she has drunk the blood of a sacrificed sheep, which allows her to recover speech and memory. She explains to her son why he cannot
embrace her: "Once life has departed from our white bones ... the soul slips
away like a dream and goes fluttering on its way."[10] Anticleia thus explains the
importance of animal blood in sustaining full human soulhood.

In contrast to *psychē*, the unconscious and posthumous soul, the living,
conscious human soul is designated by the words *thymos, noos, and menos* in
Homer. These kinds of souls account for the active, conscious personality; all
of them are extinguished upon death, with only the ghostly *psychē* surviving,
which is an impoverished form of the soul. *Thymos* is shared by humans and
animals, as is evident in the passages concerning the death of Elephenor and
the sacrificed animals cited earlier. It is the source of the emotions of fear, joy,
and revenge. Odysseus "speaks to his proud *thymos*," and Hector admonishes
Paris to join the battle: "Fool, wrongly you stored up bitter anger in your *thymos*."[11] The *thymos* was located in the chest and is often described as filling the
phrenes, an organ identified by modern scholars as the lungs or the diaphragm,
presumably because the Greeks associated strong emotions with either plea-
surable or constricted breathing.[12] Further insight into the Greeks' sense of
the physicality of mental life can be gleaned from examples of another mental
organ, the heart *(kardia)*. When Achilles becomes angry he declares, "My *kardia* fills with *cholos* (gall)."[13]

Another part of the Homeric soul is the *noos* (mind, intention, plan), also
located in the chest, but never defined as a physical substance. *Menos* is a mo-
mentary impulse that takes hold of the mind and body and inspires warriors
to acts of superhuman strength. There is also *lyssa*, literally, the "wolf's rage,"
a berserk passion that possesses soldiers in battle. "Hector, exulting greatly in
his might, rages vehemently, relying on Zeus and holding no one in respect,
neither men nor gods. And the powerful *lyssa* has entered him."[14] This type of
becoming-animal is frequent in Homer, for whom war is a cataclysmic, cosmic
event. The first clash of the Greek and Trojan armies is evoked in geological
terms: "Wildly as two winter torrents raging down from the mountains, swirl-
ing into a valley, hurl their great water together, flash floods from the well-
springs plunging down in a gorge and miles away in the hills a shepherd hears
the thunder—so from the grinding armies broke the cries and crash of war."[15]
Homer next uses animal metaphors to describe the ferocity of war: "The savage

work went on, Achaean and Trojans mauling each other there like wolves, leaping, hurtling into each other, man throttling man."[16] In another passage Diomedes is described as a beast of prey: "Triple the fury seized him—claw-mad as a lion some shepherd tending woolly flocks in the field has just grazed, a lion leaping into the fold, but he hasn't killed him, only spurred his strength; and, helpless to beat him off, the man scurries for shelter, leaving his flocks panicked, lost as the ramping beast mauls them thick and fast, piling corpse on corpse, and in one furious bound clears the fenced yard—so raging Diomedes mauled the Trojans."[17]

In Homer, animals are always endowed with *thymos* and *menos*, and sometimes with *noos* and even *psychē*. These multiple, overlapping, shared souls capture the animality of humans in battle and death, and they reveal a shared mental life, especially the strong emotional decisions of the warrior. Many of the thought processes and actions of the warrior are due to a psychology and a physiology shared with animals. The soul of the epic hero is an animal soul. The hero consents to spill his blood and lose his *psychē* for the cause of the group. The animality and mortality of the human warrior is wagered defiantly against the gods, who control human destiny. Calling upon various animal and human souls, the Homeric hero reaches full potential in battle, in this life, not the next, where the soul loses its animality and becomes but a shadow of itself.

PLATO: THE TRIPARTITE SOUL

Under the influence of Greek philosophy, the word *psychē* absorbed the other words and meanings for the soul in archaic texts, in parallel with the emergence of a unified self in Greek culture at the end of the fifth century B.C.E. This drive toward a unified soul is evident in Plato, who uses the concept of soul to present an ordered vision of nature and the entire universe. In the *Timaeus* Plato offers a model of the universe, which he conceptualizes as the actualization of a single perfect model, conceived in the mind of a Maker, a perfect totality that, by definition, contains matter, life, and thought. The entire universe is imbued with *psychē*, whose primordial characteristic is self-motion. The first and highest creations of the Maker are the fixed stars, divine beings whose circular motion is changeless and eternal, thus possessing more *being*, as opposed to the imperfect and transitory creatures caught in world of becoming, according to this metaphysical view of the world. According to Plato's philosophical myth, the Maker delegated to a demiurge the power to create other forms of life by enfolding small particles of the world soul into the bone marrow of living creatures.

The god produced the purest fire, water, air and earth; these he mixed in due proportion to produce marrow, as a kind of universal seed for

mortal creatures of every kind. ... And he moulded into spherical shape
the part of the marrow that was to contain the divine seed and called it the
brain. ... The rest of the marrow that was to contain the mortal parts of
the soul he divided into long, cylindrical sections called by the general
name "marrow" to which the whole soul was anchored.[18]

Thus is formed in humans a tripartite soul, linked together by bone marrow,
containing a divine, astral particle in the brain, and two mortal parts: one in
the chest, "the seat of courage, passion and ambition," and a lower, vegetative soul, situated below the diaphragm, responsible for appetites and reproduction.[19] This part of the soul is referred to as a "wild beast" that must be
fed. The tripartite division of the soul, which was dominant in the West until
the Cartesian revolution, insisted on the shared traits of humans and animals,
which becomes especially apparent in the Platonic version of the derivation of
the sexes and the relation between humans and other species.

According to a familiar pattern in Greek thought, women were conceptual-
ized as imperfect men. In Plato's version of this idea in the *Timaeus*, the souls
of men who live "cowardly or immoral lives" are reincarnated as women, in
response to which the gods decided to create anatomical differences between
the sexes. This was accomplished by perforating the spine of each sex and allowing the soul contained in the marrow to flow outward, through the genital
organs of each sex. "So a man's genitals are naturally disobedient and self-
willed, like a creature that will not listen to reason, and will do anything in
their mad lust for possession."[20] The anatomical animality of women is even
more pronounced in Plato's famous description of the uterus: "The matrix
or womb in women is a living creature within them which longs to bear children. And if it is left unfertilized ... it causes extreme unrest, strays about the
body."[21]

In the thought of Plato, animals, like women, are also imperfect and de-
generate men. Birds devolved from men who began to grow feathers instead
of hair, "from harmless, empty headed men, who were interested in the heavens but were silly enough to think that visible evidence is all the foundation
astronomy needs."[22] Land animals come from men who followed the lower
animal soul in their abdomens; as a result, "their fore-limbs and heads were
drawn down by natural affinity to the earth."[23] Fish, "the most unintelligent
and ignorant of all," are not worthy of breathing air, which the higher forms of
soul are identified with. Completing this view in Plato is the idea of reincarnation. The souls of men who have not used reason to point their souls toward
the celestial realm of being will be incarnated as women or animals.

Moving from the Homeric soul to Plato's tripartite soul, with its origins in a
celestial realm of Ideas, the soul is unified and hierarchized according to an a
priori metaphysical plan. In Plato, the full realization of the human soul lies

beyond the animal body, although there is still a strong sense of the animality of humans in the account of sexual difference and reincarnation. There are literally animals within the Platonic body and lessons to be learned as an animal in future lives.

What is also noteworthy in Plato's metaphysical view of the souls of men and beasts is that it is knowledge-driven and order-driven. In a Darwinian universe, animals use all means at their disposal simply to survive and reproduce. Advances in knowledge and skill serve only to facilitate survival and reproduction. In Plato's myth, the soul comes from a higher plane of knowledge and seeks to return to its origin. A metaphysical drive to knowledge is embedded in the soul.

ARISTOTLE: THE SOUL BELONGS TO THE BODY

A similar drive toward knowledge and order appears in Aristotle's account of the soul, which follows the tripartite scheme of vegetative, sensitive, and intellective faculties. Aristotle's soul, like Plato's, is a substance, but an invisible substantial *form* that Descartes and others will later reject. In *De Anima* and other of his works, Aristotle uses a constructivist metaphor to describe plants, animals, and humans as though they were similar to a building or a piece of furniture built by a carpenter, composed of matter (*hyle*) and form (*morphe*). The form is like a blueprint that gives shape and form to organic matter. In animals the male's sperm contributes the form while the female's menstrual blood supplies the matter. The constructivist model also allows Aristotle to use the doctrine of the four causes to explain the soul. The organic matter of the body is the material cause, while the soul provides the three remaining causes: (1) the formal cause, the structure or blueprint for the body; (2) the efficient cause, which, in the constructivist model, is the carpenter who actually builds the structure; and (3) the final cause, the purpose and goal of the organism. The soul is thus the abstract plan, the plan's actual implementation, and the goal and purpose toward which the organism strives. Another metaphysical distinction, the opposition between potentiality and actuality, is used to define the soul as "the first actuality of a body with organs."[24] This means that the soul is the actualization or performance of life.

De Anima uses a striking organic metaphor to stress the active nature of the soul and to restate the doctrine that the soul is a substance: "For if the eye was an animal, then sight would be its soul, being the *substance* of the eye that is in accordance with the account of it" (my emphasis).[25] The same passage extends the visual metaphor to underscore the unity of the body and soul: "So just as pupil and sight *are* the eye, so, in our case, soul and body *are* the animal. It is quite clear then that the soul is not separable from the body, or that some parts of it are not, if it is its nature to have parts."[26] In *De Anima* Aristotle declares several times that thought is generated by a soul that must reside in a physical body. In a long passage summing up his metaphysical definition of the soul, the philosopher states that the soul is a substance—as the form of the body—and that this substance must be united with a body.

> For substance is, as we said, spoken of in three ways, as form, as matter, and as the composite, and of these matter is potentiality, form actuality, and since the composite is in this case the ensouled thing, it is not that the body is the actuality of the soul but that the soul is the actuality of some body. And for this reason they have supposed well who have believed that the soul is neither without body nor a kind of body. *For it is not a body but belongs to a body,* and for this is present in a body of the appropriate kind (my emphasis).[27]

The intellective soul therefore depends on the body in order to think. "If one perceived nothing, one would learn nothing and understand nothing."[28] Aristotle does leave the door slightly ajar, however, concerning the separability and possibly the survivability of the intellective part of the soul. Everything the mind knows, it does so through its attachment to the body, yet it operates at the level of abstraction and "things without matter."[29] "In the way then, that things are separable from matter in general, in that way are things connected with the intellect."[30] Aristotle speaks in very concrete terms about mental "things," but because he is wedded to the idea that in perception and intellection, "the like is affected by the like," the mind comes to be viewed as a pure form that houses other forms. There is one sentence in *De Anima* in which the mind seems to become the immaterial objects that it contemplates: "It [the intellect] is itself thinkable just as the thought-objects are, for in the case of things without matter, that which thinks is the same as that which is thought."[31]

The Aristotelian universe is a divinely designed, fixed order, constructed in measured increments from plants to the pinnacle of the natural order—man. The result of such metaphysical design, reaching from the bottom to the top of nature, however, is to keep humans and animals much closer than they would be following the Cartesian rupture. Aristotle envisages a logical progression from the lowest to the highest souls analogous to the increasing complexity of polygons, "shapes," beginning with the triangle, adding one side to form a square, etc. "It is clear then that there will be one account of soul in the same way that there will be one account of shape. For in the case of shape there is no shape in addition to the triangle and those in series from it, and in this case there will be no soul in addition to the ones we have mentioned."[32] The higher faculties of the soul—the perceptive and intellective faculties—are modeled upon and recapitulate the lower forms. Thus perception is *like* nutrition, and thinking *like* animal perception. Nutrition involves the ingestion of the matter and form of external bodies; perception, the extraction of only forms from external objects; and reason the contemplation of forms within the soul itself.

The movement from plants to animals to men, and, most important, the appearance of mental phenomena in a purely material universe are unproblematic. Ideas are already inscribed in things, and the human being is just that animal who is capable of sifting out these ideas. This is evident in a passage from the *Metaphysics* in which Aristotle describes how humans live in close proximity to animals but are capable of extracting universal judgments out of their experiences:

> The animals other than man live by appearances and memories, and have but little of connected *experience;* but the human race lives also by art and reasoning. Now from memory experience is produced in men; for the several memories of the same thing produce finally the capacity for a single experience. And experience seems pretty much like science, but really science and art come to men *through* experience; for "experience made art," as Polus says, "but inexperience luck." Now art arises when from many notions gained by experience one universal judgment about a class of objects is produced.[33]

Animals seem very close to reason. They have memories, which are the precursors of experiences, which give rise to universals. Animals, because of the scale of nature, seem to be on the way to human reason in Aristotle.

> They [animals], all of them participate also in a kind of knowledge, some more and some less, and some very little indeed. For they have sense-perception, and this is a kind of knowledge. If we consider the value of this we find that it is of great importance compared with the class of lifeless objects ... For against the latter the mere participation in touch and taste seems to be practically nothing, but beside absolute insensibility it seems most excellent; for it would seem a treasure to gain even his kind of knowledge rather than to live in a state of death and non existence.[34]

Aristotle's notion of the soul is thus highly complex, actually anticipating certain discoveries of modern biology, such as DNA, which operates in the body much like a formal cause.[35] What remains very different from modern biology, however, is the nature of drives encoded in the Aristotelian soul-form. At the very bottom of the scale of nature, in the nutritive soul, which governs growth and reproduction in plants, animals, and humans, there is a deep metaphysical striving at work. Animals and plants reproduce their own kind so that they can achieve a kind of immortality through the permanence of the species, "so that in this way they may partake in the eternal and the divine."[36] Purposefulness and design (*entelechy*) are inscribed in all living creatures. Each animal soul contains a final cause for which it was designed, this in stark contrast to the modern view of biological structure evolving as a result of chance mutation and natural selection.

If the idea of animals striving for immortality is no longer acceptable in scientific terms, it is not without appeal as a poetic, secular image of immortality that confers beauty and meaning on the lives of animals, even if today we would probably add that, in striving for biological immortality, animals (and humans) commit their genes to a future of uncertainty and evolution.

The Aristotelian soul is thus an extremely ambitious and operative concept, a sort of biological and mental black box that unifies plant, animal, and human life. Its most important role was to make mental life a natural phenomenon that emerges seamlessly from animal life. At its highest reaches, the soul-form makes humans capable of quasi-divine thought. The nutritive and the perceptive parts of the soul are responsible for a great deal in this project. They are the glue that ties the human mind to the physical world. The strong physicality of the Aristotelian soul, just as much as its openness to immateriality, left its mark on medieval Christianity. According to Thomas Aquinas, the soul would be rejoined to the body in the afterlife because it could not reach its perfection without the body.[37]

THE ANIMAL SOUL IN THE BIBLE

In the book of Genesis human life is both identified with and separated from animal life. Land animals are created "out of the ground," and all possess a "breath of life."[38] Adam, whose name is related to the Hebrew word for earth, receives the breath of life directly from God. "Then the Lord God formed man (*adam*) from the dust of the ground (*adamah*) and breathed into his nostrils the breath of life (*nishmat hayyim*); and man became a living soul (*nefesh hayyah*)" (Gen 2.7).[39] This personal, intimate contact between man and the Creator is the first of many distinctions humans enjoy over the beasts. Adam is created in the image of God and has dominion over the animals; he has language, which is first put to use in naming the animals. Immediately following this naming, God creates a partner for Adam in a way that distinguishes human sexuality and human naming from animal sexuality and naming. As if God had a sense of humor or wanted to test Adam, Eve is presented to him, as though to be identified and named, as the other animals, at which Adam breaks forth in the first example of sustained human speech in the Bible: "This at last is bone of my bones and flesh of my flesh; this one shall be called Woman (*ishshah*), for out of Man (*ish*) this one was taken" (Gen 2.23). As Bible scholars have noted, the first name for man, *adam*, meaning earth, and relating man to all of the other land animals, is modified with the creation and naming of woman. Adam finds in Eve a part of his own flesh and adopts a new name (*ish*), echoing the name for woman (*ishshah*), meaning that, in addition to divine resemblance and language, man is distinguished from the beasts by sexual loyalty and intense subjective mirroring.

In Genesis 9.4–5, God tells Noah, "Only you shall not eat flesh with its life (*nefesh*), that is, its blood. For your own lifeblood I will surely require a reckoning: from every animal I will require it and from human beings, each one for the blood of another." There is a taboo surrounding animal blood, which is the life or soul of the animal. To consume this soul is akin to homicide, and, in these verses, animals themselves are held accountable and are equivalent to humans if they commit a crime, "from every animal I will require it." There is a strong link between humans and animals based on a shared life-principle of blood. In addition, as is evident in the creation of Adam, humans also have received the divine breath to animate them.

DESCARTES: THE GREAT REIFICATION

The metaphysical principles of what would become known as the *bête-machine* hypothesis—the idea that animals have absolutely no souls nor any intrinsic principle of life distinguishing them from machines—first appeared in the *Traité de l'homme* (Treatise on Man), written between 1629 and 1633. *L'Homme* was not published until 1662, posthumously, because at the time of its completion Descartes feared the Inquisition, which had recently condemned Galileo. *L'Homme* is the second part and conclusion of *Le Monde* (The World), Descartes' mechanistic account of the origin of the universe and its functioning according to the physics of Galileo.

Proof that the thirty-three-year-old French philosopher adhered to the new physics can be found early in *Le Monde*, when he gives a purely mechanical, atomistic (although, to be exact "corpuscular") description of fire, a phenomenon that will be central to his biology as well as his physics.[40] Descartes is hostile to Aristotle and derides the concepts of Aristotelian physics: "Let them [the Aristotelians] imagine ... that there is in a piece of burning wood the *form* of fire, the *quality* of heat and the *action* that burns it ... for myself, I am content to see in this phenomenon only the movement of particles" (my emphasis).[41] For Descartes, Aristotelian substantial forms, qualities, and actions confusedly apply human mental categories to the material world and material concepts to the immaterial soul.[42] For a mechanist, the sensation of heat is not a *quality* of fire but an artifact of the human nervous system, one of many cases in which perception in no way resembles the thing perceived. In Aristotelian physics, the form of fire gives it the qualities of heat and dryness and a natural movement upward; fire is also the most active of the four elements, giving it a kind of agency that allows it to impress its form on other matter. Descartes rejects all of these quasi-mental characteristics of fire and insists on a strictly mechanical account. Fire, like all matter, is composed of particles, whose only innate qualities are extension in space, shape, and movement.

L'Homme attempts to apply this mechanistic vision of the world to biology. The overall scheme of the two books is a grand narrative of the evolution of the universe from a primary chaos to an ordered cosmos with revolving stars and a planetary system, including Earth and its life forms, all unfolding as a result of the nature of matter and the operation of simple laws of motion. Descartes is careful to note that the actual world was probably created by God in all of its detail; however, in a fictive world, God could simply have created a mass of matter and allowed it to evolve, governed by no other principles than the three laws of motion: inertia, the conservation of energy, and the persistence of linear movement. (There is no gravity in Descartes' universe, but rather a vortex force that moves matter in circular patterns.) Such an elementary chaos could have evolved into the actual world, replete with animals devoid of souls or any special animating force. The fiction of a universe evolving out of inert particles is meant to prove that the present-day bodies of humans and animals are machines and that the operation of each vital organ can be explained in strictly mechanical terms. Even though the microscope had not yet been invented, Descartes hoped to show that what transpires in biology can be broken down into utterly simple corpuscular processes, as in the case of fire.

In *Le Monde*, Descartes gives an elaborate, and because of his reliance on the vortex principle, fantastic account of how elementary matter could have evolved into a universe; but he was unable to explain, "according to cause and effect," how nature had produced "seeds" from matter, and, eventually, animals and humans.[43] In order to fill this gap in the fictive world of *L'Homme*, God intervenes and creates "Men, composed, like us, of a soul and a body."[44] In the *Discourse on Method* (1637) Descartes makes perfectly clear the intent of the fable by altering the situation and stating unequivocally that the artificial men "have no reasonable souls nor anything else functioning as a vegetative or sensitive soul, except that he [God] placed in their hearts a heat without light."[45] The bodies of the fictive men are "statues or earthen machines" that look like humans. They "walk, eat, and breathe" as humans do, but without the benefit of a soul, relying only on internal organs that function like "clocks, fountains and mills."[46]

There is no mention, as in Genesis, that the first humans were formed in the image of God. Descartes' robots only resemble humans. Nor does an anthropomorphic God breathe the spirit of life into the artificial men, establishing a physical intimacy between God and man. The physicality of creation and the spiritual significance of the body in Medieval and Renaissance Christianity can be immediately grasped by viewing a stone carving of the creation of Adam in the north portal of Chartres cathedral. Adam kneels with his head in the lap of a fraternal Christ figure, who strokes his hair and creates Adam with his own hands. In this statue Adam is submissive and animal-like in his intimacy with Christ, suggesting that, as in Genesis, the human-divine relationship is modeled on a human–animal relationship. The relation between God and Cartesian man occurs at the level of the soul. There is a Platonic disregard for the body in Descartes, except as a challenging engineering project.

To show to what extent automatons are capable of human-like behavior, Descartes refers to "diverse machines ... in the grottos and fountains of our kings."[47] A particular fountain that Descartes describes featured a statue of Neptune that spewed water into the faces of unsuspecting visitors who trod upon a hidden lever.[48] This purely mechanical sequence illustrates the reflex arc that occurs in humans and animals without any conscious thought. The visitor stepping on the lever is analogous to a sensory stimulus, and the automatic release of hydraulic pressure in the hidden valves followed by the movement of the statue and the spurting water is like the flow of animal spirits into a muscle, causing an appropriate motor response.

Figure 1.1 one of Louis de La Forge's illustrations for *L'Homme*, shows a robotic-looking woman who seems to embody Descartes' ambiguity about whether the artificial humans in *L'Homme* and *Le Discours de la méthode* have souls or not: Does she or does she not have a soul? The woman's actions are dictated by the flow of animal spirits from her pineal gland, so named because of its resemblance to a pine cone. In Cartesian physiology the pineal gland is the place where the immaterial soul is supposed to contact the body by monitoring the flow of animal spirits in the gland. In this illustration, the woman tilts her pineal gland forward to ensure that the nerve openings corresponding to the two separate rods will cause a flow of animal spirits from two separate locations on the surface of the pineal gland, thus giving her the sensation of two separate rods instead of one.

According to this hydraulic model, plants, animals and humans have no unique structures, no intrinsic organizing principles that would distinguish them from machines. All of the movements characteristic of life—nutrition, growth, reproduction and autonomous movement—result simply from the channeling and coordination of the same corpuscular motion that Descartes described in the flame. Everything in the physical world and in the body is the result of shape and movement. "*Tout se fait par figure et mouvement*" became the motto of Cartesian physics and physiology. Whereas in traditional Galenic medicine, the various organs of the body possessed irreducible "faculties," in Cartesian physiology each organ functions according to a clearly understandable variant of the movement and filtration of small particles.

In *L'Homme* Descartes explains the major functions of the body according to this corpuscular model, starting with digestion. Food is broken down in the stomach by heat and digestive "liquors," whose small, rapidly moving particles

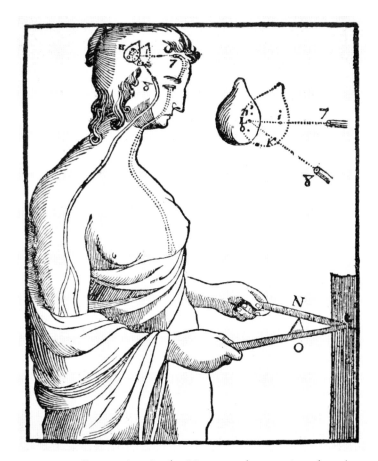

FIGURE 1.1: Pneumatic animal spirits create the sensation of touch on the surface of the pineal gland, Woodcut in René Descartes, *L'homme et un traitté de la formation du fœtus, avec les remarques de Louys de La Force*, Paris, 1664. Courtesy of the Division of Rare and Manuscript Collections, Cornell University Library.

slip into the interstices of the food and break it apart. Large particles descend through the digestive tract, while the more "subtle" parts are filtered by "an infinity of small holes," through the stomach wall and into the lactiles.[49] From there chyle passes to the liver, where it ferments and turns red, like claret. The newly formed blood flows through the heart and is heated by a "fire without light," which agitates certain particles in the blood to the extent that they become *esprits animaux* and travel to the brain by means of the carotid arteries.

The expression "*esprits animaux*" is easily misunderstood because the animal spirits have no spiritual or animal characteristics in the traditional sense of these words. The *esprits* are simply highly mobile particles with pneumatic forces; they are not spiritual in any sense. The spiritual realm is confined to the immaterial soul in Descartes' metaphysics. Nor are the *esprits* animate in the Aristotelian sense of being parts of a soul or a structure unique to living organisms.

Upon arrival in the brain, the larger particles of animal spirits are diverted to nourish the brain, while the smallest, most vigorous particles pass through the pineal gland and are distributed into the nervous system, which Descartes conceived of as a vast a network of pneumatic tubes, each containing a small filament. The filament played the role of the sensory nerve. In Descartes' physiology, a stimulus from the outside world literally pulls on the filament, causing it to open a valve or pore at the other end of the nerve. The nerve openings line the interior walls of the brain, forming a lattice structure surrounding the pineal gland. When a nerve tube opens, animal spirits flow from the surface of the pineal gland into the tube, traveling to the muscles and provoking contractions by means of pneumatic pressure. Figure 1.2 shows the pineal gland, centrally located in the "cavities of the brain," with lines indicating the outward flow of animal spirits from small holes on the surface of the gland into the surrounding nerve tubes.

The pineal gland is the most ingenious piece of engineering in the animal or human body. It is simultaneously an imaging device, a complex valve system, and a calculator that continuously and unconsciously uses "innate geometry" to measure the relative distance of visual and tactile objects. The gland begins to look like reason itself, which Descartes will define as a universal, polyvalent tool. But the pineal gland is an impasse. It does not allow Descartes to make a distinction between humans and animals. *Au contraire.* With the pineal gland, we are at the problematic juncture of human and animal nature in Descartes. Animals have exemplary pineal glands, as Descartes makes clear in a letter to Mersenne, noting that animals have larger glands than humans, "in humans it [the pineal gland] is smaller than in animals just the opposite as for the other parts of the brain."[50] Because of the difference in size, animal pineal glands were easier to see during dissection. So, what we are looking at, in fact, in the illustrations for *L'Homme,* are actual animal glands, according to Descartes' illustrator, Louis de La Forge, who reports that he drew the human gland larger in his illustrations than it really is, as if, in his words, "the *animal* were alive," clearly indicating that animal glands were used for the drawings.[51]

However, the pineal glands of animals do not house immaterial souls. That is the invisible, metaphysical gap between animals and humans that Descartes created, giving a mile, as it were, to take an inch, conceding so much similarity between the human and animal body, only to revoke this similarity completely with the metaphysical distinction between body and soul that could only be proven by subtle speech tests and observations about the creative activity of humans and animals. So similar, humans and animals, even to the point of exchangeable pineal glands, yet so different, as Descartes would reveal in

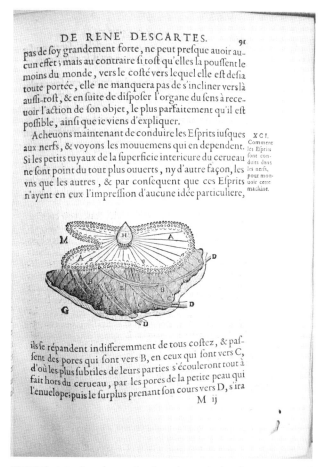

FIGURE 1.2: A schematic drawing of the human pineal gland, based on animal dissections, Woodcut in René Descartes, *L'homme et un traitté de la formation du fœtus, avec les remarques de Louys de La Force*, Paris, 1664. Courtesy of the Division of Rare and Manuscript Collections, Cornell University Library.

the *Discourse on Method* (1637), published four years after *L'Homme* was completed.

Before looking at the definitive, metaphysical gap between humans and animals outlined in the *Discourse*, it is worth considering a few other functions in the mechanical body. At the end of *L'Homme,* Descartes cites almost triumphantly a list of phenomena he has explained without recourse to a "vegetative or sensitive soul," relying solely on the "the fires that are in inanimate bodies" to give movement and sensation to human and animal bodies.[52] The list includes "digestion, … the beating of the heart, … respiration, … wakefulness and sleep, … the reception of sound, odors, tastes, heat and other qualities by the external sense organs, … the impression of such ideas on the organ of common sense [the pineal gland], ... movement, ... the passions."[53] Three items on this list merit further attention to fully grasp the materialism of Cartesian psychology and its reversal of the traditional Galenic account of the humors and passions.

The description of vision is a rehearsal of the pneumatic body at work. Light rays, which Descartes understood to be tiny corpuscles (which he compared to tennis balls bouncing off reflective surfaces) pass through the eye and physically trace an image on the retina. This physical contact pulls on the filaments inside the bundle of optic nerves, opening a number of pores on the nerve ends facing the pineal gland, as seen in Figure 1.2. When the optic nerve tubes open, they attract a stream of animal spirits that exit the surface of the pineal gland and move into the tubes. The pattern of these exiting animal spirits forms an inscription of the original object on the surface of the pineal gland. This is the actual inscription the brain "sees." Descartes calls this inscription an "idea," declaring that such material "ideas" allow the hand to point toward an object the brain sees, without thinking about it or involving the immaterial soul. "Observe that the *idea* of this movement of the hand is constituted entirely by the way the animal spirits exit the gland, and it is this idea that causes the movement."[54]

The idea or impression can be stored in the memory, which Descartes imagines as a purely physical process. The network of nerve endings forming the interior wall of the brain is like lead or wax, capable of preserving the inscription of a sensation that has passed through the network. Thus animals have physical memories and imaginations, allowing them to recall prior experiences and make associations between experiences. Anticipating Pavlov, Descartes describes a dog that, if whipped while violin music is being played, will, in the future, show the physiological signs of fear at the mere sound of a violin.[55]

Descartes also outlines in *L'Homme* a mechanistic account of the humors and the passions. In traditional Galenic and Renaissance medicine, physical and emotional health was ensured by a balance of four *natural* elements (blood, black bile, choler, and phlegm), each possessing qualities specific to living organisms. Descartes substitutes a corpuscular theory of the humors and the passions. In the prior system, mood and "temperament"—the word itself refers to a characteristic temperature of the body—were influenced by the predominance of one of the humors. In Descartes' system, mood is dictated by the rate of flow of animal spirits. An "abundant" flow of animal spirits through the pineal gland produces "confidence, bravery, love, goodness, and liberality"; if the spirit particles are large and coarse, a man or beast will feel "confidence and courage"; uniform spirits produce "constancy"; and agitated particles result in "promptness, diligence and desire." If the spirit flow is weak, the resultant mood is "malice, timidity, inconstancy, tardiness, and ruthlessness."[56]

By means of the passions, the human or animal body is also capable of complex self-regulation. A painful stimulus, such as exposure to fire, sends animal spirits along several pathways at once: some produce muscular contractions to save the body from further injury, some are directed to contract the facial muscles or produce a cry of pain, while a certain quantity of animal spirits are used to produce "internal movements," which are the passions of the body. By this Descartes meant that some animal spirits, in reaction to an external stimulus, are directed toward the heart to change the composition of the blood. By contracting or dilating the heart, animal spirit production could be increased or decreased. Elevated levels of animal spirits in the blood produce feelings of "confidence," "courage," or "desire," allowing the animal or human to muster the appropriate emotions in a given situation. Thus Descartes' pneumatic version of self-regulation replaces the prior humoral system posited by Galen and Renaissance medicine.

One must bear in mind that, at the outset, Descartes had insisted that all of this was possible in a mechanical body without a soul. A machine that is auto-regulating, that responds to stimuli by elevating or diminishing its energy level, is certainly plausible. One could even imagine an angry machine capable of stoking itself with additional pneumatic forces in response to a hostile stimulus. But some of the Cartesian moods seem qualitatively beyond a machine: "goodness," "liberality," "malice," "love."

There is, of course, always a subtle doubling going on with a human being. The immaterial soul, hidden in the pineal gland, continually monitors all of the purely mechanical sensations and passions. And Descartes insists several times in his work, "it is the soul that feels and not the body," implying that human experiences of pleasure, pain, and the passions are entirely different from those of animals because of the presence of the soul.[57] Presumably, an animal or a machine would experience all of these events as mere pressure differentials and patterns in the flow of animal spirits across a perforated membrane in the brain. There would be purely pneumatic versions of "goodness," "liberality," or "love" allowing animals or machines to function optimally.

VERSACHLICHUNG

Before discussing language and reason, the phenomena that set humans and animals apart, metaphysically, in Descartes, I feel compelled to make an observation and indulge in some general speculation about the radical mechanism of *L'Homme*. The opening myth of a parallel world where God could make humans and animals with mechanical bodies has a Promethean aspect to it. The human or animal body becomes an object of technology; humans appropriate for themselves the divine power of understanding the workings of the body and manufacturing it. The project of understanding the body according to simple mechanical principles was audacious and proved to have a limited application in physiology. As Chapter 5 by Anita Guerrini in the present volume makes clear, mechanism was rendered obsolete as a biological theory by the discoveries of Bichat, Haller, Stahl, and others.

Culturally and psychologically, however, the *bête-machine* hypothesis has been endlessly suggestive and is prophetic and true on some level. It presents itself as an immense and shocking reification of human and animal nature. The sense of organic life itself is lost as well as the distinction between plants, animals, and humans. There is something analogous and perhaps causal between this phenomenon in Descartes and what Marx termed reification (*Versachlichung*). This was the word that Marx and Georg Lukács used to characterize the mechanical tendencies of social relations under capitalism, as human beings are alienated from the fruits of their labor, and their living and creative agency is stolen from them by factories, the state, and the market. The worker's productivity and creative agency is alienated from him or her and assumes a separate, autonomous existence. In this process there is an uncanny exchange of animate and inanimate qualities, as humans lose their organic qualities and become reified, while the commodity is charged with magical, fetishistic qualities. In *Capital* (1867), Marx describes the logic of the commodity: "There is an antithesis, immanent in the commodity, between use-value and value, between private labor ... and a particular concrete kind of labor that counts as merely abstract universal labor, between the conversion of things into persons and the conversion of persons into things (*Personifzierung der Sachen und Versachlichung der Personen*)."[58] Further in *Capital* Marx describes how machines intensify reification: "Collective unity in cooperation, combination in the division of labor, the use of the forces of nature and the sciences, of the products of labor, as *machinery*—all these confront the individual worker as something alien, objective, ready-made, existing without their intervention, and frequently even hostile to them" (emphasis in original).[59]

It is very possible that all of this is foreshadowed in the *Traité de l'homme*. One of the primordial characteristics of life in Aristotle had been its ability to reproduce. This is precisely the function that mechanism has trouble with. The mechanized body can produce, but not reproduce. Just as the alienated worker under capitalism can produce but not reproduce himself or herself in work. Labor becomes alienated and detached from the worker, like so many machinic processes, lacking the organic unity of a living body. There is perhaps also the idea that the machine body creates value, not the soul. There was certainly great enthusiasm for the ability of machines to multiply human force in the time of Descartes.[60] The machine is extremely ingenious in Cartesian physiology; it accomplishes much of what had been the domain of the soul before Descartes. It is not hard to imagine that there is a straight line running from the machine in Descartes, through reification in Marx, to contemporary versions of alienated cyborg labor in Fritz Lang's *Metropolis* (1927), Ridley Scott's *Blade Runner* (1982), and Luc Besson's *The Fifth Element* (1997).

THE SOUL AS THOUGHT AND LANGUAGE

The main "characters" of the *Treatise on Man* are the artificial men, although Descartes points out several times that the body he is describing is also that of "several animals without reason."[61] The *Discourse on Method* revisits the subject of *Le Monde* and *L'Homme* and dwells more on the consequences of radical dualism for animals. In a development that does not figure in *L'Homme*, Descartes proposes that it would be impossible to distinguish between an artificial monkey and a real one. "We would have no way of determining whether they [the false monkeys] were of the same nature as animals."[62] In the case of an artificial human, however, there would be two infallible criteria: speech and reason. The latter reveals itself in the ability to accomplish many tasks reasonably well, instead of one task perfectly well, an example being a watch, which keeps time much better than a human, precisely because it is a machine designed for a single task.

Concerning speech, Descartes declares that a sophisticated automaton could never "use words or other signs as we do, arranging them to declare our thoughts to others."[63] The same is true of animals, "parrots can proffer words as we do, without however being able to talk like us ... by showing that they *think* what they say" (my emphasis).[64] Descartes says that we must not take the signs animals *proffer* as an indication of reason, but rather understand that such manifestations are the signs of mechanical, bodily passions. In a letter to the Marquis of Newcastle Descartes specifies that when animals are trained to talk or perform, such activities are "only the expression of their fear, their hope or their joy, which they are able to do without thought."[65] Descartes' radically materialist physiology allows him to interpret the passions expressed by animals as unthinking, unfeeling responses to their environment.

Human language, on the other hand, proceeds from an immaterial soul. With Descartes, in fact, thought and language become the only true qualities of the soul, a break that separates Descartes from the long tradition of unifying mental and organic life in the soul. Alone in Amsterdam, "among the crowds of a great and active people," but living, paradoxically, "as solitary and withdrawn as in the furthest desert," Descartes conducted his great thought experiment, radically doubting the truth of his senses and suspending belief in all truths, assuming that he could not be sure if he were awake or dreaming, or even had a body. There is a limit, however, that fantasy and hallucination cannot cross: "I could not fantasize that I did not exist, and, on the contrary, by the very fact that I doubted the truth of things, it followed very evidently and certainly from this that I existed."[66] From this discovery, Descartes draws the conclusion that he is a "substance whose entire nature is to think and which, to be, needs no space nor depends on any material thing."[67] Thus the soul becomes, with Descartes, only thought—thought about thought—housed, problematically, in the pineal gland.

The only mechanism capable of linking the two separate substances (body and soul) is in fact language, and that is why the distinction between human and animal language is so crucial. Descartes characterizes the human speaker as being able to respond to "meaning" and "arrange [words] diversely."[68] Humans understand, intuitively, that words have multiple meanings and that meanings change according to grammatical context. Even the most extreme madmen ("*insensés*"), a word reserved for the severely mentally ill who were confined in the Salpêtrière, are capable, according to Descartes, of "arranging words and ... making their thoughts (*pensées*) understood."[69] *Thought* is what truly human language expresses, not the passions. Embedded in all human language, even in that of a madman, is the conception of the self as an immaterial thinking substance. Descartes makes these crucial distinctions between human and animal speech in Part 5 of the *Discourse*, following the definition of the soul as pure thought (*cogito ergo sum*) in Part 4. The discussion of human language as referencing thought is thus sustained by the concept of *pensée* outlined in the preceding chapter. *Pensée*, in Descartes, has a pure self-evidence about it; it is what a human cannot deny about himself or herself, even in the most extravagant state of madness; it is, apparently, something that never occurs to animals; it is what gives human language its dexterity and polyvalence, and it is somehow always present, always referenced, in human speech.

Language is thus the tool humans dispose of that is even more ingenious than the pineal gland. It is the tool that reaches across the metaphysical divide. Language is co-extensive with thought, since all of Descartes' most extravagant thought experiments occur within language and remain discursive and recountable. The *cogito* is a spoken formula that grants existence to the thinker. "This proposition, *I am, I exist,* is necessarily true, every time I pronounce it or conceive it in my mind."[70]

Language has both immaterial and material efficacy. It is able to shape the thoughts and give existence to the disembodied thinker, but also, as sound, strike the eardrums of humans and animals and convey to these listeners either thoughts or physiological stimuli. Géraud de Cordemoy, a follower of Descartes particularly interested in making distinctions between human and animal speech, offers a purely mechanical account of how animals produce sounds and emit cries. "When, for instance, a wolf howls, the noise sets in motion the animal spirits assembled, let us say, in the ear of a near-by sheep. These jostle the brain with their vibrations and set into circulation a new flow of animal spirits to the muscles, putting the sheep to flight. The same vibrations which make the beast run cause it to emit cries."[71] "In words, however, there are always two things, namely, the production of the voice, which can only come from the body, and the signification of the idea, which is attached to the voice and can only come from the soul."[72]

THE ANIMAL SOUL DEBATE

The theological "mileage" Descartes derived from depriving animals of speech and life was to preserve and distinguish the human soul from any confusion with animal life and death. Immediately following the automaton passages in the *Discourse* Descartes presents the spectacle of animal death as something that should not worry humans. The "weak minded" might be inclined to fear that we have no more hope for eternal life than "flies or ants."[73] But, having understood how much the human soul differs from the animal soul, how it is "of a nature entirely different from the body," the believer concludes that "the soul is not subject to die with the body."[74]

In the century and a half following the publication of the *Discourse on Method,* the beast machine hypothesis became one of the most important test cases of Cartesianism. It was defended and utilized by Catholic apologists (Arnauld, Bossuet), scientists (Regius, Rohault, Louis de La Forge), and philosophers (Malebranche, Cordemoy); and attacked by traditional Scholastic thinkers, empiricists, and Epicureans (Gassendi, Cureau de La Chambre).[75] The animal machine hypothesis encountered resistance among pet keepers at court such as Madame de Sévigné and Mademoiselle de Scudéry, and La Fontaine argued in his *Fables,* following Gassendi, that animals had a material soul composed of subtle matter that they shared with humans. In England, a widespread current of Neo-Platonism resisted the Cartesian deanimation of nature. Ralph Cudworth, one of the Cambridge Platonists, maintained that "plastic nature," an autonomous force distinct from God and beyond the laws of inert matter, was responsible for the instincts of animals and unconscious phenomena in humans.[76]

It is revelatory of the widespread interest in the debate about the animal soul that Bossuet, the personal tutor of Louis XIV's son, outlined the animal soul controversy for the Dauphin in his *Traité de la connaissance de Dieu et de soi-même* (Treatise on the Knowledge of God and Oneself) and left it up for the young prince to decide whether the Cartesian or the Scholastic position on animals was right.[77]

Descartes was able to answer some of the attacks against his doctrine in his own day. In a letter to Mersenne he affirmed the idea that animals do not feel pain.[78] This idea was further justified on theological grounds according to the notion that a just God could not let animals suffer pain as punishment for original sin, since they had not committed this sin. Another theological point focused on the meaning of animal death. Although Descartes had argued that his theory established a clear distinction between human and animal death, some argued that proving that all animal behavior was the result of hydraulics and blood particles would convince most people that human mental life was also the result of purely material processes. Descartes replied energetically in the Sixth Responses to the *Meditations* that humans have an intuitive sense that *they* think, "it is not possible that we do not experience every day in our selves that we think."[79] If such humans, with an intimate and "infallible" sense of their own thought, are shown that animals do not think, they will never react logically by concluding that they themselves don't think and have only a mechanical life, like animals.

Some of Descartes' ideas prevailed. The Scholastic idea of substantial forms in nature was definitively rejected because of Descartes. The rigorous Cartesian idea of matter as pure extension was upheld by the "winners" in the debate (Bayle, Voltaire, the Encyclopedists). The metaphor of the machine persisted as well, even in thinkers who championed sentiment in animals, such as Rousseau. But Descartes' strict dualism, which separated thought and matter and reserved an immaterial soul for humans, was deconstructed. Empirical evidence began to mount that life was more complex and fundamentally different from machines. In 1694 Nicolas Hartsoeker (1656–1725) observed "animalcules" in semen through the lens of a microscope in Amsterdam, convincing him to oppose mechanist biology for the rest of his career. Bernard le Bovier de Fontenelle (1657–1757) pointed out another explanatory gap in Cartesian biology with the mocking observation if two clocks were left in a box alone together they would fail to produce a little offspring clock.

Philosophically, two key ideas that eroded Descartes' concept of the soul were those advanced by Pierre Bayle (1647–1706) and John Locke (1632–1704). In a series of articles in his *Dictionnaire historique et critique* (1697), Bayle agreed with the Scholastics and empiricists that animals do indeed have some form of mental life. He also argued that sensation implied self-consciousness: "[E]very being that has sensation knows that it has it ... and all the acts of the sensitive faculty are ... reflexive upon themselves."[80] This argument undercut Descartes' idea that self-consciousness is strictly a human prerogative resulting from immaterial thought contemplating itself. Locke, in *An Essay Concerning Human Understanding* (1693), advanced arguments that further undermined Descartes' dualism. Locke reiterated Bayle's idea that sensation *is* self-awareness and argued that thought arises in humans through "sensation ... this great source of most of the ideas we have, depending wholly upon our senses, and derived by them to the understanding."[81] In Locke's system, animals are capable of forming "particular ideas," arising directly from the senses, but not abstract ideas.[82] Nevertheless, the Cartesian metaphysical barrier between humans and animals is destroyed if ideas come from sensation, as Locke argues.

And, indeed, Locke's ideas were persuasive. Voltaire, in his *Lettres Anglaises* (1734) was an early champion of the English philosopher's ideas, and we can hear echoes of these ideas in Voltaire's comments about the soul, written in 1764, with which we began this chapter. "It would be nice to see one's soul. 'Know thyself' is an excellent precept, but only God can put it into practice. Who else but God can know his or her essence? We call soul that which animates. ... Three fourths of the human race doesn't go any further than this, and doesn't worry about the 'thinking being'; the other fourth is still looking; nobody has, nor ever will, find the answer."[83] As Voltaire mockingly dismisses metaphysics on empirical grounds ("it would be nice to *see* one's soul") and declares absolute self-knowledge to be an illusion, he announces a world where animals will be closer to humans, as they once were, prior to Descartes, closer than ever, because the invisible metaphysical barrier of the soul has vanished.

CHAPTER TWO

The War against Animals

The Culture of the Hunt in Early Modern France

AMY WARTHESEN

The highly ritualized tracking, pursuit, and killing of game animals was an identity-defining experience in early modern France. In the broadest sense, the hunt enacted human superiority over animals, but it also defined various categories within the human as well. Future kings learned discipline and courage through the hunt, as homosocial bonding and mastery over animals served as a prelude to courtship and the domination of women—although hunting was not an exclusively masculine pursuit; Diana, after all, was the patroness of the hunt, and there were notable women hunters during the Ancien Régime. The royal hunt was a hierarchical court ritual that meted out rank and privilege; the monarch leading the pack was celebrated by Louis XIV's propagandists as an apt metaphor for the king unifying the nation in an organic whole. Cultural representations of the hunt, in art, literature, and philosophy were also occasions to reflect upon pathological violence and the link between violence against animals and violence against women.

Starting with an overview of the actual practices of the hunt, this chapter will examine some of the symbolic and identity-forming aspects of hunting and trace a movement from great enthusiasm for blood sports at the end of the Renaissance to growing unease about the cruelty of this practice and the dubious pleasure of killing animals. This ambivalence is reflected in two entries in the *Encyclopédie,* one providing readers with detailed instructions and exquisite illustrations of the equipment of the hunt (including a musical score of the horn music to be played while chasing animals through the forest), the other echoing Montaigne's antihunting sentiments and calling into question the "war that we wage against animals."

JACQUES DU FOUILLOUX'S HUNTING MANUAL

First published in 1561, *La Vénerie de Jacques du Fouilloux* was one of the most popular hunting manuals of the late Renaissance and early modern eras. A large portion of the book is devoted to dogs and their history, breeding, training, and care. Another large portion is devoted to deer hunting, and smaller sections to the hunting of hare, wild boar, fox, and badger. There are many woodcut illustrations accompanying the text, and, after all the chapters of didactic information, Du Fouilloux ends the text with a lengthy lyric poem, ostensibly autobiographical, entitled "L'Adolescence." Du Fouilloux's text offers insight into the highly structured process of the traditional French hunt.

The first chapter recounts the origin of hunting dogs in France. Surprisingly, it begins with a descendant of Aeneus, Brutus, murdering his father in a hunting accident and fleeing to Gaul: "as [Brutus] and his father were in a forest, hunting a deer with their pack, they were surprised by the night, and, seeing the deer before them being forced by the dogs, approached it to kill it. Fortune came upon Brutus (as God wanted it) that as he thought he was killing the deer, he killed his father, Sylvius."[1] After the accidental murder, Brutus flees, first to Greece, where he frees some fellow Trojans, and then for Gaul and Britain, where the Trojans bring with them *"une grande quantité de chiens courans et levriers"* ("a great quantity of hunting dogs and greyhounds").[2] Since the origins of the French monarchy were also traced to the son of Hector and Andromache (known as Francion or Astyanax), Du Fouilloux's desire to create a similar lineage for the dogs who become the king's allies in the "noble art" of hunting seems appropriate.[3]

Du Fouilloux's descriptions of different races of dogs center mainly on the color of the fur, without many specific characteristics that would distinguish the breeds. Dogs that are entirely black, white, brown, or tan are better hunters than dogs with spots who come from the same litter.[4] He gives detailed instructions on the breeding and care of puppies, and on training dogs to hunt together in a pack. He advocates tying them together in pairs, the youngest ones tied to older females so that they will learn from their example, and taking them for morning exercise. The pack, tied in pairs, should walk past grazing domestic animals, and those who show an interest in running after them should be spanked to deter them from making it a habit. Du Fouilloux advises that they be trained early on to pursue one type of animal (deer, hare, etc.) so that they do not lose focus during the hunt.

In his chapters on deer, he describes how the hunter can glean various types of information about a particular animal from its tracks, its droppings, its trails, and the flattened areas in the brush where it has lain down. Once the hunter *(veneur)* has heard from his lord *(seigneur)* or king in what area he wishes to hunt, he should get up very early in the morning and go out with a *limier* kept on a short leash, to find a suitable deer.[5] Once he has chosen a particular animal, he should determine where its resting places are, and where it eats, drinks, and defecates morning and evening, in order to better predict where it will head when it is pursued by the pack. The hunter should *jeter ses brisées:* break branches to mark the deer's dwelling place *(son fort)* and leave signs to guide the hunters later. Du Fouilloux also recommends hiding in a tree to get a good view of the deer in a particular area, and then to choose the most worthy animal, making a note of its defining features. When he encounters droppings from the selected animal, he should evaluate them, and then collect them and store them in his hunting horn for safekeeping.

The day of the hunt, after the hunting party gathers and has a meal of wine and meat, the various hunters make their reports to the king or *seigneur,* each presenting his collection of deer scat on green leaves and giving information about his chosen animal. The illustration of the hunter making his report to the king indeed shows the kneeling hunter placing a pile of deer droppings on the king's table as he eats, next to the meat and bread. (See Figure 2.1.) After hearing all of the reports, the king selects one of the deer. Having described this process, Du Fouilloux says that he wishes to explain how a report should be made to the king, and suddenly switches from prose to verse.

> Before the King I come to make my report,
> As I greet him, all must be quiet:
> When I pull the dung from out of my horn,
> On green leaves I have presented them to him:
> Sire, this is a handsome, ten-point deer,
> That I believe has gone to a certain place.[6]

The switch to verse indicates a more formal, artful mode of address appropriate for the subject addressing the king. The poetic way he subsequently describes various aspects of the well-formed excrement seems risible to modern readers, but is perhaps necessary for elevating such a discussion topic to a discourse suitable for the royal table. It shows the hunter's artfulness and expertise, and is also consistent with the didactic nature of the hunting manual; as hunters learn the various skills involved in training dogs and stalking animals, they must learn the specialized vocabulary of the hunt and its usage. The chapter following the poem about the *rapport* is entitled "Of words and terms of venery that the hunter must understand in order to make his reports, and to speak

FIGURE 2.1: A hunter presenting the king with fumets as he makes his report, Woodcut in *La venerie de Iacques du Fouilloux*, Paris, 1635. Courtesy of the Division of Rare and Manuscript Collections, Cornell University Library.

before good masters." It is apparent that social class is implicated in the choice of vocabulary.

During the hunt, the hunting party pursues only the designated animal, who flees the dogs with different *ruses:* efforts to throw them off of the trail by going through water, getting far ahead, crossing the tracks of another animal, or doubling back on its own tracks.[7] Du Fouilloux gives information about different stages of the chase, including the roles of the *valets* and the *piqueurs*, and musical transcriptions of the various coded horn blasts that should be given to indicate the actions of the deer to other members of the hunting party. The dogs, if all goes well, eventually exhaust or corner the animal and it is considered to be *aux abois*, at bay. At this point, the hunter steps in to kill the deer, using a knife *(un dague)* or a sword, but he must be exceedingly careful and swift; this is the most dangerous part of the hunt, since the deer, as a last defense, may gore people or dogs with its antlers.

The ritual of gutting and butchering the deer follows. Once everyone is assembled at the site, the dogs should be recoupled (tied in pairs) and the *veneur* should first cut off the right front foot of the deer and offer it to the king or master, giving him "the honors" of the hunt. Du Fouilloux's illustration shows the *veneur* deferentially kneeling and presenting the foot to the king, just as he offered him the fumets earlier. (See Figure 2.2.) The deer is then lain on its back on a bed of leaves, and the testicles cut off and added to the *fourchette*, a forked tree branch such as the one in the foreground of Figure 2.2 onto which go "the finest pieces" *(les menuz droitz)* that by rights go to the king or to the lord of the hunt.[8] Du Fouilloux gives all the details for skinning the deer and, respecting a social hierarchy, which cuts of meat and organs go to the lord or king, to the *grand veneur*, to the *veneur* who led the hunt, to the other hunters, to the *valet de limier,* and to the other *valets.*

Next comes the description of the ritual of the *curée*, the reward for the hunting hounds. Du Fouilloux specifies that the dogs should be watching as the hunter cuts up the deer, with the best-performing dogs having the best view. Again, we see a hierarchy in effect; beginning with the chosen hunter's *limier,* he gives this dog the *premier droit,* bringing him the *massacre,* or head of the deer, and the heart. The other hunters then present the head to their *limiers,* and then the hunters go have a drink and leave the rest of the *curée* to the valets; this involves putting the deer's head in the center of the hide (*le cuir*) and serving leftover deer parts on the hide to the pack. Charles Bergman gives a reading of the butchering and *curée* of the deer as it is told in Gottfried von Strassburg's *Tristan and Isolde.* The way the deer is disassembled in this account differs from Du Fouilloux's instructions; most notably, the deer parts are taken ceremonially back to the castle by horsemen in order (the horns first, then the breast, then the ribs, etc.) and "reassembled into a new, artificial shape."[9]

This ritual of the *curée* is the ceremonial recognition of the superiority of the domesticated animal over the wild one; the top dogs in the hierarchy are put face-to-face with the head of the animal they have just chased, eat part of its heart, and then walk on its disembodied back and eat its insides. It also recognizes the dogs' animal essence while reinforcing their subordination to man. Du Fouilloux specifies that the dogs should be allowed to attack the deer at first, as we see in Figure 2.2, then be called off and subdue their urge to jump on the raw meat as they watch the humans begin to carve it up. The king or seigneur then blows his hunting horn and all of the valets begin whooping and exciting the dogs before they are finally given the signal to rush in and eat. And then, any disputes between dogs over meat, as normally occur with a feeding pack, are ended by the *piqueurs* who intervene with their whips. For these loyal, domesticated animals, the reward for the hunt is transferred from the

FIGURE 2.2: The ceremonial offering of the foot and the curée, Woodcut in *La venerie de Iacques du Fouilloux*, Paris, 1635. Courtesy of the Division of Rare and Manuscript Collections, Cornell University Library.

"natural" *jouissance* of attacking the deer they have been chasing to the ritual of being praised by the humans who then *allow* them to eat their designated share of the deer.

Reading Du Fouilloux's text, it is clear that he holds deer in high respect, and that following his strict protocols and rituals of the royal hunt maintains the deer's status as the most noble quarry and adversary of the hunter. His motivation for writing the hunting manual is to further codify and pass on what he sees as the proper methods of hunting. He remarks: "Today, young hunters take more pleasure in the bottle than in their craft," and "I see that these days one doesn't take the deer in the manner that he merits."[10] Remigereau remarks on the spirit of Du Fouilloux's text that "It is by mastery, not by treachery, that one must defeat such a worthy and valorous adversary."[11]

HUNTING AND KINGSHIP

Hunting is one of the things that define a monarch's relation to the natural world, an important indication of his sovereignty. Several of the Vallois kings have hunting associations whose verisimilitude—sometimes dubious—is less important to our inquiry than their enduring hold on the French imagination. François I (r. 1515–1547), whom Du Fouilloux calls *le père des veneurs*, left his mark with the great hunting lodge at Fontainebleau. His power over animals was reaffirmed when a wild boar, fenced in for a court spectacle, broke through the barriers and ran up a stairway to the spectator's seating area, heading straight for the king. François, although not prepared for combat, stabbed the boar in the chest; it went down another staircase and fell dead.[12] Charles IX (r. 1560–1574) was an accomplished hunter, and showed the depth of his knowledge by writing a hunting treatise himself, *La chasse royale*. Tales of his overexposure to the blood of animals are sometimes linked to the amount of Protestant carnage he generated in his government during the wars of religion. Alexandre Dumas's flair for the dramatic had this author of hunting books (who most likely died from tubercular pneumonia) ironically die from licking his fingers to turn the pages of a poison-coated treatise on falconry in his novel *La Reine Margot*. Ambroise Paré, celebrated physician to the Vallois family attributed his death to hunting, "having greatly fatigued himself by blowing the horn and hunting, which was too much for his poor body,"[13] a gloriously bizarre cause of death that puts Charles IX in league with the eponymous hero of the epic *Chanson de Roland*. Henri III, his successor, disliked hunting, and instead of *limiers* and bloodhounds, the only dogs he is reputed to have liked were lapdogs, rumors about his ambiguous sexuality and ability to govern only worsened because of his lack of interest in hunting and his distaste for violence in general.

The Bourbon kings had this legacy of animal-king relations to build on. Louis XIII (r. 1610–1643) showed an interest in hunting from the earliest age, even as an infant, he was often brought by his governess to be present at the royal hunt of his father Henri IV. His first education in music was to play the hunting airs and rhythms from *La Venerie de Jacques du Fouilloux*.[14] In 1617 Charles d'Arcussia, the writer of an early modern treatise on falconry whom

Daniel Fabre describes as the "interpreter and mythographer" of Lous XIII's extreme love of birds, writes: "It seems that the king has some secret intelligence on birds, and a power unknown to men," and that when he exits the Louvre to walk to the Tuileries, all sorts of small birds "come to land in the cypress and hedges bordering the paths, envious of one another, as if they were all trying to be the first to fall into his hands."[15] Fabre cites the parallels between the supernatural powers in these statements about the king by D'Arcussia and the mythology of both Orpheus and Jesus. During Louis XIII's coronation ceremony, as the crowd cried "*Vive le roi!*" hundreds of birds were released inside the Cathedral of Reims. Fabre states "the meaning is there, transparent: on this day which consecrates him, his empire over birds, who also come to recognize him as their sovereign, manifests itself."[16]

Antoine de Pluvinel, the master of early modern horse training, wrote his treatise on the subject in the form of an expository dialogue between the king, Monsieur Le Grand, and himself. Richly illustrated with engravings by Crispin de Pas, readers could gaze into (imagined) scenes from the monarch's education in horsemanship as they read Pluvinel's theories.[17] Pluvinel explains to the king why horsemanship is a necessary skill for a sovereign, and a "science whose perfection is not only for the body, but also for the mind":

> your Majesty can see how this good exercise is useful for the mind because it teaches it, and accustoms it to execute cleanly and with order all of these functions [of dealing with animals] amid troubling conditions, noise, agitation, and the continual fear of peril, which is a step in the process to render it capable of performing these same operations in the presence of weapons and in the middle of the hazards one comes upon.[18]

Equitation is good for the body, because it "obliges a man to live a sober and disciplined life; it frees him in all of his parts, and makes him avoid all sorts of excess and debauchery that could trouble his health."[19]

LOUIS XIV AS APOLLO THE HUNTER

The theme of hunting in a literary context is often put in relation to love, the pursuit of the beast seen as a natural precursor to the pursuit of women. Certainly, hunting is connected to masculinity, and the varied depictions of hunting that we find in the seventeenth and eighteenth centuries reflect cultural anxieties about either insufficient or excessive masculinity, misplaced masculinity, and either a dearth or excess of interest or violence toward the opposite sex resulting from a great passion for hunting. For Louis XIV, the Apollonian iconography used in his early reign valorizes the paradigm of the young male hunter, uninterested in love, who undergoes a sexual awakening and begins to pursue women, like the young Apollo who, filled with pride in his archery skills for having killed the terrible serpent Python, offends Cupid and is soon struck with his arrow and pursues Daphne. In the early part of his reign, the king performed the role of Apollo in a theatrical production for court, *The Wedding of Peleus and Thetis,* where he opened the play with these lines:

> More brilliant and better built than all the Gods put together,
> The Earth and the Sky have nothing that resembles me,
> With immortal rays my head is crowned:
> In love with only the beauties of victory,
> I ceaselessly chase after glory
> And do not chase after Daphne.

> I have defeated the serpent Python who was desolating the world,
> That terrible serpent that Hell and the Fronde
> Had seasoned with a dangerous venom:
> Revolt is a word that can no longer bother me,
> And I preferred to destroy it
> Than to chase after Daphne.

> Nonetheless, it has to happen, it is a universal Law,
> That means that sooner or later I chase after someone,
> And even though I am a God I find myself condemned to this:
> O, how my first sighs of love will draw a crowd!
> Is there a Muse, Queen, or Goddess
> Who would not want to be Daphne?[20]

Python, as described in Ovid's *Metamorphoses,* was a huge, monstrous serpent, formed by the uncontrollable fecundity of nature and the excess moisture and slime left on the earth after the great flood. In royal iconography, Python comes to represent unrest and disorder in many different contexts. In these lines, it is linked to the *Fronde,* a series of nobiliary and parliamentary uprisings resisting absolutism that threatened Louis XIV during the vulnerable regency of his childhood.[21] This episode taken from classical mythology is a particularly fitting vehicle for crafting the royal image; the young Louis—age fifteen when this ballet is performed—has overcome the revolts of the Fronde, but is still young, not having to be concerned with marriage and duties of dynastic continuity for a few more years. The author, Benserade, evokes the enviability of the young king's position and his desirability by giving him this discourse of the proud Apollo basking in his glory after the slaying of Python. Apollo refers to his preference for killing Python over chasing women, then reluctantly refers to the "law" that mandates that he must "sooner or later" pursue someone.

Charlotte Elizabeth of Bavaria, Duchess of Orléans, known as the Princesse Palatine, was the second wife of Louis XIV's brother, known as Monsieur. She had much in common with the king; they shared a sturdy constitution, gourmandise, and a love of outdoor sports. Her letters written to her relatives offer a foreigner's perspective of the French court in frank detail, particularly the hunt. Her remarks about the king and his brother attest to the abiding associations between hunting and masculinity:

> No one would have taken the king and Monsieur for brothers. Monsieur was fond of dress, took great care of his complexion, loved feminine employments. The king, on the contrary, did not like dress, was passionately fond of hunting, and had every masculine inclination. He loved to talk of war and Monsieur did not. ... Monsieur looked upon women as pleasing companions only, and, as such, was very fond of them. The king sought for more, and had not the most honorable views.[22]

This association between a dislike of hunting and a "feminine" disposition that colors accounts of the reign of Henri III in the sixteenth century lives on into the eighteenth century. The Princesse Palatine also connects hunting and "masculine inclinations" with the king's love of war and pursuit of women.

The *Devises pour les tapisseries du roi* (1668) is a crucial text in the official propaganda of Louis XIV. The beautifully illustrated book has paintings by Bailly of large tapestry plans for the Gobelins factory for each season of the year, as well as many *devises*—emblems each with a descriptive and a poetic text and a colorful miniature by Bailly between them, in the center of the page, that constitute the visual component of the emblem. These emblems cleverly laud different aspects of the monarch's character and liken them to different objects and elements of nature that glorify his reign.[23] For example, Louis's magnanimity is compared to a flowing river and a spurting fountain (which in turn reminds us of his massive undertakings in the area of water engineering, land draining, canal building, etc.). Among the emblems in the *Devises*, the team assembled to create this encomiastic work created an emblem of a hunting horn for the season of autumn, attesting to the importance of hunting in Louis XIV's court. In the text by Charles Perrault, the hunting horn, the "soul of the hunt" is likened to the king—"the soul of his kingdom"—for its ability to direct and encourage the pack, and to command obedience.

> The horn assembles, directs, and encourages the pack, and is like the soul of the whole Hunt. It is the same with his Majesty who is the Soul of his whole Kingdom, and particularly of his Armies, who make no movements but those that he gives them.[24]

The hunting horn in the emblem is a particularly apt symbol of his cultural agenda, not only for the poetic possibilities of similes with the king's character, but also because the music of the hunt, and the form and sound of the hunting horn, was greatly refined during his reign. His horns represented a great improvement over the horns of the early seventeenth century, and many fanfares were composed by André Philidor, who held the title of *Musicien de la Grande Ecurie*—Musician of the Royal Stables.

Hunting is often underestimated in its importance to court culture, taking up most afternoons of the week, sometimes mornings and evenings as well. Beginning in Louis XIV's reign, there was a prehunting and posthunting ritual of putting on and taking off the king's hunting clothes, the *botter* and *débotter du roi* (literally, the "booting" and "un-booting" of the king) that mirrored the ceremonies of the royal *lever* and *coucher*, but on a more exclusive and intimate scale. The space of the hunt offered opportunities for introduction to important people and for catching the gaze of the king, and offered the ambitious another way of showing their merit and ascending the social ladder of court. Although the royal hunting parties generally included more men than women, women of court regularly participated actively in the hunt, whether watching from carriages, or following the dogs on horseback. The truly gory parts of the hunt, such as the throat-slitting or disemboweling of the animal, while not considered inappropriate for women and small children to watch, were usually performed by men.

Versailles, the emblem of the French monarchy in the seventeenth century, in fact, has its origins as a hunting forest where Louis XIII finally had a small chateau built so that he could come on overnight hunting trips. It was this hunting lodge at Versailles that Louis XIV chose to expand to massive proportions and to make the icon of his reign. The statue of a *limier* taking down a stag by Jacques Houzeau is one in a series of four animal combat statues in two garden cabinets close to the chateau that flank the central steps that descend into the gardens.[25] (See Figure 2.3.) These statues illustrate the domestic animal winning the fight against the wild—the hound over the stag—or the kingly lions triumphing over other big game, and allude to Versailles' origins as a royal hunting park.

The court traveled to hunt at Fontainebleau, Saint-Germain, Marly, Compiegne, and other places. But Versailles remained the capital of the royal hunt, in a sense, because it is there that the king built his stables and kennels, as well as his government. The king's equine population at Versailles—about six hundred horses—was divided into two palatial stables, the Grande Ecurie for the king's war and hunting horses and the Petite Ecurie for carriage and draft horses, whose location across the *cour d'entrée* from the chateau and whose form and appearance mirror those of the palace attest to their importance. Located just

FIGURE 2.3: *A Hound Taking down a Stag,* by Jacques Houzeau, Statue in bronze. Versailles, Château de Versailles Gardens. Photo by author.

behind the Grande Ecurie, the royal kennels, the *Chenil,* like the Menagerie and the stables, had a rational system for the containment and observation of animals; the dogs were sorted in various pens by breed and age. The *Chenil,* built in the 1680s under Louis XIV, housed two to three hundred of the king's dogs. A select few of his favorites had their portraits painted by Alexandre François Desportes, the official painter of the royal hunt. These favored canines got biscuits from the king's pockets and had luxurious doghouses made out of ebony, painted white and gilded, with red velour mattresses inside and on the top of the house.[26] Under Louis XV, the kennel was expanded to house twice the number of dogs.[27] Many people also lived in the *Ecuries* and the *Chenil;* those with higher ranks lived in apartments or rooms, those with lower ranks in barracks.

"LE CHAT BOTTÉ": HUNT OR BE EATEN

"Le Maître Chat, ou le Chat botté" appeared in Charles Perrault's now-classic *Contes du temps passé* in 1695. "Puss in Boots" can be read as an allegory of social advancement, a theme found in some of the other *contes* in the collection, such as the rags-to-riches story of Cinderella. But in "Le Chat botté," there is no fairy godmother who magically facilitates climbing the social ladder, and the despairing young hero is not particularly virtuous or filled with inherent princely qualities. Instead, we have a crafty feline who uses his wit and hunting skills *(l'industrie et le savoir-faire),* as the tale's moral indicates, to create a noble persona for his master, making the master a prince and himself a *grand seigneur* by the end of the tale.

The story begins with the death of a miller, whose youngest son inherits nothing but the family cat. Not realizing the potential the cat represents, he foolishly thinks about eating him. The cat, in an act of self-preservation, asks for hunting equipment—a sack and a pair of boots—to allow him to hunt game larger than his usual targets, mice and rats. When he receives the boots, he bravely puts them on and uses the sack to trap an unsuspecting young rabbit "still ignorant of the ruses of this world";[28] *ruses* here designates not only the moves animals make to evade hounds, but also the schemes and manners of court society. The cat offers the rabbit to the king for his table, on behalf of his master the "Marquis de Carabas." After the rabbit, he moves up to two partridges, and continues building favor with the king by bringing him game for his table regularly.

The cat eventually plants his bathing master on the route of the king's promenade, and exclaims that the marquis is drowning. "Hearing these cries, the King put his head out the door of the carriage, and recognizing the Cat who had brought him game so many times, he commanded his guards to go quickly to the aid of the Marquis de Carabas."[29] The game offerings that the cat has made finally pay off. They have given credibility to the noble status of his master fabricated by the cat—hunting being the exclusive privilege of nobility—and have earned him admission into the king's circle of favor. Moreover, the king gives the Marquis one of his most beautiful suits to wear.

The cat runs ahead; he gets peasants to attribute the field they are working to the "marquis" by threatening to "grind them up like pâté meat," and, arriving at the chateau of the estate, he uses flattery to manipulate the menacing ogre owner into changing himself into a mouse, which the cat then expertly hunts down and eats. The king and princess are so impressed she becomes engaged to the faux-marquis, making him a veritable prince. The tale ends: "The Cat became a great Lord and no longer ran after mice, except for his amusement."[30] The cat's hunting activity indicates his social standing; he has gone from hunting rats and mice for sustenance at the mill, to hunting small game in the field to curry royal favor, to hunting only at his leisure on his own estate, as pure entertainment and no longer for nourishment, indicating his place in the aristocracy. The cat is so clever with his discourse and skillful in the art of hunting that the reader has the impression he might have risen to the rank of king, if he were able to marry into the royal family himself.

"GRISELIDIS": THE CRUEL HUNTER-HUSBAND

Perrault's tale in verse, "Griselidis, ou la Marquise de Salusses," is an example of the literary trope of the hunter indifferent to love. Unlike Apollo, his resistance to love is not based on his youth and a lack of interest in the fairer sex, but a deep mistrust of women and a fear that no matter how kind and virtuous they might seem, they always turn bad after marriage because of a desire to rule. Aside from his misogynistic proclivities, he is a wonderful prince, a beneficent and just ruler, and his people entreat him to get married and produce a male heir to continue his bloodline. The instability of a government with an uncertain path of succession is a constant threat in many Ancien Régime narratives.

Despite his genuine wish to fill the request of his people, he cannot bear the idea of marriage. "In the woman gifted with the most rare merit, / He saw a hypocrite soul, / A mind drunk with pride, / A cruel enemy unrelentingly aspiring / To take a sovereign empire / Over the poor man in her clutches."[31]

Hunting is the prince's chief occupation; after he is finished with the details of governing in the morning, he spends the rest of the day with his hunters. The text juxtaposes hunting and the avoidance of women. "The other half of the day / Was destined for hunting / Where the wild boars and the bears, / Despite their fury and their arms / Gave him less alarm / Than the fairer sex that he always avoided."[32] Here, women are portrayed as monstrous creatures potentially more harmful than wild boars and bears. When his people, desperate for an heir to the throne, come to the palace *en masse* to convince him of the importance of their cause, the prince addresses his people and gives a list of the worst feminine stereotypes from the world of court: the joyless melancholic; the scolding religious *dévote*; the insatiable, cheating coquette; the arts-loving, snobbish *précieuse*; and the ruinous compulsive gambler. He explains that these variations in behavior have the same cause: the desire to rule (*"de vouloir donner la loi"*). He offers his people this compromise:

So, if you wish that I engage myself in marriage,
Look for a young beauty
Without pride or vanity,
With perfect obedience,
Whose patience has been proven,
And who has no will,
I will take her when you find her.
The Prince having ended this moral discourse,
Brusquely mounts his horse,
And rides as fast as he can to join
The dog pack awaiting him in the plain.[33]

Once again, the text emphasizes the prince's fear of feminine power, his belief that all women have a desire to be the sovereign lawgiver in the marriage, and by extension, in the government of the country. He requests a woman with no will of her own (*"qui n'ait point de volonté"*), whom he will "take" when they find her.

Hunting and women are again put in opposition by the text when his discourse abruptly ends and he rushes off to join his hunting party. It is as if his anxiety about marriage and a woman who might upset the "natural" hierarchy of his rulership over her is so threatening, he seeks out the obedient, domesticated animals—the horse and the dog pack—to reassure himself of his dominion over nature, and to kill some prey. He pushes the horse's obedience, making it run as fast as it can "at a breathtaking speed" as he flees to his homosocial world of the hunt where he is comfortable and confident of his prowess. As they pursue a deer, the text uses the loud noise of the hunt to emphasize the aggressive way they tear through the natural environment, filling the space with masculinity. "All arise and all alert / Make the denizens of the forest tremble with their horns. / The barking family of the dog pack, / Here, there, glistens in the brush."[34] The hunting horns, neighing horses, and barking dogs "penetrate" "deeply" "into all the hollows" of the forest, "filling it with tumult" and making its denizens "tremble." The unmistakable rhetoric of sex and domination is a clear subtext to the cynegetic enterprise.

But then, despite the cacophony of the hunt, the prince ends up lost on a path alone, and soon he can no longer hear them at all. The tone of the poem changes. Suddenly it becomes bucolic; he stops hunting, notices the beauty of his surroundings, and enters a dreamlike state. "The place where his bizarre adventure led him / Clear of streams and somber of shade, / Seized the spirits with a secret horror; / Simple and naïve Nature / Made herself seen to be so beautiful and so pure / That he blessed his erring a thousand times over."[35] Nature is figured as a woman, who, with "secret horror" (*"d'une secrète horreur"*), seduces him with her beauty, just as he feared a woman would. It is in this state that he sees a shepherdess with her sheep by a stream and falls in love. She lives alone in a simple hut with her father; this woman in the forest, uncorrupted by society, whom he discovers while he was looking for game is perhaps the only woman he would find appealing. She leads him back to the path so that he can find his way home. As they part, the tables turn and he metaphorically becomes the hunted, wounded animal.[36]

Having separated from the Beauty,
Stricken with an acute pain,
With slow steps he walks away from Her,
Burdened by the arrow that pierces his heart.[37]

The prince goes out hunting as soon as he can, this time taking the divergent path on purpose to find her again. After his second visit, he decides to marry her. Without telling Griselidis, he announces to his council and his people that he will wed a local maiden.

On his wedding day, he leads the court in a procession, and unexpectedly takes a turn and leads them into the forest. The confused spectators think he has an uncontrollable urge to hunt. "Voilà," they said, "his weakness is taking over, / And of his passions, / In spite of Love, / Hunting is still the strongest one."[38] The procession arrives at Griselidis's hut, where she is preparing to attend the king's wedding as a spectator. He reveals to her that she is to be the bride, as long as she agrees to have no independent will: "You must swear to me that you will never have / Any other will than mine."[39] She happily consents to unconditional obedience, and they proceed to the wedding.

They live happily for some time; Griselidis is a much-loved princess, but the prince's dark, pathological misogyny resurfaces when they have a baby daughter and Griselidis wants to nurse her. He suddenly loses trust in her, believes her to be unfaithful, and becomes cruel. He takes pleasure in torturing her: "He follows her, he observes her, he loves to trouble her / By the pains of constraint, / By the alarm of fear."[40] Thinking of more and more severe measures to test her obedience; he takes away her jewelry, confines her to her chamber in the dark. Finally, he realizes what will bother her the most, and has their daughter removed from court, saying she is an unfit mother, and although she cries, she accedes even to this. He later tells her the daughter has died when she has not, and many years later, he arranges to marry the daughter, divorcing Griselidis, who still obeys; then at the last moment a young seigneur comes in and marries the young princess-daughter, and the prince informs Griselidis that he has been testing her all along, and, having survived the cruelle épreuve, she is proclaimed a perfect model of the patient wife.

The tale ends there, the moral ostensibly being that infinite patience and obedience eventually bring their rewards; however, the premise for the entire tale has still not been addressed. The prince, although he did marry, never produces the male heir that his people so ardently hoped for. Like Bluebeard, whose tale we will later consider, his fear of women has resulted in a sort of impotence, and has kept him from completing his function in the monarchy. The paranoid hunter-husband of the text is hyperbolically cruel. Perrault even remarks in his dedicatory epistle that the extremity of the trials of Griselidis would seem implausible to a modern audience. But the concerns about cruelty in a prince who is overly passionate about hunting, or perhaps who is exposed too often to the killing of animals, and who might take pleasure in prolonging the chase or the suffering of the prey are real. Perrault is not likely targeting any one particular prince with his tale, but rather drawing on a literary tradition whose problematization of powerful rulers and their unbalanced passions resonates with his audiences at the close of the seventeenth century.

LA PRINCESSE D'ÉLIDE: MOLIÈRE'S COMEDY OF THE DISTANT DIANA

Molière's comedy *La Princesse d'Elide*, written for the 1664 fête "Les plaisirs de l'île enchantée" at Versailles stars a princess who adores hunting and hates men. Much like the prince in "Griselidis," she is being pushed toward marriage by societal pressures, and hunting is her manner of asserting her own, oppositional identity and resisting the world of adult sexuality and romance. Before her entrance in the play, her would-be lover characterizes her: "It is made known everywhere that her haughty soul / Holds an invincible hate for marriage, / And with a bow in her hand and a quiver on her shoulder, / Like another Diana she haunts the woods, / She loves nothing but hunting, and in all of Greece / She makes heroic youth sigh."[41] Her reasons for shunning men mirror the comments Griselidis's misogynist prince makes. "I do not want to commit myself to these people who act like slaves to serve us, in order to one day become our tyrants. All of those tears, all of the sighs, all of the compliments, all of this respectfulness are traps set for our heart, which often lead it to committing weak actions."[42] Her fear that men's personalities change after marriage and that they all ultimately want to rule within the relationship and perhaps also in government echo the abusive hunter-husband's concerns.

"BARBE BLEUE" AND THE STRANGE DÉCOR OF THE HUNT

Perrault's tale of Bluebeard, on the other hand, shows a man for whom courtship and marriage are—literally—a blood sport. He traps his victims not with a snare or a covered pit, but by luring them into his household with riches and entertainments and then testing the limits of their obedience with mysterious interdictions designed to elicit their curiosity. When the latest young bride, the heroine of the *conte*, is subjected to his test, she cannot resist unlocking the forbidden chamber of his chateau, where she finds the bodies of his previous wives.

> she took the little key, and opened the door of the room, trembling. At first, she saw nothing, because the windows were closed; after a few moments she began to see that the floor was completely covered in congeled blood, and that in this blood was the reflection of the bodies of several dead women hung up all along the walls (it was all of the women whom

Bluebeard had married and whose throats he had cut one after the other).
She thought she would die from fear.[43]

The manner in which the bodies are arranged—throats cut and hung to bleed
out—is how one might expect large game to be stored in preparation for pro-
cessing the meat. The "collection" of prey, all killed at different points in time
and mounted "all along the walls" in one room of the castle, is also reminiscent of the way hunters displayed taxidermied deer heads and antlers or
exotic stuffed beasts as decoration for their homes and trophies marking their
hunting prowess. In fact, many chateaux and hunting lodges had a hall known
as the "Salle des Massacres" with antlers lining the walls. Bluebeard's secret
chamber is a "salle des massacres" of a different kind. This cautionary tale illustrates the pitfalls of excessive curiosity and disobedience on the part of the
young bride, but also reveals a certain anxiety about the terrible effects of a
rich, landed, aristocratic-acting man who would confuse the pursuit of beasts
and the pursuit of women. This blue-bearded man, of mysterious origins, dubious habits, and deviant sexuality, transgresses the rules of society in a far more
profound and disturbing way than his wife's infraction against obedience and
curiosity. He has not mastered his passions for the hunt and the kill, nor has he
succeeded in "taming" or "mastering" women; his failure (impotence) results
in a frustration that causes him to treat women like game and to trap them and
drain their blood instead of mating with them and reproducing.

CRUELTY AND THE BEASTLY HUMAN

At the heart of human–animal relations under the Ancien Régime is the dominant European tradition of belief that animals, plants, and natural resources
are to be used and managed by humankind as it sees fit. A great deal of the
literature involving hunting—as a subject or as a metaphor for war, love, or
coming of age—turns around questions of the dividing line between humans
and animals. Keith Thomas describes the implications of such distinctions for
early modern philosophy.

> In drawing a firm line between man and beast, the main purpose of early
> modern theorists was to justify hunting, domestication, meat-eating, vivi-
> section (which became common scientific practice in the late seventeenth
> century) and the wholesale extermination of vermin and predators. But
> this abiding urge to distinguish the human from the animal also had im-
> portant consequences for the relations between men. For, if the essence
> of humanity was defined as consisting in some specific quality, then it
> followed that any man who did not display that quality was subhuman,
> semi-animal.[44]

Humanity, in defining itself in opposition to beasts, inevitably finds its own beastly members, monstrous individuals such as Bluebeard who lurk at the margins of the category.

Philippe Salvadori comments on the dark side of the royal hunt: "The dangerous confrontation with death, recurring with regularity, has its other side: if the king is by definition he who can take on these frequent encounters without risk, can every king ensure that he will retain reasoned judgment before the spilled blood? The cruelty of kings is a threatening theme, tied to the need to hunt."[45] In the case of Louis XV, cruelty to animals was a serious concern that threatened the future of France during the already-vulnerable time of the regency. Salvadori cites this incident described in the journal of Barbier, a Parisian lawyer and diligent chronicler, when the king was twelve years old.

> The bad state we are in makes us wish for the king's majority with impatience, and on the other hand, we are starting to fear that the King's character is bad and ferocious; he has an entirely serious and morose air about him, but he had a nasty adventure three weeks ago.
>
> He had a white doe that he had nursed and raised, who would only eat out of his hand and loved the King; he had her brought to the chateau of La Muette, and he said that he wanted to kill his doe. He put her at a distance from him, shot her, and wounded her. The doe ran up to the King and nuzzled him; he had her again put at a distance and shot her a second time and killed her. We found this extremely harsh. There is also a similar story told about two birds that he has.[46]

The nineteenth-century editors of Barbier's journal explain this incident he mentions about birds with an excerpt from the Marquis de Dangeau's memoirs:

> As early as the age of six, one seems to have taken on the task of drying up the font of good feelings within him. ... In a vast room filled with a thousand sparrows, some birds trained for falconry that were released in his presence made easy carnage of them, and provided him with the amusement of their fright, their screams, the destruction of the victims, and the rain of their blood and their debris falling down.[47]

These alarmingly cruel incidents are all the more disturbing when one thinks of this boy who delights in carnage being given absolute power as the ruler of France upon his majority. Not only does this seem cruel to the modern reader, but Barbier frames the story by calling it a "nasty" adventure that the witnesses found "extremely harsh." The shooting of the deer is unsettling because it violates one of the hierarchical distinctions at the heart of the "noble art" of hunting: he doesn't distinguish between a domestic animal raised as a pet and a wild animal eligible to be prey for the hunt. This lack of discernment is heightened by the doe's reaction to the initial blow, which was to run to her master and seek comfort by nuzzling him. Gratuitous killing of loyal, hand-raised pets for amusement violates the idea of man as the rightful steward of animals and natural resources that underlies the ideology of hunting and makes the killing of game acceptable. Garry Marvin's anthropological study of the conventions of hunting describes this important distinction: "The death of a wild animal in the hunt must be achieved in very different ways from those in which the death of a domestic animal is achieved. In an important sense, its death must be won from the animal rather than simply being imposed on it."[48]

The king's previous experience at the age of six with the sparrows suggests that this indifference to suffering animals has developed over time, and Dangeau speculates, perhaps with baffled irony, that such a scene might have been set up with the express goal of "drying up" his emotions. Delighting in killing birds trapped in a room is hardly much of a challenge for a hunter, nor does it represent any realistic situation one might encounter in the field, thus, like killing a tame deer, does not offer an opportunity for perfecting hunting skills as much as it does for inuring the child to bloodshed. One cannot help but think of the expression "*tirer sa poudre aux moineaux*," to "use one's gunpowder shooting sparrows," indicating vain effort spent on an unworthy cause.[49] Dangeau's reference to the sparrows as "victims" indicates an empathy for the birds that is far from Descartes' sensibilities toward animal suffering. Thomas notes that, among those who cautioned against the cruelty of violence toward animals in the early modern era, the safety of animals was not the primary concern, but rather the safety of people: "moralists normally condemned the ill-treatment of beasts because they thought it had a brutalizing effect on human character and made men cruel to each other."[50] This certainly echoes Dangeau's observation about the dulling of young Louis XV's sentiments and Barbier's doubts about his moral character.

In Michel de Montaigne's essay, "On Cruelty," the author meditates on men's faults and virtues, proclaiming cruelty to be "the most extreme of vices."[51] After expounding on the monstrosity of his compatriots during the Wars of Religion who "murder for the sole pleasure of murdering," and "delight in the pleasant spectacle of a man dying in agony," he moves straight to the subject of hunting, and the spectacle of animals dying:

> As for me, I have never been able to see the pursuit and killing of an innocent beast, which is defenseless and does not bother us, without displeasure. And as it commonly happens that the deer, feeling out of breath and weak, having no other solution, throws himself toward us and surrenders himself to us, the very ones who are chasing him, begging for our mercy with his tears ... it has always seemed to me to be a very unpleasant

spectacle. I almost never capture a live animal without returning him to the field.[52]

Montaigne is shocked by examples of cruelty that he sees around him, and does not want to inure himself to such spectacles, for, as Thomas indicates, Montaigne fears that becoming accustomed to cruelty makes people brutish and inhuman. He continues with an example from the fallen Roman Empire: "After one had trained oneself in Rome for seeing spectacles of the murder of animals, one went to men and gladiators. Nature herself has, I fear, attached to men some instinct of inhumanity."[53] As earlier, when he describes the desperate deer with tears in his eyes begging for mercy, Montaigne's language here emphasizes the interrelatedness of the human and the animal. *"Apprivoiser"* (to tame) is typically said of animals, not of humans; likewise, the slaying of an animal is not usually termed a "murder" as it is here. Finally, the humans, not the animals, are the ones associated with nature and "instinctive" behavior, and that, to "inhumanity."

L'ENCYCLOPÉDIE ON HUNTING

Diderot and d'Alembert's *Encyclopédie, ou Dictionnaire raisonné des arts et métiers* reflects the diverse views different contributors held toward hunting. The entry for *cruauté* owes much to Montaigne's essay on cruelty, citing the progression from hunting to animal cruelty to human cruelty, and further linking Charles IX's penchant for spilling animal blood to the massacres of Huguenots during his reign. The *Encyclopedia's* entry for *chasse* begins: "This term taken generally could include venery, falconry, and fishing, and designate all sorts of wars that we wage against animals."[54] In its "common sense" explanation of the history of hunting, it states "it benefited us in more than one manner to destroy harmful animals *(des bêtes malfaisantes)*: we hardly examined what right we had over the others; and we killed them all indiscriminately, except those from whom we could expect great services by preserving them," and "our fathers, much more ignorant than us, were much bigger hunters."[55]

The entry for *chasses*, on the other hand, gives extremely detailed information about hunting with dogs for various types of quarry, hunting with traps, decoys, and nets; it describes for a wide audience all of the secrets about hunting and trapping previously held among elite circles distinguished by class. In this kind of attention to the tools, vocabulary, and methods of hunting, the entry for *chasses* has the same spirit of democratizing knowledge as those for rope making, surgery, drawing, or furniture gilding. The entries, accompanied by twenty-three plates of illustrations such as the one of the *curée* in Figure 2.4, are written by hunting professionals, high-ranking officers of the royal hunt.

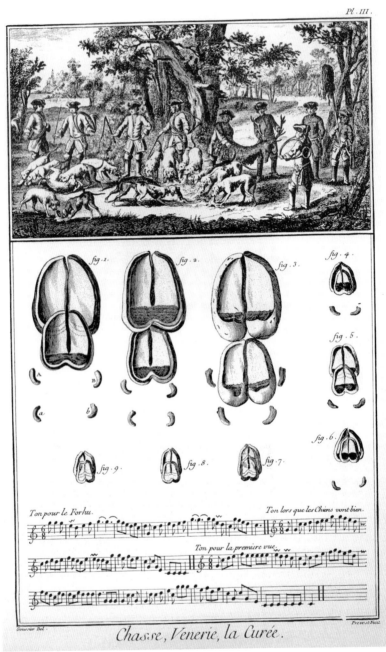

FIGURE 2.4: *Chasse, Venerie, la Curée* (Hunt, Venery, the Curée), Engraving by Bonaventure Louis Prévost after drawing by Louis-Jacques Goussier, Pl. III from the entry "Chasses" in *Recueil de planches, sur les sciences, les arts libéraux, et les arts méchaniques: avec leur explication*, Paris, 1762. Courtesy of the Division of Rare and Manuscript Collections, Cornell University Library.

OUDRY'S PAINTINGS OF HUNTING ANIMALS

Jean-Baptiste Oudry was perhaps the most famous member of the group of painters classified as *peintres animaliers* in the eighteenth century. Painting both animals from life and still lifes of game, his talents were appreciated by Louis XV, and he was commissioned to paint the exotic animals of the Ménagerie, scenes of Louis XV and his hunting parties, and a series of "bizarre" irregularly formed antlers culled from the royal hunts that Louis especially prized. His large-format oil painting *A Wild Sow and Her Young Attacked by Mastiffs* (*Laie et ses marcassins attaqués par des dogues*, Figure 2.5), presented at the Salon of 1748, was a great success. Critic Hal Opperman remarks "As was the case for many of Oudry's paintings, the *Sow* was highly admired in the eighteenth and nineteenth centuries, and rarely commented upon in ours."[56] Oudry's aesthetic—the academic style, the subject of a dog eating a young animal in front of its mother—does not resonate with our modern sensibilities. One critic especially appreciated the "imagination," the "truth," and the way the "character" of the animals is rendered in their movements.[57]

Indeed, Oudry's painting glorifies the characteristics of both species of animals. The dogs are strong, obedient specimens with well-delineated muscles and sublimely fearsome teeth and claws, closing in on their prey, who has thrown one of their pack to the ground. The wild sow, however, is humanized because of her relation to the piglets. Without the tusks that a boar would

FIGURE 2.5: *A Wild Sow and Her Young Attacked by Mastiffs*, by Jean-Baptiste Oudry, 1748, Oil on canvas, 276 × 405 cm. Caen, Musée des Beaux Arts. Photo © Martine Seyve, Musée des Beaux Arts, Caen.

have, she seems less of a threat. Although she is being bitten on the neck, she is turned toward her offspring, hearing the noise that one of them is making as a mastiff sinks his teeth in, not wheeling around to throw off her attacker. The six *marcassins* stay together, all of them in the lower right quadrant of the composition. Their vulnerability is accentuated by their variety of responses to the threat; one cowers beneath the sow, some run in opposite directions, and one looks out of the picture plane straight at the viewer. The sow is trapped, forced by the dogs, but Oudry chooses not to show her attacking the dogs. The dogs' unleashed natural fury—only one wears a collar—as well as the ribs we clearly see through their coats, show them attacking the porcine household in their least domestic light.

   Bitch Hound Nursing Her Pups (Lice allaitant ses petits), completed in 1752 is quite different in tone from *Wild Sow*, but evokes a similar maternal theme. (See Figure 2.6.) The *lice* (a term used only to designate female hunting dogs) is not pursuing prey, but nursing her vulnerable young brood. Like the *Wild Sow*, this painting was extremely successful when Oudry exhibited it at the Salon, critics praising both its affective quality and its technical merit. Opperman

FIGURE 2.6: *Bitch Hound Nursing Her Pups*, by Jean-Baptiste Oudry, 1752, Oil on canvas, 103 × 132 cm. Paris, Musée de la Chasse et de la Nature. Courtesy of Musée de la Chasse et de la Nature. Photo © Nicolas Mathéus, Musée de la Chasse et de la Nature, Paris.

discusses the reception of the painting in terms of evolving beliefs about the souls of animals: "By Oudry's day it was generally accepted that animals, to varying degrees, possessed interior qualities of sentiment and thus could enter into social intercourse with man. ... More than one critic calls the bitch 'la mère,' humanizing her; another likens the puppies to the famous sculptures of infants by François Duquesnoy; one says that Descartes (who denied a rational soul to animals) would have renounced his system if he had seen Oudry's paintings."[58] The rustic setting, the light coming in from the window, and the vigilant maternal gaze are all elements this painting shares with conventional depictions of the Nativity. As Masumi Iriye has written: "That a painting of animals could give rise to a comparison to history painting, and to a specific scene in the life of Christ, would have been unthinkable before the eighteenth century."[59]

THE VIOLENT DEATH OF THE ROYAL HUNT

Louis XVI, like his predecessors, was an avid hunter; his journal meticulously notes where his party hunted and the numbers of animals killed. Budgetary concerns in the decades leading up to the Revolution prompted Louis XVI to prudently downsize the costly personnel and trappings of the royal hunt. Not surprisingly, hunting rights, the exclusive right of nobility and wealthy landowners, became a hotly contested issue in revolutionary France, particularly the *droit de suite*, the right to follow the hunted animal across property lines even if it meant trampling crops. Hunting rights along with other noble privileges were revoked toward the end of the eighteenth century.

A pamphlet from 1789, "The Hunting of Smelly and Ferocious Beasts," decreed that a number of dangerous animals were terrorizing the countryside around Paris. Instead of the rabid skunks or wolves that the reader might expect to be targeted in such a decree, we find a listing of exotic beasts such as "a tiger raised in the Ménagerie at Versailles ... that has escaped after causing horrible damage," and an "extremely dangerous" "fifty-five-year-old lion, raised at Isle Adam, an impressive chateau belonging to the Prince de Conti."[60] Citizens were encouraged to reduce the population of "snakes, lizards, and bats" that are "to be found in great number around Versailles, Parliament, and the Archbishopric."[61] It becomes clear that it is not animals, but nobility and high-ranking church and government officials, who are the "smelly, ferocious beasts" in question. The ritual and ceremony of the royal hunt that reinforced the supremacy of the sovereign over wild, resistant animals as well as trained, obedient animals and human subjects by extension, is overturned by the revolutionaries who use the language of the hunt to make the king their ultimate quarry.

CHAPTER THREE

From Sheep to Meat, From Pets to People

Animal Domestication 1600–1800

KAREN RABER

I will make the case that to explore and affiliate with life is a deep and complicated process.

—E. O. Wilson, *Biophilia*

PET KEEPING AND/VERSUS LIVESTOCK DOMESTICATION

The cultural history of domestication in the period 1600–1800 appears at first glance to be a divided one. Domestication, the process of taming, adapting, and manipulating animals to make them both dependent upon and more useful to humans, accelerated in the latter part of the eighteenth century in response to a variety of scientific and technological advances. However, in terms of the cultural conceptualization and representation of domesticated animals, that acceleration seems to have had two distinct consequences: the vast majority of livestock animals became more objectified, more distanced from an investment of human emotion, while certain privileged animals, usually pets but also on occasion certain special livestock animals, were increasingly endowed with quasi-human subject status. In the most significant study of these two trajectories to date, Harriet Ritvo argues that the way to connect both is through a focus on human manipulation, material and ideological, of animals. In pre-modern society, animals were a threat, a source of danger: "At the beginning of this period, people perceived themselves to be at the mercy of natural forces, at the end, science and engineering had begun to make much of nature more vulnerable to human control."[1] "People systematically appropriated power they had previously attributed to animals, and animals became significant primarily as the objects of human manipulation,"[2] Ritvo notes, and concludes that once nature was defanged, "it could be viewed with affection and even, as the scales tipped to the human side, with nostalgia."[3] Love of pets and pleasure in wildness both led to the further management and control of nature.

In this chapter, I intend to extend Ritvo's analysis to the earlier early modern moment that sees the birth of the Victorian context; I also hope, however, to adjust the terms by which we think of animal domestication as a historical process. I wish to offer the reader a few first steps toward a deep-ecological argument that connects the fates of both pets and livestock, yet does not merely fall into a privileging of a paradisal wild past. If "deep ecology" can be roughly understood as the attempt to remind people about their responsibility for the natural world of which they are a part, it is the second half of that definition that interests me—what it means, and has meant historically to *participate* in nature, to *partake* of the natural world. There may be no "paradisal" wild past, and human beings may not have ever existed in perfect organic union with nature, but I will suggest that it was true, and remains true, that human identity and human psychology require engagement with the natural world, for ideological or discursive self-construction, yes, but also for a sense of purpose and connection that is not merely reducible to self-delusion or rationalization. In short, I will ultimately argue that the history of animal domestication in the seventeenth and eighteenth centuries instructs us in the twenty-first that human life requires and seeks communication "across irreducible difference."[4]

The general arc of this chapter travels through an analysis of livestock domestication that foregrounds totalizing objectification to a reading of pet culture that foregrounds the need to endow pets with human individuality. On the one hand, the erasure of distinction, on the other its creation and elaboration: two results that are connected by a human need to hold onto some simulacrum of nature while its real referent is flattened and distanced. In sum, I will argue that the treatment of pets represents an investment in "nature" that seeks to compensate for the loss of an overall embeddedness in nature, understood here as the animal world. With the transformation of livestock farming, dependency, mutuality, and community were replaced in the period 1600–1800 by alienation, rationalization, objectification, and a consequent sense of loss among the human community that required some alternative fantasy of belonging, acted out in pet relations. Remarking on the ironies and discontinuities in the evolution of attitudes toward domesticated animals, Keith Thomas writes:

> It is too often assumed that sensibilities and morals are mere ideology; a convenient rationalization of the world as it is. But in the early modern period the truth was almost the reverse, for, by an inexorable logic, there had gradually emerged attitudes to the natural world which were essentially incompatible with the direction in which English society was moving. The growth of towns had led to a new longing for the countryside. The progress of cultivation had fostered a taste for weeds, mountains and unsubdued nature. The new-found security from wild animals had generated an increasing concern to protect birds and preserve wild creatures in their natural state. Economic independence of animal power and urban isolation from animal farming had nourished emotional attitudes which were hard if not impossible, to reconcile with the exploitation of animals by which most people lived.[5]

It is this paradoxical development, applied to the cultural valorization of animals-as-nature, that this chapter charts.

A CALCULUS OF CATTLE

It has in the past sometimes been assumed by modern eco-critics and animal advocates that the history of domestication is one of progress toward increasingly humane treatment. Vegetarianism has roots in traditional Christianity as well as in many pre-Christian philosophies, but it received new attention and defense throughout the latter seventeenth and early eighteenth centuries.[6] Animal lovers of the same period began to more vocally condemn cruelty, paving the way for organizations such as the Royal Society for the Prevention of Cruelty to Animals (RSPCA) and the Anti-Vivisection League of the nineteenth century. However, this apparent historical progress is in part an illusion: while the individual moments it notes are valid, it ignores the more complex history of confusion about humans' appropriate relationships with domesticated animals, and obscures the massive scale of cruelties involved in factory farming and other modern husbandry practices. In this section I will account for the historical shifts that undergird the treatment of livestock animals. The new empirical science, religious views on animals, and the growth of capitalism did not immediately lead to vast cruelties or exploitation of livestock animals. In fact, the smaller scale of agriculture in the early seventeenth century, combined with real dependence on farm animals for subsistence, could mean that such animals were not much more poorly treated or undervalued than their human owners. Thomas notes that "[i]n many ways ... domestic beasts were subsidiary members of the human community, bound by mutual self-interest to their owners, who were dependent on their fertility and wellbeing."[7]

Of course, domestic farm animals could and did become individuals in the course of the great breeding improvements of the eighteenth century. Harriet Ritvo's work focuses on the prodigy cattle of the early nineteenth century, celebrated for their immense size in portraits and sculpture; these massive creatures participated in discourses about bloodlines, elite breeding, exemplarity, and national identity.[8] Horses, the quintessential borderline species, can be discussed in the literature of the period as pets or as livestock equally, and sometimes almost simultaneously. As I have argued elsewhere, the seventeenth-century horsemanship treatises of the Duke of Newcastle endowed horses with nascent subjectivity, portraying them as the unwitting citizens of a new, post-Civil War English artistocracy.[9] The language that came to dominate many husbandry and horsemanship treatises such as Newcastle's was the language of love and "cherishing," hardly a language that reflected alienation or blind domination. Thomas Bedingfield, for example, writes at the close of the sixteenth century with advice that a rider "please" his mount by "cherishing" him, so far as to "make him love your person."[10]

Individuation emerges even in early veterinary texts, or farriery manuals, which in the seventeenth century usually offered a compendium of venerable and bizarre treatments for common diseases of horses and cattle. One of the most prolific of such writers in England during the early and middle part of the century was Gervase Markham, who writes at length about attending to the quirks and individual behaviors of the horse as signs of approaching disease:

> As you thus acquaint your self with the complexion of your horse, which I include in this colour: so you must also have a setled knowledge in his Countenance and Gestures: and to that end you shall be careful to mark and note his countenance and behaviour in all his actions and motions, as well within doors as without; as well in his play as in his rest, at his times of feeding, and at his times of exercise; you shall note the cheerfulness of his eye, the carriage of his head and neck; which be his angry characters, and which be his pleasant; when he biteth for wantonness, or for offence, and these you shall best find out, in his Feeding, in his Exercise, and Playing, and in his Dressing; and if at any time you find any of these characters to fail on the sudden, and that his Gesture is more Impish, heavy, then call your self to account what you have done, either in exercise, feeding, airing, or ordering; for there is no doubt but there is distemperature and sickness approaching, if it be not prevented.[11]

Taking note of this elaborate set of behaviors, however, is not enough: the good owner monitors the interior movements of the horse's body.

And to this end you shall especially mark his filling and his emptying, that is, his manner of feeding, and the manner of discharging his body ... so you shall mark his qualities in emptying, as the time, the place, the substance.[12]

The good horse keeper, then, becomes a kind of psychologist and policeman, an ethnographer of the horse's "natural customs," so that interruptions of normal behavior can be registered, and a decoder of the horse's interior life: "because they [the horse's healthiest conditions] proceed most from hidden inclinations, or else accidental apprehensions, which by continuance of time grow to natural Habits: and any of these when they shall surcease or fail, are true prognostications of distemperature and sickness."[13] Horses are figured as malleable creatures, but with complex lives both internal and external that the attentive master must observe, record, and intuit.

We find the compulsion to observe, anatomize in detail, and document livestock animals everywhere in the mid-seventeenth century. Leonard Mascall's *Government of Cattel* (1662) offers a chart of the horse's body, which depicts diseases marked with small written tags attached with pen lines to individual body parts on a large-scale drawing of the horse's body. (See Figure 3.1.) Likewise the horse's body is opened to the investigative eye in Robert Barrett's *The Perfect and Experienced Farrier* (1660), spread-eagled like a dissection experiment. Perhaps the epitome of lovingly detailed anatomizing is found in Andrew Snape's *Anatomy of an Horse* (1683). (See Figure 3.2.) Figures 3.3 through 3.5 are interior views of the horse's abdomen and brain, along with an image of a foal within the womb, just three of dozens that accompany Snape's text.

The ever-expanding catalogs of animals and their diseases suggest the incursion of regularized, rational systems into every nook and cranny of the farm animal's body—or its feed and dung. The application of humoral theory to animal medicine results in the same intensification and regulation of the body that it imposes for human beings. Early moderns operated within a cosmology of likenesses, a chain of being in which the higher forms of life comprehended the lower: in Bacon's words, "man has something of the brute; the brute has something of the vegetable," and so on. Gail Kern Paster reminds us that the elements of earth, air, fire, and water, along with the qualities of cold, wet, hot, and dry with which they were associated, formed the basis not just of humoral theory for humans, but the composition of all life, and so extended into the animal world.[14] Hence, certain animals could be identified with certain humors, such as the cat with melancholy for example. "A cat's melancholy is its humor—hence a temperature, a temperament, a disposition, and a liquid of specific consistency [black bile] organizing its relations to the world," observes Paster.[15] And like humans, animals were believed to suffer disease through the imbalancing of the various components of the animal's particular

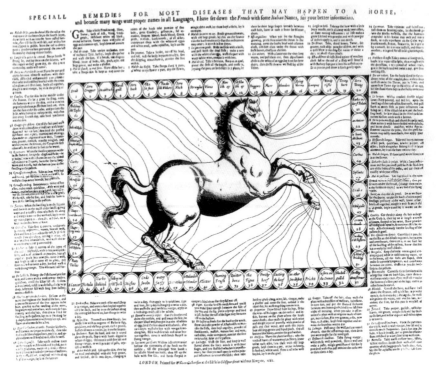

FIGURE 3.1: *Speciall remedies for most diseases that may happen to a horse,* Wood-cut included with 2nd edition of Leonard Mascall, *The Government of Cattel,* London, 1662.

qualities—feeding "hot" or "dry" food to a "cold-" or "wet"-natured animal could either inhibit natural excess and temper the creature's own bodily surfeits, or could improperly accelerate the animal's natural system. To find out what element is either missing or present in too great quantity requires extensive knowledge of the humoral system, the humors of a particular animal, the influence of region, weather, diet, and other factors, and requires intense thought and judgment about the specific individual animal as well. Such a system generates the impression of intense intimacy: after all, not only must the successful husbandman be familiar with every expression of his beasts' bodies, he must carefully weigh intangibles of individual animals' desires, choices, and conditions of life.

It is hard to imagine a more thoroughgoing form of knowledge about simple farm animals. But this kind of rationalization of the animal's body and well-being simultaneously distances the object of its scrutiny. Rather than creating a new and deeper bond between horse and owner, sheep and shepherd, cow and cowherd—rather than creating a satisfying sense of connection—such epistemological changes in animal husbandry techniques ultimately create alienation, disaffection, division for the human subject in the relationship.

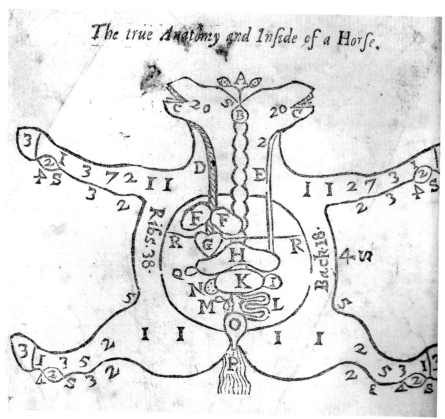

FIGURE 3.2: *The True Anatomy and Inside of a Horse,* Woodcut in Robert Barrett, *The Perfect and Experienced Farrier: Being necessary for all gentlemen-troopers, farmers, farriers, carriers, carmen, coachmen, and horse-coursers, & c,* London, 1660. Copyright © The British Library.

Although the system of similitudes embraced by the sixteenth and seventeenth centuries promised connection through analogies and knowledge, the need to investigate, to compile, to gather empirical data, turned ordinary animals into epistemological objects of the scientific gaze. When humoral theory and other early notions of bodily health and behavior disappeared, they left only the cold gaze of science to carry on.

Advances in farming in the eighteenth century have been branded an "agricultural revolution," one with far-reaching implications for livestock animals. From serving as labor, bearers of wool for weaving, and vehicles for manuring fields, herd animals during this revolution were gradually transformed from individual servants on the farm into aggregates, vast populations of meat incarnate. Sheep had been England's most important national beast, providing wool for industry as well as the platform for an entire symbolic order in the poetic pastoral. But breeding experiments in the seventeenth and eighteenth centuries and the new practice of "floating" meadows to increase early fodder

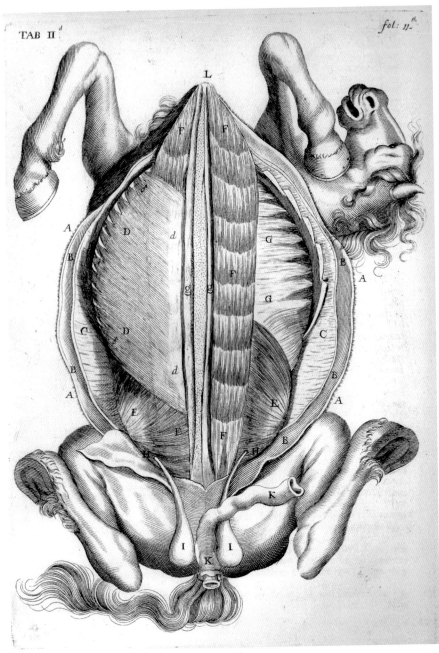

FIGURE 3.3: Abdomen of the horse, Engraving in Andrew Snape, *The Anatomy of an Horse*, London, 1683. Copy after Carlo Ruini's *Dell'Anotomia et dell'infermità del Cavallo*, Bologna, 1598. Copyright © The British Library.

TAB . XXIV.   ·   *pag.119.*

I   II

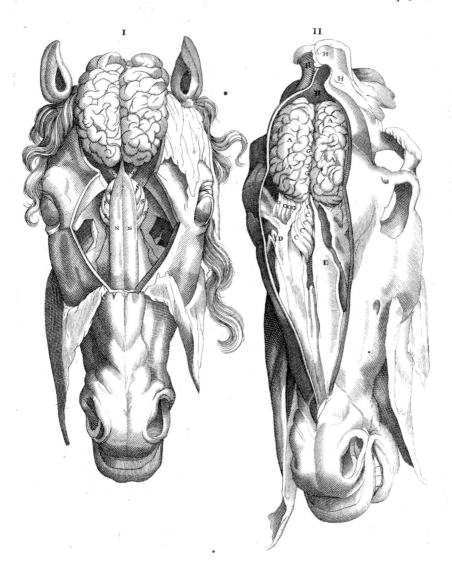

FIGURE 3.4: The morphology of the head, Engraving in Andrew Snape, *The Anatomy of an Horse*, London, 1683. Copy after Carlo Ruini's *Dell'Anotomia et dell'infermità del Cavallo*, Bologna, 1598. Copyright © The British Library.

in spring, "turn[ed] the free-ranging, slow-maturing, unprolific, bony English sheep into a closely monitored, fast-maturing, and prolific slab of 'mutton on the hoof.'"[16] By the end of our period, the sheep, Thomas Bewick tells us in his *General History of Quadrupeds* (1790), "in its present domestic state, seems so far removed from a state of nature, that it may be deemed a difficult matter to point out its origin."[17] Contradictions between the old and the new

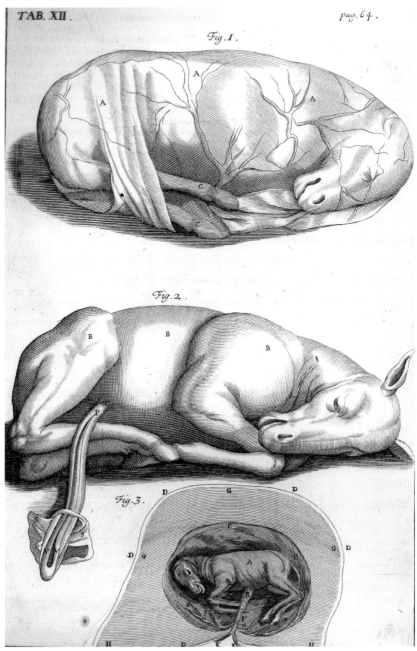

FIGURE 3.5: A stillborn foal in and removed from the placenta, Engraving in An-
drew Snape, *The Anatomy of an Horse*, London, 1683. Copy after Carlo Ruini's
Dell'Anotomia et dell'infermità del Cavallo, Bologna, 1598. Copyright © The
British Library.

version of sheep create tension in poetry on rural subjects in the period: as Goodridge notes, Dyer's *The Fleece* must negotiate the differences between the sheep's role in a "golden legacy" of the wool trade that reached back to before the Middle Ages, and its new position in "the agri-business of mass mutton production."[18]

Cows also became meat. Early modern farmers up through the late seventeenth century frequently kept cows, but in relatively smaller numbers, and often as part of a diversified household economy—often, indeed, dwelling within the house itself as part of a farm menagerie intended to address the varied needs of the household. But as crop productivity gradually improved, and pressures to feed an expanding population eased, more fodder crops could be grown and the more inefficient use of cattle as a staple food source grew. English national identity had always been associated with their favorite pets, as we will see, but in the eighteenth century Englishness became additionally characterized by beef eating. Pehr Kalm visiting from Sweden in 1748 commented: "I do not believe that any Englishman who is his own master has ever eaten a dinner without meat."[19] "Fatting" cattle became a normal concern of larger farms with herds; markets were expanded, exports increased, the systems for moving cattle to points of sale improved; and overall livestock density on agricultural lands increased. Ultimately, the work of breeders like Robert Bakewell resulted in consistently larger cattle. Unlike sheep, as Overton points out, which did see changes in size and weight on average during the sixteenth and seventeenth centuries, cattle did not show unusual changes in size until much later at the close of the 1700s.[20] It was only later, during the nineteenth century, that prodigy cattle became a phenomenon.[21] The combined function of these changes was to emphatically render herd animals as aggregates, instead of collections of individuals. Sheep and cattle that might once have registered on the rural traveler as small groups now extended past the horizon of sight, swarming to form an undifferentiated mass on the land; cattle that once might have figured in that traveler's imagination as Bessie and Daisy and Fleur,[22] now appeared merely as pounds converted to butchered meat or money. Indeed, land itself could convert into totalized notions of commodity, the distinct existence of sheep or cow entirely erased as a meditative step: W. Pitt observed of Leicester and Northampton in 1809 that "from 128 to 160 lb. per acre, of beef or mutton, is as much as can be bred and fatted on good pasture land."[23]

Husbandry manuals lag slightly behind the reality of farm density through the early and mid-eighteenth century, but we might see the problem of newly expanded livestock holdings and the changing nature of livestock uses to the farmer in the extremely general nature of George Cooke's 1771 advice on horses: "The farmer should be particularly attentive to the first sign of a disorder in his horses ... if any of them seem more sluggish than ordinary, it is a sign of some growing indisposition."[24] *The Husbandman's Magazine* (1718) likewise remarks: "And observe this Rule, that good and careful looking to, is as great a means to promote their thriving as their Provinder,"[25] but only recommends a quick check morning and evening of the farmer's various cattle and horses. More of a change can be found in John Mills's *Treatise on Cattle* (1795), which comments on the ox that "[h]e lives to a good age ... and when he is worn out with service, he is fattened, and becomes excellent food, or if he breaks a limb, he is fatted and his flesh is eaten. His skin and his suet sell for a good price. Even his horns and his gall fetch somewhat."[26] Mills also praises the sheep, which "yields greater profit to man" than any other animal, and instead of merely collecting arcane remedies for livestock illnesses, offers a historical account of how, where, and with what effects various great cattle plagues occurred in the last century, with speculation on the source of contagion from saliva in pasturage and the improper burial of carcasses. Mills's work nudges the perspective of the reader/farmer toward the increasingly totalized view of animals as profitable commodities. By the time George Culley writes *Observations on Livestock* (1786), the idea of cattle, sheep, and other livestock animals as future meat for sale is solidified in his approach: Robert Bakewell he credits with supplanting England's "large, long-bodied, big-boned, coarse, gummy, flat-sided" breed of cattle with "small, clean-boned, round, short-carcasses, kindly-looking cattle" that are

> inclined to be fat; and it is a fact that these will both eat less food in proportion and make themselves sooner fat than the others: they will in truth pay more for their meat in a given time, than any other sort we know of in the grazing way.[27]

These are no longer individual creatures, despite their "kindly-looking" quality, but aggregates of meat more profitably and easily rendered at butchering. Culley, in a method more typical of late eighteenth- to early nineteenth-century husbandry writing, offers estimates of prices per pound, and average poundage from various sheep breeds, and advocates Bakewell's sheep breeds for being "remarkable for the firmness of [their] grain" as cooked mutton.[28]

From the objects of the "new science" of the early seventeenth century to the objects of a new calculus of marketability, meat production, and statistically realizable populations, domestic farm animals become increasingly totalized and mathematized during the eighteenth century. Keith Thomas describes the changes in scientific classification during the eighteenth century, which shifted inexorably away from the anthropomorphic systems of earlier periods, so that although the human might persist in metaphors (like the Linnaean system rendered in English with its language of kingdoms, tribes, and nations), the systems themselves were distanced from anthropocentric issues of beauty, usefulness, smell, and so on: "The scientists thus gradually rejected the man-centred

symbolism which had been so central to earlier natural history."[29] Far from an
unalloyed good, however, such a distancing also had negative consequences
for how humans thought about themselves—they no longer participated in a
great organic whole, but were now clearly divisible from their nearest cousins.
Seventeenth-century Cartesian philosophy, for instance, bolstered and intensi-
fied such an experience, by dividing animals from humans absolutely at the
level of the soul: according to Descartes, matter was mechanistic—animals and
humans were machines that operated like clocks or automata, "but the difference was that within the human machine there was a mind and therefore a
separate soul, whereas brutes were automata without minds or souls."[30] While
animals might have the capacity for some kinds of reason, and while few, including Descartes, shared the view that animals could not feel pleasure or pain
at all, the broad implications of mechanistic philosophy were profound for
ensuring a gulf between human and beast, at least temporarily. In an ironically
circular process, advances in engineering that made possible new and complex
kinds of machinery undergirded a philosophy of animals that resulted in attempts to produce entirely manmade animal automata: in 1738 Jacques Vaucanson created a mechanical duck that ate grain from the hand of observers,
and then defecated a reasonable facsimile of duck guano. (See Figure 3.6.) As
Jessica Riskin notes, it is not so much the fact of a machine duck that strikes
us now as the fact that its inventor attempted to reproduce natural physical
processes such as digestion, "thereby to test the limits of resemblance between
synthetic and natural life."[31] The example of the defecating duck, Riskin argues, represents paradoxes of eighteenth-century philosophy and science that
included "the rise of a materialism that coexisted with a profound ambivalence
about mechanist explanations of nature."[32] Yet a mechanistic view of nature
settled rather comfortably and inexorably into at least one area of daily life in
the period: livestock agriculture.

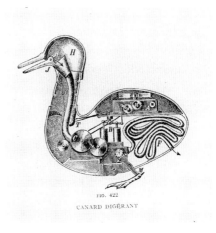

FIGURE 3.6: Reconstruction of Jacques de
Vaucanson's mechanical duck, from Alfred
Chapuis and Édouard Gélis, *Le Monde des
Automates: Étude Historique et technique*,
Paris, 1928.

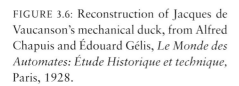

Unsurprisingly, human ideas about the animals with which they share their world extend out of, mirror, and reciprocally transform ideas humans propagate about themselves. Patricia Cahill and Timothy Reiss have described the emergence of "calculable man," often best recognized in military organization, which translates human soldiers into numerically or geometrically manipulable entities. Reiss notes that the idea of mechanism usually associated with Descartes does not adequately explain the convergence of science, mathematics, accounting, and population control practices that cast both human knowledge about the world and human subjectivity itself in a wholly new mold: "Mathematics had become a technique for adjusting the known and discovering and calibrating the unknown,"[33] allowing it to serve as the most powerful revisionist platform of the early modern world. "Mathematical reason best ordered all aspects of life, from riding horses and using firearms to more general behavior,"[34] suggests Reiss, while Cahill examines what such a sweeping assumption applied to military science did to human identity:

> As their number-laden word problems and tables make clear, these books defined men through a rhetoric of equivalence: all were imagined to consume identical quantities, to carry out the same amount of work, and to be virtually interchangeable. In this way, the military books constituted a norm based on measurement and enumeration: one that translated individual men into ordered multitudes and physical bodies into abstracted social embodiment.[35]

As with humans, so with animals: the gradual invasion of individual bodies by the scientific gaze, by quantification, by systems of knowledge, slowly permits the assimilation of the individual animal body into an aggregate, a totalized entity that translates into the abstraction of numbers, prices, pounds per acre.

Cahill argues that humans experienced this transformation into "calculable man" as a form of violence, so that literary works actually figure numbers as the instruments of attack and assault in and by themselves. That violence, I would argue by extension, migrates into animal husbandry practices, so that human alienation is made increasingly concrete by the assault on animal carcasses through breeding manipulations, expansion of herds, and the redefinition of domestic "service" by these animals as death and profit. Carolyn Merchant has suggested that the work of Baconian science and its heirs is to reduce dangerous, feminine Nature to slavery: "The new man of science must not think that the 'inquisition of nature is in any part interdicted or forbidden.' Nature must be 'bound into service' and made a 'slave,' put 'in constraints' and 'molded'" by the mechanical arts.[36] Like women, domestic animals exist to supply the matter of patriarchal domination; like feminized nature, domestication becomes the target of the dehumanizing violence inherent in dawning modernity. To some degree, early moderns observed this process at work: Bewick comments, not entirely triumphally, that "We have seen in the history of the Cow and the Sheep that those animals which have been long under the management of man never preserve the story of nature in its original purity."[37]

The more nature is enslaved, it turns out, the more humanity is enslaved to its own violation; if, as Merchant points out, "The world we have lost was organic," it is fair to say that the process of loss has occasioned pain and mourning.[38] Pets, the subject of the next section, are the sign of that pain, and the consolation of that mourning.

PET PERSONHOOD

Pet keeping was not new in the period 1600–1800. Companion animals are recorded throughout human history; England's Middle Ages saw upper-class men and women doting on small dogs, cats, birds, and other species kept as personal pets, while horses and dogs, the two breeds that consistently straddle the boundary between utility and pure indulgence, were celebrated for beauty, loyalty, and a general capacity for attachment to humans throughout English history. But, as Thomas remarks, "[b]y 1700 all the symptoms of obsessive pet-keeping were in evidence."[39] In particular, early modern pet keeping made inroads among the middle classes: "It was in the sixteenth and seventeenth centuries that pets seemed to have really established themselves as a normal feature of the middle-class household, especially in the towns, where animals were less likely to be functional necessities."[40] Beyond the traditional types of pets, a small group of other animals, such as squirrels, monkeys, and other exotic animals, achieved pet status.

Cats served an important household function as cleanliness became a virtue more universally prized; dogs too could hunt small vermin and provide household protection, while horses of course were a principal means of transport. But it is the emotional attachment to the pet animal, the qualitative as well as the quantitative aspect of pet keeping, that changes significantly in the period. Love of pets has probably always existed; but pet love was *invented* as a social and cultural force in the seventeenth and eighteenth centuries—both the excessive love of people for their pets and the assumption that human affections were returned by the pet in question. In the sixteenth century Thomas Bedingfield wrote that a rider should make his horse love him in order to more effectively train the beast; but by the eighteenth century, many people were deeply convinced that their pets could and did love them, and returned the feeling with passion. This phenomenon was initially more often the target for satire than for approval: Alexander Pope skewers shallow Belinda in his *Rape of the Lock* for her love for her lapdog Shock; the fact that "[n]ot louder Shrieks to pitying Heav'n are cast, / When Husbands, or when Lapdogs breath their last" (III, ll) not only signals Belinda's specifically questionable values, but it also resonates with wider cultural issues of gender, individuality, agency, and attachment.[41] Women's affection for lapdogs in the eighteenth century evoked fears, argues Jodi Wyett, precisely because the dog could serve, paradoxically, "as both a repository for the lost agency of pre-modern animals and a stark reminder of the lost agency of some early modern humans."[42]

Yet, as we will discover, women were not the only lovers of their pets, nor were all cases of pet love held in similar suspicion. Pet love and pet person-hood evolved among members of both genders, and in the middle as well as the upper classes. One way of registering this evolution is by looking at the representation of pet animals in portraiture; another is through the reflection on the status of pets we find in pet elegies. The remainder of this section does both.

In the first years of the seventeenth century we find an example of one fascinating pet emerging as a subject of cultural observation in its own right, achieving something very close to the status of independent individual. John de Critz's portrait of Henry Wriothesley, Earl of Southampton, painted in April of 1603, commemorated the earl's release from prison; Wriothesley was a co-defendant with the Earl of Essex in the latter's 1601 rebellion against Queen Elizabeth, and by his release had spent two years in the Tower. Wriothesley was famous before his involvement in the Essex affair for his close relation-ship with Shakespeare and other poets, for his sexual ambiguity (he was sus-pected of homoerotic or homosexual attachments to other men, but also made a scandalous marriage), and generally for being headstrong, self-indulgent, and a bit chaotic in his personal and political behaviors.[43] (See Figure 3.7.)

FIGURE 3.7: *Portrait of Henry Wriothesley, Third Earl of South-ampton in the Tower,* attributed to John de Critz, the Elder, Oil on canvas, 104 × 87 cm. The Buc-cleuch Heritage Trust, 1603.

The upper right corner of the portrait contains a painted view of the Tower from outside, and a chronology of the earl's incarceration accompanied by the motto *In vinculis invictus* ("Though in chains, unconquered"). The soberly dressed Southampton stands by a window in the Tower, accompanied by his cat. Because the earl is surrounded by messages, textual and symbolic, about his character and career, the cat might be seen as merely another of these inanimate accoutrements. Cats are rarely, if ever, found in early modern English paintings, and almost never depicted with the clarity and intensity of Southampton's. This very traditional English cat sits with its feet tucked neatly together, given prominence in the portrait by its size (it may be a small cat, but it dominates its space) and its gaze (locked onto the viewer's, head cocked, slightly cross-eyed). Since it is the only other living creature in the portrait, however, Southampton's cat becomes a main character, attached to the earl physically by the blending of black fur into black sleeve, and in every other way by the intensity of its personality. This is, I would argue, an early instance of an animal moving from margin to center—becoming a subject, not an object in art.

Cats as pets are treated by early moderns as uncanny. They are literally *unheimlich*—Edward Topsell's *History of Four-Footed Beasts* ascribes poisonous influences to cats, who "consume the radicall humour and destroy the lungs."[44] Sleeping near them causes fevers and "hectick consumptions," while eating them can cause frenzy and loss of memory. Straddling boundaries between natural and supernatural, domestic and public, even just night and day, cats are *unheimlich* also for the manner in which they defy efforts to demarcate and differentiate, especially efforts to stabilize the human/animal boundary. Unlike dogs and horses, or even apes and monkeys, cats are emphatically alien. They are abject, powerless, tiny, vulnerable, and yet they are invested with mythic capacity for evil and mischief. Cats' eyes "glister," according to Topsell, "especially when a man commeth to see a cat on the sudden, and in the night, they can hardly be endured, for their flaming aspect."[45] Their agility and skill at hunting, their placidity interrupted by extreme physical antics, motivate some to praise and admire them, but inspire fear and revulsion in others. Only in their speech do cats seem to mimic a human characteristic, and in that they exacerbate the problem. "At the time of their lust ... they have a peculiar direfull voice."[46] Cats' range of vocalization is not found in many other domesticated mammals; they sing, one might say—they growl, howl, yodel, warble, shriek. Cats are, finally, sexually ambiguous. Rapacious, given to intrusive displays of passion, indiscriminate in their partners, cats are often used as touchstones for human infidelity in early modern culture (as well as in our own). All cats, if not specifically named male, are assumed to be female—indeed, calling a cat a "she" is the common default in early modern texts such as Topsell's.

Cats are domestic animals, not merely in the sense that they cooperate with humans and are integrated into human culture, but in the sense that they privilege place over person: "The nature of this Beast," according to Topsell, "is to love the place of her breeding, neither will she tarry in any strange place, although carried very farre, being never willing to forsake the house for the love of any man, and most contrary to the nature of a Dogge, who will travaile abroad with his maister; and although their maisters forsake their houses, yet will not these Beastes beare them company."[47] Wriothesley's cat is unusual for its voluntary presence with him, if indeed it is no simple Tower ratter, since its dedication to person over place emphasizes a depth of loyalty of which it is not supposed to be naturally capable. But its predetermined status as both promiscuous and effeminate resonates with Wriothesley's reputation for gender-bending and sexual latitude.[48]

The cultural work of Wriothesley's cat, then, is extremely complex: the cat implicitly mounts a defense of the earl, whose own perceived loyalties to his convicted patron, the traitorous Earl of Essex, were conflicted and not well understood by his masters; its presence is also a rebuke to those whose own loyalties fell away upon the earl's imprisonment, leaving him ill in prison and without friends. In fact, Wriothesley's cat speaks both for him and about him: its generic characteristics, derived from cultural constructions of feline identity and behavior, reflect the earl's self-conscious embrace of his own reputation whether for sexual promiscuity or for narcissistic self-indulgence; the cat's marginality, alienness, and abjectness reflect on the earl's immediate position as imprisoned traitor. These two aspects of the cat's significance are mutually constitutive—had the earl not been in some sense *unheimlich* in reputation, had he not been uncannily ambiguous in his person and actions, he might possibly have escaped the opprobrium and suffering of his conviction. But the cat also testifies on the earl's behalf: its uncharacteristic devotion to one master, its willingness to share the suffering and melancholy of prison, its steadfast gaze at the viewer of the portrait, all insist on the earl's worthiness despite his ill fortunes, and revel in the justification of the earl's nature conveyed in James I's complete pardon and Southampton's impending return to court life.

At the same time, however, that the earl's cat testifies for its master, and precisely because, in part, of that capacity, Wriothesley's cat remains to some extent opaque, not fully available to the viewer or the critic. Unlike the other two-dimensional symbolic items with which the earl has surrounded himself in the portrait, the cat is not so reducible; it thinks its own thoughts, it makes apparent its own interiority—its separate thoughts, its capacity for independent confrontation with the viewer—via its posture, facial features, and eyes. It is not merely a mirror of the earl; its complexity is not merely a mirror of his. Erica Fudge has argued that the boundary between humans and animals in the early modern world remained problematically porous: "In the early modern period, as now, animals were not easy beings to contemplate. They raised the specter of human limitation; they provoked unease about the distinct nature of humanity; they undid the boundaries between human and beast even as they appeared to cement them."[49] The irreducibility of Wriothesley's cat invites the portrait's viewer to consider just such consequences of its inclusion in the earl's act of self-representation.

Wriothesley's cat is an initiating example of how a pet might move from anonymous accoutrement in a piece of art to potentially self-contained individual in its own right. It is not yet the sole occupant of the visual field—that is, the painting is still a portrait of a human, not of an animal. It is not, however, a portrait of an animal dominated by, even physically transformed by its connection with a human, as are, for instance, the famous Van Dyck portraits of Charles I, one of which shrinks the horse's head to render it smaller than the king's, and another of which lowers the horse's head so that the rather short Charles standing next to it will still look superior.[50] By the eighteenth century, individual animals are memorialized with great frequency in portraiture and poetry, signifying the rise of sentimental attachment to companion animals and a corresponding tendency to consider each and any pet an individual. In art, the English learned to privilege pets from Continental examples,[51] especially the aristocracy and nobility who began to commission portraits and sculptures of favorite pets. Elite pets of royalty signified respite from the pressures of office, and their unique or exotic origins, breeding, and deportment could reflect status and refinement. However, ordinary pets also emerged in portraiture and art: Hogarth's pug Trump, called by MacDonogh one of the earliest models for dog porcelains, also loomed large in Hogarth's life and work: at first portrayed with his master, Hogarth's pug soon merits his own engravings, ultimately standing in (insultingly) for the artist in political satire.[52] Dogs in general, observes Ronald Paulson, served Hogarth in many ways, representing "something of the unacknowledged underside of eighteenth century life"[53] and upsetting the superficial niceties of formal social order.

The most famous animal portraiture painter of the eighteenth century is George Stubbs, whose horse portraits are now much reproduced in print form. Stubbs, however, gravitated from human to animal anatomy (he authored a book on anatomy and provided illustrations for a midwifery book), and also focused on wild and exotic species. Horses were traditionally used in portraits of the nobility to emphasize royal control and authority through the rider's dominance of the horse; Stubbs's work, and that of other "sporting" artists like him, emphasized instead the individual animal, although still often intended to demonstrate wealth and prestige. Hence, Stubbs's portraits of named horses such as the Marquess of Rockingham's Whistlejacket (1762), Earl Grosvenor's Bandy, or the harness-racing progenitor, Mambrino (1790).

Whistlejacket's portrait is a fascinating example of the pet literally replacing the human subject as the focus of the work. In this painting the horse is arrested in a low levade, forelegs raised, crouched on hindlegs, muscles bulging. (See Figure 3.8.) Such a pose is unusual in Stubbs's oeuvre, which mainly offers famous horses posed statically, standing at attention rather than in motion; in fact, the movement in Whistlejacket's portrait is more reminiscent of Stubbs's other famous work, *Lion Devouring a Horse* (1763), which captures a moment of wild conflict against a natural background. Whistlejacket, however, is abstracted from nature, with no background at all. Its head turns slightly back toward the viewer, ears perked forward, and eyes highlighted to give the impression not only that the horse regards the observer, but that it is slightly wild-eyed despite the extreme control necessary for its pose. The size of this painting (115 in. by 97 in.) makes the horse nearly life-sized, ensuring that its engagement with the viewer will be direct and nearly real. It is reported that Whistlejacket was a rambunctious animal: during the process of painting, the artist placed the horse's portrait against the barn wall where a groom was walking Whistlejacket up and down in order to see his progress from a distance. The horse, catching sight of himself in paint, went wild and lashed out at what he presumably thought was a challenger.[54] Whether or not this incident actually happened, or is merely an invention, it indicates that artist, and perhaps owner and audience, wanted to believe in this animal's particular personality and capacity for engagement with his own image. The moment is both oddly human (the idea that an animal would recognize painted images for what they are meant to represent) and not-human (unlike human beings, a horse cannot distinguish between image and reality).

FIGURE 3.8: *Whistlejacket*, by George Stubbs, ca. 1762, Oil on canvas, 292 × 246 cm. London, National Gallery.

What I think is yet more significant about this portrait as a key moment in the cultural history of pets and animal favorites is the story of its initial conception. The horse's pose and the lack of background were apparently the consequence of the first plan to use Whistlejacket as the basis for a portrait of George III on horseback, one that would have figured the monarch in the traditional posture of so many rulers in similar paintings. A vast array of statuary and paintings of mounted monarchs use the levade in particular: it is a movement from the *haute école* of horsemanship, very difficult for both horse and rider to achieve, and so signals the elite skills of the rider that can then be extrapolated to the skills necessary to rule effectively.[55] The plan may have been to have Stubbs paint the horse, another artist render the background, and even a third paint the monarch's portrait. The explanation for the unfinished state of the painting is George III's diminished political appeal; yet another possible explanation is that Stubbs, and possibly his patron the Marquess of Rockingham, found the painting more aesthetically pleasing as it now is (and for the Marquess, more personally pleasing, given the sole subject).[56] Whatever the facts of the case, the consequence is striking: a horse here displaces the human utterly from the painting, takes over the central and solitary status of portrait subject, and becomes famous in his own right. Pet personhood grows until it supplants not merely individual personhood of human beings, but the very centrality of the monarch himself. It is as if Wriothesley's cat took over his Tower room, and squeezed the earl so far toward the margins that the human figure simply disappeared. Between 1603 and 1762, this is essentially what has happened.[57]

About another famous portrait, of John Wootton's *The Bloody-Shouldered Arabian* (1724), Donna Landry has argued:

> The Arabian struck many English people as such a reasonable being that he might be considered a confidante or friend as well as a loyal servant. Youatt records the traveler Major Denham's account of the "degree of derangement" he suffered at the death of his Arabian in Central Africa, an emotion akin to "grief" of which he felt "ashamed," but justified because the horse had been his support and comfort—"nay I may say, companion, through many a dreary day and night." Such an exceptional horse transformed the notion of "companion species" into "second self."[58]

Indeed, grief and mourning for pets is a general signal that they have been endowed with personhood, that they have, in Landry's words, become "second selves" to their human owners. Nowhere is more evidence of this found than in the poetry of the eighteenth century that concerns itself with pets.

Writing about ordinary, everyday pets became generally more common during the late seventeenth and eighteenth centuries. Alexander Pope found his

dog, Bounce, worthy of poetry: "Bounce to Fop," subtitled "An heroick epistle from a dog at Twickenham to a dog at court," sings the praises of a good
old-fashioned household dog whose simplicity and excellent virtues reflect his
owner's: "My Master wants no Key of State, / For Bounce can keep his House
and Gate."[59] William Cowper's poems on his pet dog, cat, and hare use these
household pets as witty mirrors of human folly, but without obscuring a sentimental kernel of affection throughout. In "The Retired Cat," Cowper's self-
absorbed housecat is trapped in a dresser drawer:

> Awaken'd by the shock (cried Puss)
> "Was ever cat attended thus?
> The open drawer was left, I see,
> Merely to prove a nest for me,
> For soon as I was well composed,
> Then came the maid, and it was closed."[60]

Cowper's poem recalls the moment of a cat in jeopardy in a poem written forty years earlier, Thomas Gray's "Ode on the Death of a Favourite Cat,
Drowned in a Tub of Goldfinches."

> Eight times emerging from the flood
> She mewed to every watery god,
> Some speedy aid to send.
> No dolphin came, no Nereid stirred;
> Nor cruel Tom, nor Susan heard.
> A favourite has no friend!
>
> From hence, ye beauties, undeceived,
> Know, one false step is ne'er retrieved,
> And be with caution bold.
> Not all that tempts your wandering eyes
> And heedless hearts, is lawful prize;
> Nor all that glisters gold.[61]

In contrast to Gray, Cowper allows the rescue of the endangered cat so that
she may continue to vehiculate meditations on human foibles.

Although Gray's account of poor Selima's death is a satirical gesture in
which the cat represents beauty's self-absorption, rightly punished by drowning, the real cat it commemorates was a genuinely coddled pet of Horace
Walpole. Satirical pet elegies suggest a degree of discomfort with the genuine
mourning of dead pets. As people become more comfortable with sentimen-
talizing pets throughout the eighteenth century, poetry responds by becoming

more serious and committed to pet eulogies, elegies, and memorials. Cowper, for instance, grew attached to a wild hare rescued and raised by him; the hare arguably mirrors Cowper's sense of himself.[62] Yet Cowper recognizes the limits of anthropomorphization in his elegy, and he also suggests the real "work" of companionship the hare accomplished:

> Here lies, whom hound did ne'er pursue,
> Nor swifter greyhound follow,
> Whose foot ne'er tainted morning dew,
> Nor ear heard huntsman's halloo;
>
> Old Tiney, surliest of his kind,
> Who, nursed with tender care,
> And to domestic bounds confined,
> Was still a wild Jack hare.
>
> Though duly from my hand he took
> His pittance every night,
> He did it with a jealous look,
> And, when he could, would bite.
> . . . .
> I kept him for his humour's sake,
> For he would oft beguile
> My heart of thoughts that made it ache,
> And force me to a smile.

In contrast to the gentle and reticent claim of grief in Cowper's poem, we might set Byron's unapologetic and extreme epitaph and elegy for his dog Boatswain, engraved on a substantial monument (larger than Byron's own):

> Near this spot
> Are deposited the Remains of one
> Who possessed Beauty without Vanity,
> Strength without Insolence,
> Courage without Ferocity,
> And all the Virtues of Man without his Vices.
> This Praise, which would be unmeaning Flattery
> If inscribed over human ashes,
> Is but a just tribute to the Memory of
> BOATSWAIN, a DOG
> Who was born at Newfoundland, May, 1803,
> And died at Newstead, Nov 18th, 1808.

When some proud son of man returns to earth,
Unknown to glory, but upheld by birth,
The sculptor's art exhausts the pomp of woe,
And storied urns record who rest below:
When all is done, upon the tomb is seen,
Not what he was, but what he should have been:
But the poor dog, in life the firmest friend,
The first to welcome, foremost to defend,
Whose honest heart is still his master's own,
Who labours, fights, lives, breathes for him alone,
Unhonour'd falls, unnoticed all his worth,
Denied in heaven the soul he held on earth:
While man, vain insect! hopes to be forgiven,
And claims himself a sole exclusive heaven.
Oh man! thou feeble tenant of an hour,
Debased by slavery, or corrupt by power,
Who knows thee well must quit thee with disgust,
Degraded mass of animated dust!
Thy love is lust, thy friendship all a cheat,
Thy smiles hypocrisy, thy words deceit!
By nature vile, ennobled but by name,
Each kindred brute might bid thee blush for shame.
Ye! who perchance behold this simple urn,
Pass on—it honours none you wish to mourn:
To mark a friend's remains these stones arise;
I never knew but one,—and here he lies.[63]

In Byron's poem we find hints of the construction of pets that Kathleen Kete observes in nineteenth-century Parisian pet keeping in her *The Beast in the Boudoir*: fidelity, love, loyalty in dogs represent all that is lacking in bourgeois human urban society; poetic fantasies of pet love such as Byron's are summaries of the depredations of modernity—"pet-keeping describes the fault-lines of individualism,"[64] the isolation of the human from rewarding social communion. Boatswain's heroism must go unremarked because the traditions of heroic representation do not extend to animals. The valiant dog, who embodies all the virtues that should, but do not characterize humans, is excluded from heaven, which becomes a lonely prison for the dead souls of men. The reversals (humans become insects, debased dust, while dogs have souls on earth, if not in heaven) and self-disgust Byron articulates suggest the use of the pet to explore the failures of triumphal materialist ideologies. No longer, as Major Denham was, ashamed to love an animal, Byron marks with this elegy the transition from Landry's notion of pets as "second selves" to the full supplanting of human by pet personhood.

ANIMAL NEEDS

Erica Fudge observes that "the notion of character and individuality is carried from one sphere into another. As one type of animal leaves the human domain, another takes its place."[65] Although Fudge's comments are directed at the relationship between women (the "animal" replaced by the pet) and domestic pets, the idea of substitution holds promise in thinking about patterns of domestication in our period. "Beasts," Thomas points out about sixteenth-century farm life, "were relatively more numerous than they are today; and they lived much closer to their owners. ... The animals were also less sharply segregated."[66] Evidence indicates a prolonged period of communal habitation, shared space, shared labor, and necessary communication—one might even go so far as to call it communion. Thomas quotes Joseph Hall in the latter part of the sixteenth century on the Northern farmer: "At his bed's feet feeden his stalled team, / His swine beneath, his pullen o'er the beam."[67] When men and women left the farm, and the farm turned into a waystation to the slaughterhouse, early modern England began to reinvent pet keeping as a replacement for the lost world of human/animal communion. It had to. And it mourned that loss. As much as pets are mourned by their owners in eighteenth-century verse, diaries, and monuments, pet keeping per se represents a form of cultural mourning and melancholia.

Most discussions of the purpose of pets, of their appeal to humans and their significance culturally, focus on pets as replacements for *human* intimacy. Thomas, for instance, describes pets in the usual way as "company for the lonely, relaxation for the tired, a compensation for the childless":[68]

> Today the scale of Western European pet-keeping is undoubtedly unique in human history. It reflects the tendency of modern men and woman to withdraw into their own small family unit for their greatest emotional satisfactions. It has grown rapidly with urbanization ... and the fact that so many people feel it necessary to maintain a dependent animal for the sake of emotional completeness tells us something about the atomistic society in which we live.[69]

I do not disagree at all with anything in this snapshot of pet ownership, except its relentless assumption that if humans had other humans to rely on for community, love, physical closeness, and social engagement at every level, that pets would not have become necessary—in other words, its anthropocentric view of the place of pets. While it is true that pets are a compensation, and in some respects compensatory for human "atomism," I would argue that it is equally true that pets represent an (often misguided, to be sure, and representationally complex, ideologically charged) effort to redress human alienation from the natural world. In many respects it is this aspect of pet keeping that disappears from current critical treatments of domesticated animals.

Donna Haraway expresses unmitigated disgust at the infantilizing of pet animals in modern culture: "To regard a dog as a furry child, even metaphorically, demeans dogs and children."[70] She likewise detests the assumption of their ability to render "unconditional love": the idea that "dogs restore human beings' souls by their unconditional love may be the neurosis of caninophiliac narcissism."[71] At some level, however, turning a pet into a surrogate child is a symptom of a disease that is not entirely narcissistic, one for which the pet is still, in part, the cure. As Marjorie Garber remarks, "The point is perhaps not to argue about whether dog love is a substitute for human love, but rather to detach the notion of 'substitute' from its presumed inferiority to a 'real thing.' Don't all loves function, in a sense, within a chain of substitutions?"[72]

"Loving" a pet, in Haraway's formulation, is not impossible, however: "The permanent search for knowledge of the intimate other,"[73] the effort to learn the other's language, to adapt to its needs, to provide it with joy and pleasure, requires an enormous commitment and ongoing struggle. Pets, Kathleen Kete observes, achieve "a quality of contact ... of a higher level than that between individual and most other human beings."[74] Medical literature in the twentieth century shows pets having significant physiological effects on their owners, including the reduction of pulse rates and blood pressure; the action of petting a furred animal cannot happen, researchers have found to their consternation, without attendant speech.[75] Most medical literature on pets hints that humans *need* animals in a fully fundamental, biological, psychologically compelling way.[76] There is no reason to imagine that early moderns did not experience pet love in much the same ways; the difference comes at the point of representation of what these biological needs are believed to mean. "Need" can be rewritten, as it was in the early Christian world to mean "dominate," or it can be interpreted as "empathy," as it appears in late eighteenth and early nineteenth-century literature. In the nonmaterial sense, human culture is built upon the construction of itself in relation to, distinction to, the natural world, and animals are—physically and semiotically—the most mobile members of nature.

Most recently human culture in the West has again (after *assuming* it for centuries) begun to register that if human beings need animals in so many ways, animals also need human beings. The hyperskeptical antihumanist strain in animal studies has begun to moderate and animal welfare perspectives seem to be gaining ground, supported by new evolutionary science and the "distributed" version of animal domestication (one that gives animals agency in their own co-operations with human societies).[77] Lurking in this account of seventeenth and eighteenth century animal domestication is the information that domestication has so transformed animals, not only imaginatively, but physically, through breeding (along with climate change, the shift in types of agricultural practices, the advent of First World versus Third World economic competition, and so on) to the extent that the animals "we" have created now need us for survival, for purpose, for "love" and pleasure. Haraway argues passionately for "positive bondage" reciprocal possession, and a commitment to making animals happy in "emergent nature/cultures" of training. One implication I derive from all her arguments is that they are reversible—humans not only can't escape the responsibility for the animals they have domesticated, they should not want to, since in positive bondage, reciprocal possession and training (a two-way street as any animal trainer will tell you), humans reengage with their own animal needs.

The calculus of cattle and the personhood of pets are linked, not divorced, by the fact that the two are different endpoints of a trajectory far longer than the period we consider here, from human dwelling with and among animals, to human beings' paradoxical enforcement of both distance and extreme intimacy on domestic animals.[78] The personhood of pets is no less a sign of the disease than is the calculus of cattle, just as current pampering of pets coincides with, and I would argue, must be connected directly to horrific forms of neglect and abuse in ordinary places among ordinary people. By completing the history of animal domestication, we might find a way to alleviate the needs of animals even as we alleviate our own.

CHAPTER FOUR

Inside and Outside

Animal Activity and the Red Bull Playhouse,
St. John Street

EVA GRIFFITH

During the year 1605, building work was taking place on a Jacobean play-house that went by the name of the Red Bull. The location of this theater was just off St. John Street, a thoroughfare that cut through the Middlesex sub-urbs of London. It was situated, in other words, in the eastern portion of the then-village of Clerkenwell, which has long been subsumed into modern-day London. By 1605, King James VI of Scotland, now James I of England, had managed the throne of a royally engendered "united" kingdom for two years.[1] William Shakespeare, during this year, was probably penning or about to pen at least two of his great tragedies: *Macbeth* (about another Scottish king) and *King Lear* (about a *dis*-united kingdom). During the building work on the Red Bull, Robert Catesby, Guido Fawkes, and their confederates were planning an attempt to blow up the Houses of Parliament.

During another period, long after the people of England had executed their king, Charles I, the son of King James (in 1649), and after a terrible civil war and its aftermath—by 1664, in other words—the Red Bull playhouse was end-ing its days as a venue for entertainment. At that time of a restoration of the monarchy, Samuel Pepys was writing his diaries. Within this journal, he took care to note the names of the new phenomena of the actress when engaged in his societal critiques.

There are many things one could use as historical and cultural context concerning the Red Bull throughout the period when it was a going concern. However, bearing in mind the subject of this volume, it should be stated that during all this time there was one constant when it came to context for this venue for drama. It is a curious constant for a playhouse, and, although ignored as a context before, it has always been of importance to the history of the Red Bull. The context in mind, of course, is London's animal life. Of direct relevance to the Red Bull and St. John Street, London was crowded with animal life. The most direct reason why this was so was that London needed food and its people loved meat.[2] The city was therefore supplied with meat in great quantities and this meat was supplied in these quantities through the streams of animals entering the city down St. John Street, the road just outside the Red Bull.

This chapter looks at the significance of animals to the story of this seventeenth-century playhouse: animals inside the theatre as well as outside of it. It touches on matters of interest concerning entertainment and animals in the larger London area as well as at court, and ventures thoughts on the entertainment effect of large-scale animal presence in London. The exploration of these topics will alight on different time periods, and I will need to address historical circumstances that were in place *before* the erection of London's playhouses in particular. However, because the Red Bull was a Jacobean theater, we will be concentrating on London in the early seventeenth century especially, the first significant period in the life of the Red Bull. To begin with, we must familiarize ourselves with what this playhouse was, who worked there, and the perceptions of them that have come down to us. Some of these perceptions have a direct relationship with the animal life of London at the time and are crucial to a developing understanding concerning the whole subject of this playhouse and its players. It is because of this understanding that the subject of animals and entertainment in London is so compelling.

The Red Bull theater was built to house the Jacobean acting company known as the Servants of Queen Anna of Denmark, winning, as it did, the patronage of King James's queen, a great devotee of drama. During the last Tudor reign of Queen Elizabeth, prior, that is, to that of King James the Stuart, the same actors had performed as the Earl of Worcester's men, under the patronage of Edward Somerset, the fourth earl. I was first drawn to the fact of the importance of animals to the history of the Red Bull while examining existing accounts of this theater and its company. It would be more accurate to describe this activity as "hunting" for existing accounts, as the places where such information was found were sparsely located. Frustratingly, where information emerged, it was imbued with a wholly dysphoric or subjective perception of both company and venue. It was as if the playhouse was lacking in both literary worth when it came to the entertainments performed there and moral fiber when it came to the people who took part in them. With reference to the latter, much is mediated through scholars about the net effect of *legal* evidence against the Red Bull's actors. C. J. Sisson, in an article discussing the important case involving a widow called Susan Baskervile, used the adjective *stormy* (more than once) when he was writing about both these men and their venue. He wrote: "It is difficult to conceive a more stormy history for even an Elizabethan theatre and its company of actors than that of this theatre and this company."[3] Then, at the end of the article, writing purely of the actors involved, Sisson put the matter into context with some conviction. "When we think of what is sordid, self-seeking, or petty or cunning, in these people," he quipped, "we should not forget that in the year in which the actors and Susan joined battle in Chancery, in 1623, the great First Folio of the works of Shakespeare was published."[4]

This, perhaps, indicates the nub of the problem of perceptions here, but in terms of theater history, it gives us some cause for thought. The Jacobean playing company known as "the Servants of Queen Anna" represents a historical collection of actors who had won royal patronage from a universally acknowledged entertainment-loving queen. On the other hand, it is by and large agreed that Shakespeare's company—the King's Men—were given patronage by a monarch who, unlike his wife, much preferred hunting to drama. However good Shakespeare's company was, therefore, we may state the case that weighing preadjudged morals concerning the Queen's Servants, as Sisson did, against the retrospectively admired publication of only some of the King's Men's repertoire (Shakespeare was not the only playwright who wrote for the king's company) is unjustified. In today's historical climate it is surely the case that many factors concerning the history of an acting company—their fullest circumstances and the variables of life that affected them—would need to be taken into account before we could say that their enterprise was better or worse than another's. It is also true to say, however, that very little of what is available among the legal documents of the company would seem to aid the Queen's Servants' rescue in terms of reputation. Evidence is laid bare in particular, for instance, concerning the one-time actor-manager of the company, Christopher Beeston, and his behavior over the funds used to build the Cockpit theater in Drury Lane. At one time the actors of his old company, the Queen's Servants, were under the impression that these funds belonged to them and that the Cockpit, when built, would be their indoor playhouse, just as the Blackfriars had been for the King's Men. This is the same Christopher Beeston, one of the first real and thrusting theatrical entrepreneurs of his age, who was accused of rape in June 1602.[5] Records do not exist of the outcome of this court case, although his friends, the actors, were noted at the time for their rowdy behavior in court. What we can be sure about is that he did not complete any prison sentence, as his activities as a budding actor-manager seemed to continue unabated after this hearing.

Based on the available evidence, Christopher Beeston remains a fascinating if vaguely questionable character, but the quandary about the moral stability of the rest of the original company that he managed at the Red Bull should not be affected by the question mark that hangs over him. In the instance of the company's troubles concerning St. John Street in particular, any value judgments made about their difficulties—their inability to keep the road outside the Red Bull in good condition, for instance—is, I would argue, wholly unfair.

With reference to this particular problem of roadway management and upkeep that was expected of Jacobean residents and businesspeople, we know that in 1617 the Queen's Servants' company agreed to extra taxes for not keeping the highways outside the playhouse in the best repair. We know this because on October 3, 1622 there was reference made to a Sessions of the Peace of 2 October that year that made a judgment about it.

> Whereas Christofer Beeston, Thomas Hayward, Richard Perkins, Thomas Drew, Richard Harrison and Ellis Worth have bene hertofore presented at severall Sessions of the Peace for not repayringe the Highwayes neere the Red Bull in the parishe of Clarkenwell, and afterwards upon their peticion, at the Sessions of the Peace holden secundo die Octobris anno Regni Regis Jacobi decimo quinto ..., the Court taking notice of the great charge they had bene at in repayringe the said waies, It was ordered that further proces shold be staied upon those presentmentes, But forasmuch as the footewaies neere the said Red Bull, which ought to be repaired by the persons aforenamed are nowe very farre out of repayer, and they doe obstinatelie refuse to amende the same, It is therefore Ordered that Proces de Novo be awarded against them upon the former presentments.[6]

In another record published in John Cordy Jeaffreson's edition of the Middlesex Sessions Rolls, a memorandum of 1616 notes that "Christofer Beeston and the rest of the players of the Red. Bull are behinde five pounds, being taxed by the bench 40s. the yeare by theire owne consentes."[7] Beeston was threatened with being outlawed in that following year, 1617, which was recorded in an entry that refers to a previous session of April 1612.[8] Although this outlawing has often been cited as the only evidence of Beeston's putative recusancy, it could be that the problem was derived from elsewhere. It could have been his obstinate refusal to be liable for debts concerning the company with whom he was licensed to play that got him into such trouble. It is possible that his personal dismissal of such orders could have brought about his outlaw status at that time. It may also have had something to do with the very difficult situation he was entering into over some building works he had undertaken in Clerkenwell and/or other places. Putting aside such alternative conditions, for the Red Bull scholar, all these difficulties in terms of his company, specifically here the nonpayment of taxes for road repair, are tantamount to an additional "nail in the coffin" for current-day historical perceptions. We never hear of Shakespeare's company, the King's Men, being reprimanded for nonupkeep of the Bankside roads outside the Globe, and therefore, it may be claimed, we have no other option but to judge the Queen's Men as irresponsible. Such records, in other words, seem to compound innate suspicions concerning companies other than those with whom Shakespeare is associated, while confirming our best thoughts for the King's Men's already overenhanced profile. But could it be, perhaps, that St. John Street was tangibly different from Maiden Lane where the Globe was built?

As this chapter has already suggested, London needed meat and loved meat and was supplied with meat in great quantities. And this meat was supplied plentifully through the crowds of animals entering the city via St. John Street, the thoroughfare upon which the Red Bull innyard was converted into a playhouse in a period beginning in 1605. As William Pinks never-bettered nineteenth-century work on *The History of Clerkenwell* states: "St. John Street, which at first was a packhorse road, very soon became an important highway." And here is the central concern: it was "so much traversed that it frequently became out of repair."[9] Evidence abounds of the truth of this statement. St. John Street was the direct route in and out of the city for all kinds of living goods, human and animal. However, it was the only direct route for livestock making their way into the city via Smithfield, which was an area, in turn, that was the only space set aside for the sale of such livestock.[10] William Fitzstephen, the chronicler, mentioned Smithfield in 1174 where he described the "smooth field" where "every Friday there is a celebrated rendezvous of fine horses to be sold, and in another quarter are placed vendibles of the peasant, swine with their deep flanks, and cows and oxen of immense bulk."[11]

Herded from far-flung places all over the island mass of Britain, the animals would be taken first to this noisy space where they would be assessed and then sold to butchers for slaughter and profit within the city walls. Important to the history of this livestock market, its associated trade, and the thoroughfare that took the animals down to it are the Smithfield "Bars," barriers denoting civic jurisdiction, which were set up at the bottom of St. John Street before the beginning of the market. These had been consolidated as a legal entity in 1222 and this time, presumably, marks an important moment along a journey where the area that was technically outside the City of London's walls was to be regarded as subsumed into the city as part of Farringdon Ward.[12] By 1393 this enormous section of the city was considered of too cumbersome a size and was divided in two, the ward that included Smithfield becoming the "Ward of Farringdon Without."[13] The "bars" were literally a combination of chain and wooden pole where a visitor would encounter a control point, assessing the person, and, if there were any, animals as well. At the market, tolls and taxes were chargeable, for one was now entering London even while remaining, technically, outside its walls. It was here, at these bars at the bottom of St. John Street, that the ward structure "without" the city walls began and therefore the city itself ensued—where the Middlesex suburbs ended, and where London life opened out. Once in Smithfield, the drovers were charged for their stock: one penny on each ox or cow and a similar sum for twelve sheep in the thirteenth century. The animals would be displayed and bought at the market and then led on into the city proper through the gate of Newgate to St. Nicholas Shambles.[14] This was one usual place in London set aside for the slaughter of livestock by London's butchers.

Now one would assume that it would serve the country farmer and drover well to get the best price for their goods well outside the city before coming into the "suburbs" that Clerkenwell and St. John Street represented. By doing this they would have avoided the tolls, etc., and we know that it may have suited the free butchers of London too if they had been able to do this, entitled, as freemen are, to bring their newly bought animals into the city without charge. But the city wanted its tolls, and buying animal stock outside the city was strictly forbidden.[15] In 1439 the butchers' guild made an ordinance. It stated that "no freeman of the craft should ride to fairs in Essex or elsewhere to buy cattle of drovers on their way to the market of Smithfield." It also declared that no one should "buy and sell at the second, third or fourth hand, by which re-sales prices were raised to the grievous hurt of the citizens." This offense was known as "regrating."[16]

Records also exist that demonstrate to what extent the purchase of any livestock outside the city's walls in Smithfield, which had to be brought within the walls to the butchers' property, was a trial to those concerned. This was particularly pertinent to the matter of what the butchers of London did with the livestock after purchase and removal to their slaughter areas. For instance, in 1361, the first ordinance of Parliament was passed "for the slaughter of all great beasts outside the City" and Knightsbridge was suggested as the area where both the killing and the cleaning of the animals should take place. This act was reenacted and confirmed on several occasions, the concern about the flouting of these matters resulting in writs and orders from the king to the mayor and aldermen.[17] However, slaughtering and cleaning the carcasses *outside* the city was regarded as an inconvenient idea and was resisted by the butchers. Perhaps this is no surprise in view of the fact that, because of city interests, they had been forced to buy the animals from a site *inside* city jurisdiction. It may have added insult to injury to expect them to take them outside again to be processed.

From the foregoing account I hope we may begin to see to what extent Smithfield, and therefore St. John Street, was a busy place in terms of animal life. Market days at Smithfield were recorded as Wednesdays and Fridays;

however, animals were driven along the street outside the gates of the playhouse all week in preparation for sale.[18] In April 1612 a Monday market was agreed at a time when the suburbs just to the north of the bars were truly burgeoning. Hicks Hall, a courthouse serving the whole Middlesex area, suburbs, and county, was completed at the bottom of St. John Street in that same year.[19] Sir Hugh Myddelton's New River venture, supplying fresh water to London, was soon to be opened the following year, 1613, at the northern boundary of Clerkenwell.[20] At this time the Red Bull playhouse had been up and running for at least six years. Ostensibly, the company who played there was financially managed by Christopher Beeston; however, up until this time it had been led by Thomas Greene, its clown, and Greene, unfortunately, died during 1612.[21] While the suburban area where the theater was located was growing and finding its feet, the fortunes of the Red Bull and its company were taking a turn for the worse. However, it was not all smooth sailing for the meat trade either.

Such was the business of butchery at this time that, unfortunately, disputes about the activity of freemen and nonfreemen had flared up from the beginning of the century with different times argued when freemen and nonfreemen could start trading at the London market. Because of time restrictions favoring the London butchers, it was said that nonfreemen were going to Barnet Market to make their purchases, affecting sales at Smithfield. By 1631, the people from around the Barnet area were accusing London butchers of buying their own grazing land outside the city, thereby controlling elements of the livestock coming into London to be bought. The attorney general of the time found, after complaints about the suppression of Barnet Market by the London butchers, that this was indeed the case. Evidence exists that London butchers became substantial graziers into the later seventeenth century.[22] However, in many cases, it may well have been true that the butchers' ancestors had been farmers in the first place. The citizens of London of whatever trade were made up of one-time apprentices, many of whom started their lives outside the city in the nation beyond its jurisdiction. It has been noted that the origins of London apprentice butchers in the late sixteenth century can be easily traced to areas of livestock breeding and trading. These include areas such as the Midlands, Wiltshire, and Somerset, and surprisingly few from counties closer to home such as Hertfordshire, where objections to London butcher grazing activity were mounted, or other bigger areas such as East Anglia.[23] We may therefore acknowledge a situation where the lines of community contact for London butchers in the country at large bore some significance when it came to "home counties" complaint. Many butchers had no point of reference with communities closer to the city and therefore it is unsurprising that farmers nearby found it easy to complain. It also means that if many of the London butchers were originally from farming communities in the Midlands, in particular, and "indulging" in grazing animals in the fields outside the city to their benefit inside it, they were not, at least, without knowledge of the farmers' skill in grazing. In turn this means that whether they were illegally cutting out the middlemen or not, they were supposedly entitled to feel familiarly appropriate to the task.[24] More evidence exists of butchers going even further afield for livestock—to Northampton, Hanging Houghton, Boston, and Sleaford, for instance.[25]

The Red Bull playhouse, then, named after an animal not unrelated to farmer interests and placed not far from other self-referentially drover-related places such as "Cowcross Street" and "Turnbull Street," was sited amid all the noise and bustle of this animal and human activity. And it is likely that the inn associated with the yard that was converted into the playhouse catered much of the time to the people involved in the trafficking of these animals. It is even possible that before its playhouse conversion, the Red Bull's yard accepted herds of animals before the drovers entered Smithfield bars.[26] However, this is speculation, and we have, as yet, only touched on one area of the animal action that took place around, about, and possibly inside the theater.

Smithfield not only sold livestock for London consumption but also sold horses for transport purposes and prominently so. When it comes to depicting Smithfield, for example, on the much-cited "'Agas' map of the 1560s, it is not the butchers' interests that are displayed but the horse-buyers."[27] (See Figure 4.1.) A few "farmyard" animals are shown in the area marked as "Schmyt Fyeld" with a suggestion of drovers and stalls. However, most prominent among the beasts depicted is an illustration of a man mounted upon a rearing horse, the animal's front legs pointing toward "Litle Britaine," the street leading to Aldersgate and the city beyond. Of interest to historians in subject areas such as the nobility living in London's suburbs, the literary activity of people in and around the Red Bull, and the subject of horses is the fact that the Duke of Newcastle possessed a residence near the site of the playhouse. William Cavendish and Margaret, his wife, are both known as writers as well as remarkably expressive characters from history, William spending much of his time training horses at the Cavendish great house, Welbeck Abbey in Nottinghamshire. When in London, however, Newcastle had a home at Newcastle House, built in the 1630s and located on the ruins of the cloisters of St. Mary's nunnery. The St. Mary's nunnery land also supplied the post-Reformation once-monastic site for the Red Bull.[28] It is not known if the Cavendishes attended performances at the Red Bull or, indeed, if any of their plays were ever performed there, and we only have evidence of both of them staying at Newcastle House as a couple in 1667.[29] However, it is a happenstance too obvious to ignore that the Cavendish household was near to Smithfield, the foremost horse market in the country, and that this must have had an effect upon the Duke's activity there. Time and again in the considerable span of history that includes the life of William Cavendish, mention is made of his talent with horse management or the skill of horse "manège." His skill in horsemanship was well known—he taught Charles II how to ride—and friends received advice on the buying and breeding of horses and their training. It is said that of all his works his "real labour of love" was a book on horsemanship, published in French for a continental audience, called *La Métholde Nouvelle et Invention Extraordinaire de Dresser les Chevaux*.[30] With reference to horses too, Thomas Bedingfeld, a relative of the leasehold owner of the Red Bull, translated an Italian work about equine matters, which he called *The Art of Riding, Conteining diuerse necessarie instructions, demonstrations, helps, and corrections apperteining to horssemanship, not heretofore expressed by anie other Author*. At the time of its publication in 1584, he had been a Gentleman-Pensioner to the Queen from 1567 and held a share of the playing cards monopoly with one Ralph Bowes (he gave up his share to Bowes in 1585). In 1603, in the same year he gave up his position as pensioner, he became Master of the Tents and Toils.[31] Interestingly, this was a position associated with that of the entertainment-centered "Revels" office because it involved the storage of court materials that might have been used for entertainment-related occasions.[32] The buildings where these materials were kept, and where, for example, the Master of the Revels looked over scripts and saw rehearsals of plays, was located at the old St. John's Priory in Clerkenwell only a little way from both Smithfield and the Red Bull. This was also where the Master of the Tents and Toils held an office-related residence. As well as this, there was also a long-term Bedingfeld residence at St. Bartholomew's, directly adjacent to Smithfield, although it is not known exactly where this residence was or which sixteenth-century Bedingfeld lived there.[33] Not far away in Cow Lane, a street leading off Smithfield to the west, the dramatist John Webster and his family were engaged in their coach-making business, again horse-related. Webster's father, made free of the Merchant Taylors' company in 1571, undoubtedly chose the spot as useful for his business. Webster's dramatic work, which found a home at the Red Bull on a number of occasions, may well have been undertaken in parallel with his own participation in the family trade. He himself was admitted into the Merchant Taylors through patrimony in 1615 after his father's death the year before.[34]

Apart from human beings with horse-related interests, the horse, too, had an undoubted bearing upon the very nature of the Red Bull. For, as a one-time yard to an inn, for the majority of the time certainly, it had been the place where horses were kept while their owners stayed at the Red Bull inn proper. Once this is acknowledged, along with the possibility of more active drover-use of the Red Bull's yard (and as one must attempt to do in the cases of other converted innyards such as the Boar's Head in Whitechapel and the first innyard playhouse conversion that we know of, the Red Lion), a certain sense of playhouse ambience is recognized. It is understood that when

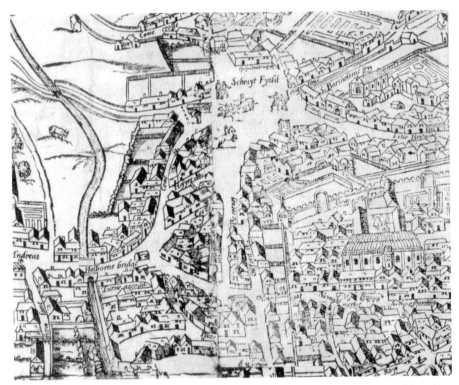

FIGURE 4.1: The Smithfield and Newgate areas, detail from "Agas" map of London, ca. 1562. Guildhall Library, City of London.

drama entered the innyard, it was the animal that presided there *first*, and a realization that animal activity once took precedence within a space makes imagining that space an action that carries a sense of a continuum. Perhaps to illustrate this idea further, it might not be a complete surprise to hear that by the early nineteenth century, the site that was once the Red Bull yard had reverted to a place that catered to animals. Not as a place to keep beasts but as a place for storing their hay.[35]

In the early seventeenth century, then, one may imagine a London and its suburbs permeated with necessary animal/human activity of all kinds, but the most obvious animal/human activity that must be of interest here is that found within the entertainment world itself. Very little evidence exists of whether real "live" animals or men dressed up as animals appeared upon the English stage in Shakespeare's time.[36] However, there are many references to animals and one or two animal appearances—even manifestations—in texts. As for those kinds of animal entertainment that took place outside the playhouse, it would appear that sixteenth- to early seventeenth-century audiences were well acquainted with them. One such animal entertainer was Morocco, the famous performing horse, managed by "Banks"—first name uncertain—who led the animal to practice tricks and stunts before audiences in London and all over

Europe.[37] Morocco or Marocco, as the horse's name was sometimes spelled, was able to pick out people named by his master, count money, and climb steps. This last feat found its zenith when the horse climbed the steps to the top of St. Paul's Cathedral in about 1600. First recorded in Shrewsbury in 1591, by 1598 he appeared in an epigram in *Chrestoleros* by Thomas Bastard: "*Bankes* hath a horse of wondrous qualitie, | For he can fight, and pisse, and daunce, and lie. | And finde your purse, and tell what coyne ye have. | But *Bankes*, who taught your horse to smel a knave?"[38]

According to a pamphlet published in 1611 and entitled *Tarlton's Jests*, Banks exhibited his horse "of strange qualities ... at the Crosse Keyes in Gracious-streete." In an earlier pamphlet of 1595, *Maroccus extaticus*, "or Bankes Bay Horse in a Trance" (which was more a satirical note of the times than a description of the horse's tricks), he was performing at the Belsavage without Ludgate. Both these innyards had been used as venues for human dramatic performance, but here, perhaps, the point should be remembered that horses occupied these spaces first; they were intended for them, and therefore, in a sense, Morocco was much more appropriate to the entertainment performance arena and occasion.[39] In 1601 Morocco was taken to Paris where he met with some difficulties in terms of the country's understanding of what a trick-performing horse might mean. A magistrate of the city thought the tricks could only be possible by nefarious magic and both trainer and horse were imprisoned for a time until Banks demonstrated to the authorities how he controlled Morocco by signs. He is also recorded as a horse that could find people in the crowd with religious symbols about them, and this was also interpreted as akin to devilry. Trainer and horse also visited Frankfurt and Brunswick-Wolfenbuttel early in the new century; and references to Morocco continued well into the period long after the original animal must have died.

The exotic beast, too, found its place in Jacobean society. Ben Jonson's play, *Bartholomew Fair*, dated to the year 1614, is set in Smithfield, and references to animals and their entertainment potential abound within the play, from eating pigs to horse coursing and hobbyhorse selling. The play takes its fullest inspiration from the summer fair held once a year at the livestock market around the feast of St. Bartholomew (August 24). But before the play proper, the stagekeeper of the venue where the play is performed makes a speech referring to "a juggler with a well-educated ape." The animal in question, one that was recognizable to an audience in 1614, could "come over the chain for the King of England, and back again for the Prince, and sit still on his arse for the Pope and the King of Spain!"[40] The animal and self-referential nature of the speech is compounded by the fact that the venue for the play was the Hope playhouse—a Philip Henslowe managerial enterprise that doubled as a bear-baiting arena. The capacity of the stagekeeper is clear, for the Book-holder who speaks with the Stagekeeper after his speech is amazed at his presumption in sharing his "judgement" with the audience: "Your judgement, rascal? For what? Sweeping the stage? Or gathering up the broken apples for the bears within?"[41]

The appropriateness of a bear-baiting arena to evoke the atmosphere of an August fair held at the site of the city's livestock market needs no further comment; however, it is worth noting that this is another instance where drama was enacted at a place where animals presided *first*.

The Red Bull too, apparently, was a venue where at one time horses and possibly other animals had been installed and where—once converted into a theater—plays were performed that included both vivid imagery associated with animals and representations of members of the animal kingdom. With reference to the former, early modern drama was fond of using the imagery of animal disease, especially the term the *staggers*, which, in the *Oxford English Dictionary*, is defined as "a name for various diseases affecting domestic animals, of which a staggering gait is a symptom." It was therefore used more generally to denote a giddy feeling as in Shakespeare's *Cymbeline* (V, 5) when Posthumous strikes Imogen disguised as his page:

> *Pisanio*:
> O gentlemen help
> Mine and your mistress! O my Lord Posthumous,
> You ne'er kill'd Imogen till now! Help, help!
> Mine honor'd lady!
> *Cymbeline*:
> Does the world go round?
> *Posthumous*:
> How come these staggers on me?
> *Pisanio*:
> Wake, my mistress![42]

In Thomas Heywood's *The Rape of Lucrece*—a popular play about the engendering of Rome's first republic and originally performed at the Red Bull ca.1607—the character Valerius, who peppers the play with popular song, uses the word to describe the current state of political affairs. "No doubt *Colatine* no doubt," he says, "heres a giddy and drunken world, it Reeles, it hath got the staggers, the commonwealth is sick of an Ague, of which nothing can cure her but some violent and sudden affrightment."[43]

Thomas Greene, the aforementioned clown and leader of the Queen's Servants, as well as owner of half the tiring house and yard of the playhouse until his death in 1612, was apparently known for his impersonation of a baboon.[44] Greene would have also played the part of the Clown in Thomas Heywood's two-part *If You Know Not Me You Know Nobody*. This character has a particular relationship to an animal that may have been represented by the real thing. The first part of this play, written by the company's own actor-dramatist (akin to Shakespeare in nature of company membership), was directly taken from John Foxe's *Actes and Monuments*. This was the large-scale folio Protestant propaganda book that through various edicts made in the 1570s found its way into the book inventories of bishops, archbishops, and those of most London civic authorities.[45] In the book, Foxe told his tale of the heroism of the then-queen when she was only the Princess Elizabeth under her Catholic sister, Queen Mary. Popularly known as "the Troubles" of the Princess Elizabeth, Heywood made full use of Foxe's stories, especially the part where she was looked after by "Sir Henry Beningfield."[46] The real person behind the character of Sir Henry was otherwise known as Sir Henry Bedingfeld, privy councillor to Queen Mary, a dedicated Catholic beyond Queen Mary's death and the father of Thomas, the Master of the Tents and Toils mentioned earlier. In the plot of the book, Bedingfeld, vicariously spelled as "Benifield" by Foxe, is portrayed as somebody unknown to Elizabeth and somewhat frightening. In one extract he is shown to be overbearing in his care of her because of a matter concerning a goat. The man who discovers it near her room protests to the princess that he must show the beast to Bedingfeld in case it were a dangerous friend of hers. In the play the scene is extended, taking place between the Clown and a ridiculously careful "Beningfield," who takes the security threat of the goat very seriously indeed:

Enter Clown.
Clown. O, Sir *Harry!* you looke well to your office:
Yonders one in the garden with the Princesse.
Bening. How, knaue ! with the Princesse? she parted euen now.
Clown. I sir, that's all one; but shee no sooner came into the Garden,
    but he leapt ore the wall; and there they are together busy in talke sir.
Bening. Here's for thy paines: thou art an honest fellow.
Go, take a guard, and apprehend them straight. *Exit Clown.*
Bring them before me.—O this was well found out.
Now will the Queene commend my diligent care,
And praise me for my seruice to her Grace.
Ha! traitors swarm so neare about my house?
Tis time to look into't—Oh, well said, *Barwicke.*
Where's the prisoner?
Enter Clown, Barwick, and *Soldiers, leading a goat: his sword drawne.*
Clown. Here he is, in a string, my lord.
Bening. Lord bless vs! Knaue, what hast thou there?
Clown. This is he I told you was busy in talk with the Princesse. What
    a did there, you must get out of him by examination.

Bening. Why, knaue, this is a beast.

Clown. So may your worship be, for any thing that I know.

Because of this impertinence in the play, the Clown gets a beating.[47] It is presumed that a real goat was used on stage; although, as stated before, it is a
point of contention with scholars whether there is any proof that real animals
appeared or whether a man pretended to be the animal concerned. From the
debate about real bears on the public stage to the knowledge of real bears
baited or simply viewed (like those kept cheek by jowl with the lions at the
Tower of London), alongside the certainties of men who made themselves
look like animals both real and mythical, it is clear that London saw a mix of
animals both in the flesh for entertainment, and embodied in entertaining representation.[48] While goats and bears were possible on the public stages of London and bears and lions were viewed with relish by King James at the Tower,
the safety of the heir to the throne, Prince Henry, could so easily have been
seen as in jeopardy in view of his taking part in Ben Jonson's masque *Oberon*.
According to the text, he entered as the fairy prince "*in a chariot ... drawne by
two white beare*s," and some thought has gone into what kind of bear could
have been used and what age they could have been, if real bears were used.[49]
For myself, and with reference to *If You Know Not Me*, it is hard to imagine
that a *local* culture, particularly the Red Bull/Smithfield culture, so permeated
with farmyard animal life could have considered anything other than the use of
a real goat for the Heywood play. To lend credence to other possibilities, as this
first play was only published in 1605, when we know the Red Bull was being
built, it is possible that the drama was first performed at a slightly less animal-
orientated venue called the Boar's Head in Whitechapel. This was one place
we know the Earl of Worcester's men played before they became the Servants
of Queen Anna. It could have also received its first performance at another
venue associated with this company, such as the Curtain in Shoreditch, or even
the Rose on the Bankside. Neither of these last two venues were particularly
animal-related. However, with repeat publications in 1606, 1608, 1610, 1613,
and even 1623, 1632, and 1639, *If You Know Not Me* Part I was almost certainly performed at Heywood's Red Bull in the later years of the company's
time there and continued to be performed after the company had officially
come to an end.[50]

Again written by Heywood, the *Ages* plays are another instance of the use
of animals, or, at least, more creative mythological animal references drawn
from the stories of classical Greece and Rome. And here, one imagines, the
only way to evoke these animals was through manmade props, costumes,
and special effects. Thomas Heywood's *The Golden Age*, *The Silver Age*, *The
Brazen Age*, and the two-part *The Iron Age I* and *The Iron Age II* are most
immediately referred to as plays demonstrating the power of spectacle. They

border, in fact, on the masque-like in many instances, particularly with the earlier three, where the *Iron Age* plays display more muscular battle-orientated kinds of effect. Masque-like spectacle is obvious in the case of *The Silver Age* (London, 1613), for instance, where, after "*Thunder and lightning,*" "*Iupiter appeares in his glory under a Raine-bow, to whom they all kneele.*"[51] Pluto somehow arrives on stage in a chariot drawn by devils at one point in the play; the Earth rises from beneath the stage at another point as does the River Arethusa at another soon after; and Juno and Iris are somehow "*plac'd*" above in a cloud at another.[52] Most spectacular of all in the play is a scene near the end where Semele's bed catches fire at the amorous touch of Jupiter.[53] How all this was managed at the converted innyard off St. John Street is never quite explained; we are simply asked to believe that it was. For animal reference and for fancy's sake, this same play also managed to convey the idea of centaurs, those half-man, half-horse mythological inventions of classical times. These kinds of creature, evoked by actors, must have seemed more relevant, if still extraordinary and fantastical, to Red Bull audiences accustomed to the utility and character of the horse than we could be today. And with four-legged, fully qualified horses being sold at the market only a little way from the theater, something of the relevance must have seemed appropriate to the animal-orientated space. In many senses, more relevant to the subject at hand, is the animal activity displayed in *The Brazen Age* (London, 1613), where we have the following unlikely-sounding directions near to the beginning of the play. Here Hercules fights with a shape-shifting Achelous:

Alarme. Achelous is beaten in, and immediately enters in the shape of
   a Dragon.
Herc. Bee'st thou a God or hell-hound thus transhap't,
Thy terrour frights not me, serpent or diuell Il'e pash thee.
Alarme. He beats away the dragon. Enter a Fury all fire-workes.
Herc. Fright us with fire? our Club shall quench thy flame,
And beat it downe to hell, from whence it came.
When the Fury sinkes, a Buls head appeares.
Herc. What, yet more monsters? Serpent, Bull and Fire,
Shall all alike taste great *Alcides* ire.
He tugs with the Bull, and pluckes off one of his horns.
Enter from the same place Achelous with his forehead all bloudy.[54]

From large-scale mythological dragons to an actor covered in fireworks to an appropriate *Bull's* head appearing at the Red *Bull* playhouse, these metamorphoses were made to come alive at the converted animal yard with bovine herds baying and moving around just outside the door. When Jason approaches the Golden Fleece there is a bullish moment too. "*Two fiery Buls*

*are discouered, the Fleece hanging ouer them, and the Dragon sleeping beneath
them : Medea with strange fiery-workes, hangs aboue in the Aire in the strange
habite of a Coniuresse.*"[55] There is, unfortunately, no direct evidence that
butchers, drovers, and their ilk attended the Red Bull plays that were so local
to their activities, although butchers were citizens and the citizens of London
are all but universally accepted as the probable audience for Queen's Servants/
Red Bull plays. For instance, the second play of Thomas Heywood's *If You
Know Not Me You Know Nobody* was published in 1606 and centered on the
life of Sir Thomas Gresham, founder of the Royal Exchange and a tremendous
citizen hero. Heywood's previous plays were even lampooned for appealing to
the citizens, such as *The Four Prentices of London* in Francis Beaumont's *The
Knight of the Burning Pestle*. In 1699, James Wright described the companies
and some of the audiences at the different theaters:

> Before the Wars, there were in being all these Play-houses at the same
> time. The *Black-friers*, and *Globe* on the *Bankside*, a Winter and Sum-
> mer House, belonging to the same Company called the King's Servants;
> the *Cockpit* or *Phoenix*, in *Drury-lane*, called the Queen's Servants; the
> private House in *Salisbury-court*, called the Prince's Servants; the Fortune
> near *White-cross-street*, and the *Red Bull* at the upper end of *St. John's-
> street*: The two last were mostly frequented by Citizens, and the meaner
> sort of People.[56]

In Thomas Tomkis's *Albumazar*, however, a Cambridge University play of 1615,
a "country clown" called Trincalo plans his attempt to court a woman and
how he will "confound her with complements drawn from the Plaies I see at
the Fortune, and the Red Bull, where I learne all the words I speake and vnder-
stand not."[57]

Here, perhaps, from a play performed outside London, at a gentry-orientated
university, we are given a vision of a simple farmer going to see something like
the Classical Ages plays at a Middlesex suburbs theater like the Red Bull. The
satirical take on particular audience members evident in the text could confirm
something Heywood wrote for his narrator figure, Homer, at the end of *The
Brazen Age*.

> He that expects fiue short Acts can containe
> Each circumstance of these things we present,
> Me thinkes should shew more barrennesse then braine:
> All we haue done we aime at your content,
> Striuing to illustrate things not knowne to all,
> In which the learnd can only censure right:
> The rest we craue, whom we vnlettered call,

Rather to attend then iudge; for more then sight
We seeke to please. The vnderstanding eare
Which we haue hitherto most gracious found,
Your generall loue, we rather hope then feare:
For that of all our labours is the ground.
If from your loue in any point we stray,
Thinke HOMER blind, and blind men misse their way.[58]

Whether or not drovers and butchers attended Queen's Servants/Red Bull plays, animals undoubtedly made their way down St. John Street in vast numbers along with the people who were in the business of getting them to London. During the eighteenth century, when the playhouse was long gone, new rules were put in place whereby the original owners of the herds—the country drovers—were probably no longer present when their animals took their penultimate journey. Under an act of 1781 (21 Geo. III, c.67), orders were made by the Court of Aldermen between 1792 and 1855 providing for licensed drovers who wore numbered metal armbands and who sported their names and addresses on ivory tickets.[59] Official licensed salesmen, with Corporation of London approval, struck bargains with the country farmers in Islington. Taken, probably, from the area around the Angel, their cows and sheep would be led down St. John Street to Smithfield and then to their particular destiny.

But the animals came down St. John Street all the same; and in view of this burdensome situation that had existed in the highway for a very long time, it is little wonder that the actors at the Red Bull had trouble keeping up with repairs on the roads outside their playhouse. In fact, setting aside the general feeling among theater historians that this company was reprobate in some way, it is worth pointing out that in the same record of October 1616 where the company is mentioned being cited for nonupkeep of St. John Street, other locals fare similarly. This was for nonprovision of carts for the same necessary roadwork:

Lady Burley of Clerkenwell. Distrained.	6 [days]
Sir John Butler of the same, knight	6
Sir Francis Anderson of the same, knight	6
Sir Henry Minne of the same, knight	6
Rebecca, Lady Sackford of the same, widow	6[60]

William le Hardy, editor of the *Middlesex County Records* from which these records are taken, describes the problem of local road upkeep thus:

Several troublesome liabilities were placed on the inhabitants of the County, and perhaps the most irksome of these was the repair of the highways, for which every freeholder had to provide men or wagons for so many days, according to the proportion laid down by the Justices. Those failing or refusing to provide the necessary quota were naturally brought before the Court, and either bound over or fined.[61]

Le Hardy then goes on to say, however, that everybody found keeping these statutes difficult, observing that the list of "defaulters" included "members of the nobility, knights, esquires and gentlemen, and as many as twenty-five of them appear at one sitting."

The undoubtedly distinguished titles of the Clerkenwell residents of 1616 listed earlier indicate more than a little about both the nature of the area in which the Queen's Servants lived and played, and also about the status of personages living near them. It was not all drovers, butchers, and their livestock that occupied the Clerkenwell area and this is witnessed by the presence of other important people mentioned in this chapter such as the Cavendishes and Thomas Bedingfeld. The fact of the matter was (as has been indicated from the beginning) that St. John Street was a thoroughfare that was always difficult to maintain. And it was as difficult for the actors as it was for everyone else. Because it was, in every way, always associated with the animal trade that was reliant on it as the main way to market. It must have been especially hard to keep up with necessary repairs, resulting in all kinds of trouble for the residents and players alike who found the responsibility for these works rested on their shoulders. The name of the last listed for difficulties in 1616, Lady Rebecca "Sackford," is worthy of note, for she was the widow of Thomas Bedingfeld's associate in the role of Master of the Tents and Toils, Sir Henry Seckford. Henry Seckford's brother, Thomas, was a Master of the Court of Requests and had owned, during his lifetime, the land upon which the Red Bull was built. However, Thomas Seckford's story has nothing to do with animals. Both Sir Henry Seckford, Lady Rebecca's husband, and her brother-in-law, Thomas, were dead by 1616, Sir Henry while in his house at Clerkenwell. He was therefore buried in the south aisle of the parish church of St. James on October 15, 1610. Lady Seckford continued to live as a widow in Clerkenwell, dying in 1631. She was buried in the chancel of St. James, and it may only be hoped that at some point before she died she managed to contribute her share of the road repairs.[62]

It is my hope that the facts and arguments cited in this chapter will convince readers of the extent to which animals permeated the lives of Londoners both before the beginning of the seventeenth century and during it. And also how the presence of both needful meat supplies and at least a smattering of animals for entertainment purposes, both real and imaginary, may be perceived as enlivening both city and court culture in a way that is alien to us today. Most of all (for my own purposes), I hope this chapter also goes some way toward redressing the balance in terms of perceptions of the Red Bull and its actors, both as unworthy of detailed attention where noticed, and as something over which to take the moral high ground. Animals were once so important to the Red Bull as to be worthy of the status of "normal residents," occupying the yard before the playhouse ever came to be. This was the case in other instances of playhouse conversion, not just the square innyards that were converted into theaters, but the large round purpose-built bear-baiting arenas, and, indeed, small round cockpits too. For when the redoubtable Christopher Beeston built his "Cockpit" playhouse, ostensibly but not materially for the Queen's Servants, as his company's indoor private venue to match its King's Men rivals, it was a pit made for fighting cocks, situated near to Queen Anna's residence by the Strand, that was converted. This was the first theater to be founded in what we now know as "the West End" of London, and in the street that became its historical heartland—Drury Lane. And the rest is another kind of animal history altogether.

CHAPTER FIVE

Natural History, Natural Philosophy, and Animals, 1600–1800

ANITA GUERRINI

The topic of scientific uses of animals in the era of the Scientific Revolution inevitably brings to mind the Cartesian beast-machine, blood transfusion experiments, and dogs nailed to tables. But these images encompass only a portion of the scientific interest in animals in this era, and there were also many attempts to classify animals, to explain their origins, behavior, and appearance, and to seek out new and unusual examples. The latter topics are usually labeled *natural history*, a descriptive endeavor distinct from *natural philosophy*, which concerned theories of causation. Both of these are now subsumed under what we call biological science; the term *biology* was coined in the early nineteenth century. This chapter examines natural history and natural philosophy and some of the ways they intersected around animals.

The definition of *natural history* has occupied many historians. Francis Bacon, in the early seventeenth century, classified natural history as a subject of Memory, a topic concerned with the collection of information. He contrasted this to natural philosophy, a topic of Reason.[1] In this chapter, I continue Bacon's distinction, which historians of science also make, between natural history and natural philosophy, that is, between works mainly of observation and description and works of theory and generalization. But the dividing line between these two areas of endeavor was never clear-cut and became fainter as the period progressed. This blurring is especially evident in the works of writers of natural history who attempted to classify, rather than merely list, and in the works of natural philosophers who observed rather than experimented. A system of classification reflects a certain theoretical outlook, and to the new empiricists of the Scientific Revolution, observation was at least as important as experimenting. Robert Boyle's *General Heads for the Natural History of a Country*, published posthumously in 1692, implicitly distinguishes the history from the philosophy of nature. Boyle counseled the traveler to observe and record but not to draw conclusions.[2] Yet, because these observations followed Boyle's guidelines, they would not be random or naive.

Natural history and natural philosophy again merged in the work of Claude Perrault and his colleagues at the Paris Academy of Sciences at the end of the seventeenth century. The combination of natural history description and anatomy displayed in their *Mémoires pour servir à l'histoire naturelle des animaux* (1671–1676), described later, served as a model for Buffon in the eighteenth century, whose magisterial multivolumed *Histoire naturelle* (1749–1788) dominated the discourse on natural history until Darwin.

HARVEY, DESCARTES, AND THE EXPERIMENTAL TRADITION

While others before him had experimented on animals, the English physician William Harvey (1578–1657) was the first since the Roman physician Galen to develop a systematic research program based on experimentation on live animals. His discovery of the circulation of the blood, published in his book *On the Motion of the Heart and Blood in Animals* (1628), marked the beginning of medicine as a science, although the full implications of his discovery took many decades to work out.[3] He combined observation, experiments on living and dead animals, and quantitative arguments, and his methods were widely imitated in the seventeenth and eighteenth centuries. During the seventeenth century, many natural philosophers employed Harvey's methods to support their mechanistic theories about life. During the eighteenth century, the mechanical paradigm was gradually discarded, but experimentation continued.

A vitalist, Harvey would not have agreed with the view that the animal body was essentially a machine. His contemporary Descartes (discussed later) introduced this idea, which was adopted by a generation of natural philosophers who came of age after 1650. These mechanical philosophers such as Boyle, Hooke, and Malpighi adopted Harvey's methods to perform experiments that resulted in a significantly greater understanding of the human and animal body, while also greatly increasing the number of animals used in research.

Harvey's experiments were varied. He opened the chest cavities of different animals and observed the operation of the heart. At times he used ligatures to tie off certain vessels and observe the effects. He bled animals to death to measure the amount of blood in the body, and observed the differences between arterial and venous blood. He tied a tight band around the arm of a human volunteer to observe the action of the valves in the veins. Harvey repeated his animal experiments many times over a period of several years between 1602 and the 1620s. Following Aristotle's notion of the essential similarity of all animals, Harvey sought general principles applicable to all animals and he dissected hearts with two, three, and four chambers, belonging to cold- and warm-blooded animals. He assumed that nature followed certain laws, and that similar experiments would lead to similar effects. As a Christian, Harvey probably believed that miracles could occur, but they were outside the ordinary course of nature, which displayed in its lawfulness the intelligence of its creator.

Harvey's theory of the circulation of the blood overthrew the Galenic model that stated that the blood moved back and forth in the blood vessels, and that new blood was constantly being made in the liver to replace blood that was used up by the body's organs. Although anatomists in sixteenth-century Padua had disproved some aspects of the Galenic theory, it retained its credibility until Harvey. Vesalius had demonstrated in 1543 that the septum, the muscular wall dividing the left and right sides of the heart, was not perforated as Galen had claimed. A decade later, Realdo Colombo described the pulmonary circulation, by means of which the blood travels from the right side of the heart to the left by passing through the lungs. However, neither of them challenged the central premises of the Galenic model, that new blood was constantly being made and that it simply moved back and forth.

To Harvey, the pulmonary circulation did challenge those premises, and he designed experiments further to disprove the old theory. The experiments demonstrated that the blood circulated throughout the body and that it was constantly reused rather than constantly newly made. Harvey learned how to do dissection in Padua from the anatomy professor Girolamo Fabrizi, known by his Latin name of Fabricius. Fabricius was an ardent Aristotelian and Harvey followed him in this as well. After he returned to London in 1602, Harvey pursued his anatomical researches privately. He used animals as proxies for humans; only infrequently could he test his ideas on human cadavers and his experiments on live humans were not invasive. But like Fabricius, Harvey followed Aristotle's assumption of a fundamental analogy between humans and animals. Harvey presented some of his conclusions in public anatomy lectures delivered to the London College of Physicians between 1616 and 1618. Like most anatomy lectures, these included both the dissection of a human cadaver and the dissection and vivisection of several animals.[4]

Harvey's discovery of the circulation revealed the immense power of experimental demonstration, especially animal experimentation, to disclose valuable information about the human and animal body. In his second major work,

Anatomical Exercises on the Generation of Animals (1651), Harvey employed his experimental and observational skills to uncover the secrets of generation, investigating frogs, snakes, fish, insects, and a number of domestic fowl and mammals. Like many others, he traced the development of the embryo by examining the stages of development in chicken eggs, but the range of his investigations went far beyond any of his contemporaries.[5]

As a physician to the English King Charles I, Harvey had access to numbers of deer for dissection, shot by the king or his courtiers at one of his many estates. Harvey's dissections of deer as well as vivisections of dogs, cats, and rabbits allowed him to give a minute account of fertilization, gestation, and embryonic development. This close observation of large numbers of animals was as important a model for subsequent research as were the experimental techniques of his work on the circulation.

To Harvey, animals served a purely instrumental function, and if the question of cruelty occurred to him, he never expressed it. Despite his sacrifice of hundreds of animals, modern antivivisectionists and animal rights activists have largely ignored him, unlike his younger contemporary, the French natural philosopher René Descartes (1596–1650). Descartes performed few experiments on animals; modern criticism of him is based not on his experimental activity but on his philosophical claim that animals are not conscious. Therefore, he believed, they lack the ability to suffer and feel pain in the way humans do. Many modern critics have argued that Descartes' claim "appears to have been widely used as a justification for experimenting on live animals, at a time when that practice was becoming more common."[6] But in fact most of his contemporaries did not accept the claim that animals could not feel pain. Although many after Harvey experimented on animals in the seventeenth and eighteenth centuries, few used Descartes' ideas to justify their practice.

Descartes was among the first to theorize the new mechanical philosophy. Its central premise was that the universe was a machine that operated according to the laws of mechanics. The Italian natural philosopher Galileo Galilei (1564–1642) focused on the implications of the heliocentric universe proposed by Copernicus for the laws of mechanics. To Galileo, these laws must operate universally; there could be no distinction between the earth and the heavens or between living and nonliving objects on earth. Descartes in turn intended to systematize Galileo's mechanics and his mathematical approach into a new philosophy. This mechanical philosophy of nature established the primacy of material (rather than other sorts of) causation. Matter itself was no longer seen as active, but inert. Descartes wished to avoid Galileo's fate at the hands of the Roman Inquisition, and his philosophy of nature incorporated the mechanical worldview while keeping intact God's central role in nature's governance.

To Descartes, the world consisted of a collection of mechanisms, which could only be analyzed by means of mathematics and mechanics. Like Galileo, he made no distinction between what we would call the physical and biological worlds. But Descartes believed that reality did not necessarily correspond to our perception of it. The evidence of the senses did not tell the whole story. He proceeded, therefore, not primarily by experimentation but by reason. He discussed the motion of the heart in his *Discourse on Method* (1637) not in terms of experimental results, like Harvey, but in terms of mechanical necessity. Descartes did not describe experiments, but simply his conclusions. While he agreed with Harvey that the blood circulated, his account described the heart as a kind of teakettle whose motion depended on animal heat that he attributed to the chemical process of fermentation. Harvey, in contrast, said nothing about the origins of the heart's motion, which he attributed to an unknown vital force, describing only his experimental results. Descartes claimed nonetheless that his description of the heart's action was consistent with observed phenomena. The configuration of the parts, he said, dictated this conclusion much as the wheels and weights of a clock determined its motion.[7]

According to Descartes, the human body, like the animal, was a machine, but humans also possessed reason, which animals did not. Therefore humans necessarily knew God and possessed immortal souls. To Descartes this dualism of mind and body, the complete separation of matter and spirit, constituted the essence of existence, and this was a theological as well as a philosophical principle.

Descartes marveled at the clockwork automata of his time. He reasoned that if humans could make such convincing devices, how much more clever was the hand of God? In the *Discourse on Method*, Descartes argued that humans could, in theory, make a mechanical animal that would be indistinguishable from the real thing. Humans could even make a mechanical human, but unlike the animal, it could never be mistaken for a real human, because it would lack a mind. Only God could bestow a mind, and God bestowed one on humans alone. The mechanical human would lack two critical attributes of a real human: it would not be able to speak and it would lack the ability to reason.[8]

Descartes believed that animals could neither speak nor reason, and therefore they were simply body. They were machines, but complex machines, and could make sounds in response to certain stimuli, or act in certain ways. God had constructed the body, said Descartes, to do quite a lot without reference to the mind. While animals were not self-conscious or capable of reasoned thought, they did, he believed, feel pain, heat, hunger, and emotions such as fear and joy. In contrast, the mind's functions included memory, conscious perception, and most important, reason. Animals could feel pain physically but could not experience it cognitively. Theologically, this was an orthodox position; the Catholic Church did not grant immortal souls to animals.[9]

EXPERIMENTATION IN THE SEVENTEENTH
AND EIGHTEENTH CENTURIES

Descartes accepted Harvey's animal experimentation as a valid method of research, as did many more natural philosophers. Two assumptions governed much of the research in the second half of the seventeenth century: that organisms and machines are analogous, and that all vital functions can be explained by the laws of physics. Yet Descartes' notion that the animal body was a machine—the so-called beast-machine concept—was far more important as a methodological principle than as a moral principle or a description of what animals were really like. Although many natural philosophers sought evidence for mechanism in animal form and function, most did not believe that animals felt no pain, and it's not clear that any of them observed Descartes' fine distinction between feeling and experiencing.

Among the many who worked in this era, three groups stand out: the circle around Robert Boyle at the Royal Society in London, Claude Perrault and his colleagues at the Paris Academy of Sciences, and Marcello Malpighi and his circle in Italy. The Royal Society, founded in 1662, included several members who had learned experimental techniques from William Harvey. The Paris Academy of Sciences followed shortly after in 1666, with human and animal anatomy among its initial projects. Malpighi worked at several Italian universities and gained support from the Duke of Tuscany, whose Accademia del Cimento during the 1650s and 1660s included many of the most active natural philosophers in Italy. Malpighi communicated many of his findings to the Royal Society in London, where they were published in its journal, the *Philosophical Transactions*.

The Royal Society circle used many animals, both alive and dead. They followed Harvey in investigating problems that the circulation of the blood introduced, and employed such techniques as the ligature of blood vessels, the inflation of lungs or other organs to show their structure, and the injection of various substances. Among the best known of the Royal Society's experiments were those employing the vacuum pump or air-pump invented in the late 1650s by Robert Hooke (1635–1703) and Robert Boyle (1627–1691). In 1659, Boyle and Hooke placed a lark in the receiver of their "pneumatick engine" and pumped out the air. The lark died, the first of many animals—kittens, puppies, snakes, fish—sacrificed to the air-pump. Boyle and Hooke determined, among other things, that all animals need air and that fresh air had qualities that sustained life better than air that had already been respired. Immensely popular, the air-pump became a kind of icon of Royal Society science, admired and satirized in equal measure. In addition, the use of a machine may have made it easier for researchers to think of the animals they used as mere machines as well, although accounts of the experiments often remark upon the pain and suffering of the animals.

In addition to the air-pump experiments, Hooke and Richard Lower (1631–1691) performed a series of surgical vivisections in the mid-1660s to determine the mechanism of respiration. In these experiments, the thorax and diaphragm of a dog were cut away, leaving its heart visible, and the dog was kept alive by pumping air into its windpipe through a bellows. As soon as the bellows stopped, the dog's heartbeat faltered. While this experiment also showed that air was essential to life, it could not disprove the claim that the motion of the lungs (as some natural philosophers argued) was equally important. Hooke and Lower varied this experiment a few years later. Employing two sets of bellows, they kept the lungs continuously full but motionless. Air escaped from a prick in the pleural membrane. The heart continued to beat even when the lungs did not move, proving that the air, not the motion of the lungs, was the critical factor.

Some of the spectators at the Royal Society, while impressed with the results, were uneasy about these experiments; even Hooke disliked the open-thorax experiment because of its cruelty, and it took three years for Lower to persuade him to perform the variation. The Dutch lens-grinder Antoine van Leeuwenhoek (1632–1723) revealed the possibilities of the microscope, and in his book *Micrographia* (1665), Hooke expressed his preference for the microscope's nonviolent exploration of nature.

As curator of experiments for the Royal Society, Hooke performed many other demonstrations on animals. He injected ink into various animals to trace the course of blood vessels; others injected drugs, poisons, and paralytic agents. Attempts at intravenous feeding with injections of broth and milk failed, but dogs got drunk when injected with wine and beer.

In the late 1660s, experiments in blood transfusion became especially popular in England and France. Blood continued to be a mysterious substance and older ideas persisted of its status as the repository of temperament. It played a major role in the central ritual of the Christian faith, and bleeding continued to be a common therapy even after Harvey had proven the circulation, and therefore, the finite amount of blood in the body. Animal-to-animal transfusions ran between "Old and Young, Sick and Healthy, Hot and Cold, Fierce and Fearful, Tame and Wild Animals."[10] At the Royal Society, Lower began with dog-to-dog transfusions but soon moved on to cross-species experiments that included sheep and calves. Humans were next to be transfused with animal blood; experimenters argued that young calves and lambs had purer blood than humans. Moreover, the blood of the lamb had long symbolized the blood of Christ.

A French royal physician, Jean-Baptiste Denis, transfused the blood of a sheep into a young man suffering from a fever. (See Figure 5.1.) According to Denis, the young man recovered. Lower soon tried a similar experiment, transfusing sheep's blood into a young clergyman whose brain had been described as "sometimes a little too warm." The transfusion appeared to calm the young man's behavior.[11] A second transfusion on the same individual a few weeks later brought out a crowd of spectators. Shortly thereafter Denis performed another animal-to-human transfusion, but this patient died shortly after a third attempt a few months later. We now know that the humans' bodies would have formed antibodies to the foreign blood after the first transfusion, leading to more serious consequences in subsequent attempts. The death of Denis's patient early in 1668 quickly ended further attempts at animal-to-human blood transfusion, at least those publicly known.[12]

The transfusion experiments formed only a small portion of the research enterprise in this period. While most natural philosophers agreed that Harvey's theory of the circulation was true and that his anatomical methods were useful,

FIGURE 5.1: Blood transfusion from a sheep to a man, Engraving in Matthias Gottfried Purmann, *Grosser und gantz neugewundener Lorbeer-Krantz; oder, Wund-Artzney,* Frankfurt and Leipzig, 1692. London, The Wellcome Trust Medical Photographic Library.

the interpretation of his discovery varied widely. Boyle and his circle believed that the animal body could be analyzed in mechanical terms, but they did not follow Descartes in attempting to find the mechanisms of the body.

The Italian anatomist Marcello Malpighi (1628–1694) and his colleagues also experimented on animals, looking for particular mechanisms. Other notable experimenters in this vein were the Dutchman Regnier de Graaf (1641–1673) on the glands, and the Dane Nicolaus Steno (1638–1686) on the structure of the muscles. To explain physiological processes such as respiration, Malpighi investigated the microstructure of the lungs. Over several years, he and his colleague Carlo Fracassati dissected and vivisected guinea pigs, cats, sheep, frogs, and birds. (See Figure 5.2.) They injected the lungs and the pulmonary vessels with colored water, revealing the lungs as a series of small cellular vesicles separated by membranes, rather than solid flesh. They also traced the pulmonary circulation. No one had yet seen the anastomoses, or connections, between the smallest veins and capillaries, even though Harvey's theory required them, and Malpighi endeavored to find them with his injection experiments. But his injection methods encountered many problems: in dead animals, the fine vessels clogged with clotted blood, while in live animals, the blood flowing through the vessels could not easily be replaced with colored water without killing the

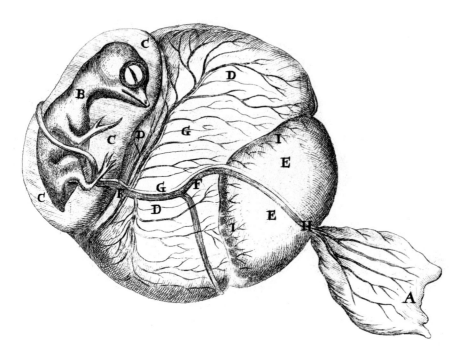

FIGURE 5.2: Development of the chick, Engraving in Marcello Malpighi, *Dissertatio epistolica de formatione pulli in ovo*, London, 1673. London, The Wellcome Trust Medical Photographic Library.

animal. Malpighi nonetheless continued, sacrificing, he said, almost the entire race of frogs.[13]

Frogs were excellent experimental subjects: their lungs are relatively simple in structure, and nearly transparent, allowing a clear view of the blood vessels within. After observing the frogs alive, Malpighi dried the tiny lungs, inflated them, and then examined them with a microscope. There he found the connections between the blood vessels. His 1661 treatise on the lungs, *De pulmonibus*, gave new prominence to the newly invented microscope, which, to Malpighi, revealed the minute subtlety of nature that atomism and mechanical theories only surmised.

Claude Perrault (1627–1688) and his colleagues at the Paris Academy of Sciences followed a third research pathway, that of comparative anatomy. In Perrault's work we see the intermingling of natural philosophy with natural history. The beginnings of comparative anatomy are usually dated to the appearance in 1551 of Pierre Belon's (1517–1564) work on the anatomy of cetaceans, soon followed by his comparison of a human skeleton to that of a bird (1555). Volker Coiter (1534–1576) established comparative anatomy as an autonomous field of study in the 1570s, and works such as Carlo Ruini's (1530–1598) landmark study of the horse, published in the late sixteenth century, established animal anatomy as an independent field of inquiry.[14]

At the first formal meeting of the Paris Academy in January 1667, Perrault proposed two projects under the rubric of *physique*, on botany and on anatomy. The anatomy project devolved into two: fundamental research on human anatomy, which followed along the lines of Royal Society experimenting and used animals as surrogates; and an examination of the anatomy of various exotic animals that came to the academy from the royal menageries.

These projects were not entirely separate; the dissection of all sorts of animals served as evidence in the ongoing debates about human and animal physiology. (See Figure 5.3.) But the exotic animal dissections aroused great public interest and descriptions quickly found their way into print, first in pamphlets, and then in a large-format book, *Mémoires pour servir à l'histoire naturelle des animaux* (1671, reissued with additional descriptions in 1676).[15] A collaborative work involving several members of the Paris Academy, in content it was a virtual menagerie, a paper zoo. Perrault's introduction established several important principles for animal observation, description, and anatomy. These principles were distinctly anti-Cartesian: Perrault refused to speculate about causes or to generalize from particulars, and he was less concerned with animal mechanism than with animal structure and behavior. Each animal he described was unique, and the duty of the natural philosopher, he said, was first to describe. Any attempt at generalization was premature. Perrault followed the model of natural history established by explorers and chroniclers of the sixteenth and seventeenth century such as Charles de L'Ecluse (1526–1609). But

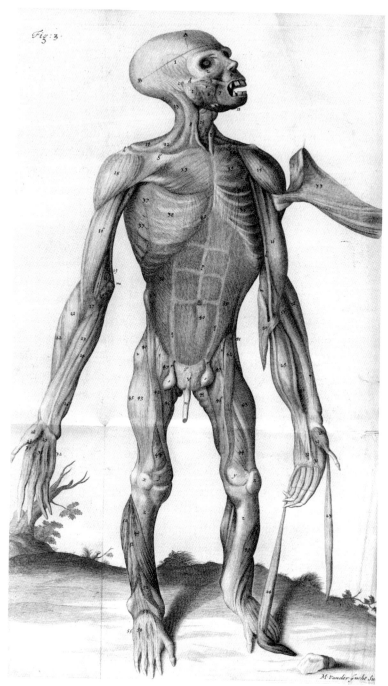

FIGURE 5.3: Dissected chimpanzee, Engraving by M. Van der Gucht in Edward Tyson, *Orang-Outang, Sive Homo Sylvestris, or The Anatomy of a Pygmie Compared with That of a Monkey, an Ape, and a Man*, London, 1699. London, King's College, Foyle Special Collections Library.

unlike his contemporaries in natural history such as Joseph Pitton de Tournefort (1656–1708) and John Ray (1627–1704), Perrault paid more attention to anatomy than to classification, carefully describing the internal structure of each specimen. He refused to attempt a classification of the motley assortment of animals he chronicled or to endorse any of the current systems of taxonomy. Not until Buffon's *Histoire naturelle,* discussed later, did anatomy and taxonomy mutually inform each other.

The collection of exotic animals, whether for research, display, or other use, lagged far behind that of exotic plants. By the end of the sixteenth century, the botanical productions of the New World had begun to fill the gardens of Europe, but New World animals remained few, their collection confined to those of culinary use such as the turkey or obvious oddities such as the opossum and the armadillo. Edward Topsell's *A History of Four-Footed Beastes* (1607) contained only a few more non-European animals than the work of which it was a revised translation, Conrad Gesner's *Historia animalium* (Description of animals) of 1551, the era's most comprehensive text on animals. On the other hand, exotic animals were a form of diplomatic exchange dating back to Roman times. Medieval monarchs established menageries such as that at the Tower of London, which during the sixteenth century included lions, leopards, a tiger, a lynx, an eagle, and a porcupine. Animals in menageries were often used for sport in the form of animal combats or baiting. Louis XIV of France established menageries at his palaces at Versailles and Vincennes. His animals included gifts from foreign monarchs and contributions from France's colonies. Perrault and his collaborators noted the origin of each animal they included in the *Mémoires pour servir à l'histoire naturelle des animaux,* and thus the volumes also served to demonstrate the monarch's power and the extent of France's colonial empire.

By the end of the seventeenth century, the animal body (and by analogy, the human) was much better known than it had been at any time in the past. Nonetheless, natural philosophers at times felt the need to justify their practices against critics who argued that natural philosophy would lead to irreligion. Perrault echoed common sentiments when he asserted that humans, as the ultimate perfection, formed the basis of comparison in his work. His teleological argument formed an important justification for the work, giving the necessary reference to the Creator without being overtly religious. Robert Boyle also defended natural philosophy in his *Some Considerations Touching the Usefulness of Experimental Natural Philosophy* (1663). A devout Christian, he refuted claims that science threatened religion, referring to Augustine's idea of "two books" that stated that the "book" of nature complemented the book of God. Boyle also revived the old concept of stewardship, the notion that God had entrusted the earth to humans to improve it and not merely to contemplate it. To Boyle, experiments on animals displayed God's approval of natural philosophy.

The experimenter gained knowledge of God's creation, as well as knowledge useful for medicine. Experiments also demonstrated the underlying purpose of the creation. To Boyle, it was obvious that God had provided animals to the anatomist to make experiments he could not pursue on humans.[16]

Boyle never denied that the animals could suffer. Although most of his contemporaries were committed to some version of the mechanical philosophy, few of them took literally Descartes' argument that if animals were machines, they did not feel pain as humans did. Boyle, for example, frequently noted the animals' distress in the course of an experiment, and a viper was "furiously tortured" under the influence of the vacuum.[17] Many other examples can be found of this kind of acknowledgment. Carlo Fracassati injected a dog with vitriol (hydrochloric acid) and noted, "The Animal complain'd a great while ... and observing the beating of his breast, one might easily judge, the Dog suffered much."[18] But all of them believed that such suffering was preferable to human suffering for the sake of advancing knowledge. (See Figure 5.4.)

There were experimenters who believed that animals could not feel pain, but they were in a minority. Members of the religious order of Jansenists, based at the Parisian monastery of Port-Royal, have often been cited for their cruelty to animals:

> They administered beatings to dogs with perfect indifference, and made fun of those who pitied the creatures as if they had felt pain. They said the animals were clocks; that the cries they emitted when struck, were only the noise of a little spring which had been touched, but that the whole body was without feeling. They nailed poor animals up on boards by their four paws to vivisect them and see the circulation of the blood which was a great subject of conversation.[19]

To these Cartesians, who also included the well-known clergyman and philosopher Nicolas Malebranche (1638–1715), the denial of animal suffering was a point of theology. While human suffering stemmed from the original sin of Adam, animal suffering could not. Since God would not create creatures who suffered for no reason, animals must not suffer. More common, however, was the view of the Danish anatomist Nicolaus Steno, who wrote to a friend, "I wish [the Cartesians] could convince me as thoroughly as they are themselves convinced of the fact that animals have no souls!"[20]

Experiments using animals continued during the eighteenth century, even though mechanism gradually waned as the dominant paradigm in favor of variations on vitalism, which argued that the phenomena of life were unique and could not be reduced to the laws of physics. The English clergyman Stephen Hales (1677–1761) continued to rely on the mechanical philosophy in experiments measuring blood pressure in horses and dogs, which he published

FIGURE 5.4: Operation to collect pancreatic fluid from a dog, Engraving in Reinier de Graaf, *Tractatus anatomico-medicus de succi pancreatici natura & usu*, Leiden, 1671. London, The Wellcome Trust Medical Photographic Library.

in *Haemastaticks* (1733). However, the public criticism he endured for these experiments by the 1730s marked the beginnings of a change in attitudes toward animals as the unease felt by some members of the Royal Society in the 1660s became more widespread. Increased popular interest in science, fueled by new magazines and other publications, also meant increased popular scrutiny of scientific practices: the poem "The Air-Pump," which appeared in the *Gentleman's Magazine* in 1740, speculated what the notorious Roman emperor Domitian would have done with such a machine:

For instance—To have seen a mouse,
Shut fast within its crystal house,
And thence the air exhausted all,
To view the creature gasp and sprawl;
At ev'ry suction of the pump

Observe him pant from head to rump,
Spew, kek, and turn him on his back—
T'had been, ye powers, a mighty knack![21]

The English artist Joseph Wright of Derby (1734–1797) dramatically illustrated such a scene in his painting "An Experiment on a Bird in the Air Pump" (1768). Wright portrays the natural philosopher as a quasi-magician, while the quivering children display both awe and that new and potent emotion of sensibility: if the experimenter has no feelings about the animal's fate, his audience certainly does.

While Abraham Trembley (1710–1784) explored the edges of the animal world in his work on the tiny freshwater hydra, the Swiss physician Albrecht von Haller (1708–1777) explored the edges of pain perception in the animal. Trembley demonstrated that the hydra was an animal, not a plant, and that it displayed a remarkable capacity for self-regeneration; cut into pieces or turned inside out, the hydra recreated a functional form. Trembley's work was an important contribution to the ongoing debate between vitalists and mechanists: nonliving tissue could not regenerate, so that the hydra showed the fundamental distinction between life and nonlife.

Haller used almost two hundred different animals in a series of experiments on the quality of irritability in living tissues, defined as the ability of tissue to respond to stimuli. He distinguished irritability, an unconscious response of the organism, from sensibility, a conscious response of tissues that have nerves. Pain was an example of sensibility. His work presupposed that animals felt pain, since he was measuring reactions to various often painful stimuli, and he apologized for his use of animals in the preface to his essay on irritability and sensibility, published in Latin in 1752.[22] His apology indicates that a new sense of responsibility toward animals was developing, evidenced by several publications from the 1690s onward, beginning with Gabriel Daniel's satirical *Voiage du monde de Descartes* (1691), which was quickly translated into English, Latin, Italian, and Spanish.

ANIMALS AND PUBLIC ANATOMY

Animals also were at the center of many public anatomical demonstrations. Public anatomy flourished in Europe between 1500 and 1800. At its peak, around 1700, dozens of lecturers dissected human and animal corpses and live animals before thousands of spectators across Europe. Public anatomy encompassed public and private demonstrations in a variety of settings. Early modern anatomists competed with each other to entertain, to enlighten, to bedazzle, and to offer moral edification as well as to educate, and animals played roles in all of these functions. Public anatomy is most commonly defined as the annual ceremonial anatomies performed at most European medical schools. These were usually free and open to anyone who wished to attend. But in addition, various anatomy courses, both private and officially sponsored, were open to the public. All of these were advertised in newspapers and broadsides. Public anatomists competed for their audiences with each other as well as with the theater and other forms of public entertainment, including animal fights, musicians, and magicians.

Animals, as well as human corpses, were essential to early modern anatomical demonstration. Live animals, in particular, could demonstrate functions that the cadaver could not. The role of animals in public anatomy has been overlooked by historians. Yet by the time of Vesalius in the sixteenth century, the ritualized dissection of a human cadaver included demonstrations on live and dead animals. Modern historians, much like early modern demonstrators, have until recently regarded animals as mere imperfect substitutes for humans, and as such unworthy of historical scrutiny. Nonetheless, public anatomical demonstrators used animals to teach particular lessons and to produce particular reactions in their audiences. The use of animals encompasses not only the scientific idea of the animal but also the theatricality of public demonstration and its moral implications. Public anatomy declined when it became socially and morally unacceptable to witness dissection and vivisection. The history of public anatomy between 1600 and 1800 illuminates the developing culture of experimentation discussed in the previous section and shows how science moved from being a public activity to one performed only for scientific peers behind the closed doors of a laboratory.

Anatomy occupied a peculiar place in early modern culture. Broadly, it was a metaphor for all of early modern natural philosophy, in which "anatomies" of many topics abounded; in the *New Organon,* Bacon claimed that his goal was to perform an "anatomy of the world" (chapter CXXIV). As a methodological principle, anatomy was equated with the analysis or taking-apart that formed one aspect of experimental practice. Early modern anatomy was also an entertainment in which humans and animals played highly ritualized roles, vying with alchemy and astronomy as delightful diversions. Annual public dissections were not merely for the benefit of medical students, and anatomy courses multiplied after 1660. By the end of the seventeenth century, for example, Paris had at least half a dozen sites where one might witness a dissection. In addition, many private entrepreneurs offered instruction to anyone willing to pay. While historians have tried to distinguish "real" science from street displays, this distinction cannot be clearly drawn in discussing public anatomy. Large and raucous crowds witnessed the blood transfusion experiments of the 1660s at the Royal Society, highlighting an essential difference between demonstrations in the physical sciences and those in the phenomena of life. Because the latter were messy and unpredictable, they were much harder to constrain into a "polite" framework.

Simon Schaffer's important 1983 article "Natural Philosophy and Public Spectacle" introduced the theme of natural philosophy as a moral spectacle. Schaffer argued that public electrical experiments in mid-eighteenth-century Britain provided sufficient drama to provoke moral effects in its audience. These experiments produced a sense of wonder and amazement that led the audience to a better appreciation of divine power and wisdom.[23] Other popular displays of the period, such as natural history cabinets, orreries, and anatomical waxes, also celebrated God's creativity.

But public demonstrations on animals, which manipulated life itself, produced the most dramatic effects by far. They also raised additional moral questions by causing pain and death in living creatures for the purpose of demonstration. Witnessing anatomy demonstrations certainly led to a greater appreciation of God's design. Anatomy lecturers frequently referred to teleology and the design of nature exhibited in human and animal bodies as proof of the existence of a Deity, an argument both familiar and acceptable to their audiences. When the Edinburgh anatomy professor Alexander Monro drew up a list of the uses of anatomy in 1739, he gave first place to natural theology. Surgery came fifth.[24] But anatomy demonstrations pushed at the limits of acceptable behavior in a society that increasingly emphasized politeness, and forced its audiences to consider the more profound issues of the meaning and purpose of life and death.

In this period, anatomical demonstration became a kind of "moral theater," a public performance intended to induce in its audience such emotions as awe, fear, and compassion, emotions similar to those provoked by religious practice. Relevant here is René Girard's analysis of the relationship between ritual sacrifice and religion. Ritualistic violence, whether real or implied, has, he argues, a necessary cathartic function for a community. In the context of ritual sacrifice, he continues, "there is little reason to differentiate between human and animal victims."[25]

The English physician Richard Lower referred to one of his experiments on dogs before the Royal Society as a "tragedy." What did he mean? Classical theory of tragedy, based on Aristotle's *Poetics*, had been rediscovered in the Renaissance. Aristotle argued that tragedy evoked in its audiences the particular emotions of pity, based on sympathy for the plight of the hero, and terror, based on the audience's participation in the protagonist's plight. The resolution of tragedy, according to Aristotle, resulted in an emotional catharsis that often expressed itself in tears. Aristotle took it for granted that the tragic protagonists would be good people whose dilemma and resolution would therefore have an uplifting effect on the audience. In the *Advancement of Learning*, Francis

Bacon commented that drama would be especially useful if it properly inspired the audience to virtue, recognizing the great power of performance.

Public anatomical demonstration shared many characteristics with dramatic performance. The construction of anatomy theaters preceded the construction of theaters for dramatic performances during the Renaissance, and some structures served both purposes. Music accompanied both public dissections and theatrical performances, and both usually required tickets for entry. The experience of witnessing an anatomical demonstration had much in common with witnessing a tragedy, particularly because, unlike in earlier eras, by the later seventeenth century the audience was becoming aware of the animal as a feeling being. The audience saw a suffering animal, and its sympathies were further engaged because the animal explicitly acted as a stand-in for a human subject. The origins of classical tragedy lay in the seasonal rites of the Greek god Dionysos, which included ritual animal sacrifice as a reenactment of the sacrifice of the god. The animals, apparently, were proxies for the humans who originally participated.[26]

Animals were thus as important to the message of public anatomy as the human body itself, and audiences understood this. Audiences and demonstrators recognized a multitude of symbolic and metaphorical meanings of animals that shaped the presentation and its response. The Roman encyclopedist Pliny recognized the didactic purpose of animals, and his use of animals to convey moral truths was a commonplace in the anatomical theater from the Renaissance onward. In the mid-sixteenth century, the Padua professor Realdo Colombo was said to have cut open the womb of a pregnant dog and removed the pups to demonstrate the force of mother love, since the dog would ignore her own pain and attempt to relieve the pups. Accounts of this experiment were repeated for at least a century and a half; in 1711, Joseph Addison cited it in *The Spectator* as a proof of animal emotion. Pain was also viewed as a means of revealing truth; the early medieval encyclopedist Isidore of Seville had defined torture as a method of finding truth by means of pain and fear. This bears certain resemblances to Aristotle's notions of catharsis, but it also reminds us of Bacon's now infamous comments on forcing nature to reveal her secrets.

As Addison's comment illustrates, what was praiseworthy in the 1550s was problematic by 1700. As an example, let us turn to the best-known anatomy lecturer in Paris around 1700, Joseph-Guichard Duverney. Duverney was a member of the Paris Academy of Sciences and had already gained a reputation as the "anatomiste des courtisans" for his demonstrations before the court of Louis XIV by 1682, when he was named professor of anatomy and chief demonstrator at the King's Garden in Paris. He had participated in Claude Perrault's *Mémoires pour servir a l'histoire naturelle des animaux* of the 1670s, performing most of the dissections for this project. By order of the King, the anatomy courses at the King's Garden were open to all. Duverney's predecessor in the

anatomy chair, the surgeon Pierre Dionis, packed in up to five hundred spectators for his course.

Even Dionis acknowledged, however, that Duverney was in a different league
than he in his expository skills. Where Dionis had confined his remarks to the
human body and apparently only employed one or two of those for his entire
course, Duverney used many animals, as well as anatomical preparations—a skill
for which he was noted—and several human bodies. Many of the skeletons
of the animals dissected by Duverney and Perrault for their academy project
decorated the anatomy theater at the Garden. The unsettling effect of the skeletons contributed to the moralizing impact of the lectures, which juxtaposed the
human cadaver with living and dead animals. The initial letters in the Perrault
folios showed Biblical scenes of animals such as the Temptation and the Ark.
In his lectures, Duverney was witty and logical, but he also constantly appealed
to teleology: to purpose, leading inevitably to the purposes of the Creator.[27]
The dead human body was often an executed criminal whose execution and
punishment were completed by the anatomist. Contemplation of this human
body, juxtaposed to the living and dead animal bodies that illustrated particular
human features, led inevitably to contemplation of the meaning of death itself.

Yet in Duverney's hands, anatomical demonstration trod a narrow line between moral edification and prurience. He matter-of-factly noted that "animals
which one opens alive ... suffer much," but went on to explain what particular
physiological phenomena were thus produced.[28] He did not comment on the
suffering; cruelty made the moral happen. But the excessive emotion provoked
by witnessing anatomy and particularly the dissection of live animals cut
against the moral purpose of the demonstration. Although in theory dissection
appealed first to the intellect and then to the emotions, in fact the emotions
of the audience were far more engaged than their intellectual faculties. The
literary critic Nicolas Boileau singled out Duverney's dissections in one of his
Satires from the 1690s for just this reason: that they appealed to prurient curiosity. Duverney was so popular that he outgrew the lecture hall at the King's
Garden, which he shared with the lecturers in chemistry and botany, and a new
anatomy theater was built by royal order in 1692.

About the same time as Duverney lectured in Paris, a new genre of entrepreneurial anatomy lecturers emerged in London. They modeled themselves not on
surgeons or medical schools but on the popular lecturers in natural philosophy
whose advertisements could be seen in the new daily newspapers. Beginning
with the 1706 lectures of James Douglas, these lecturers found a ready niche in
the crowded world of public entertainments, while their pronouncements and
advertisements attempted to defuse the increasing unease that accompanied audiences to dissections. Douglas and William Cheselden provide examples.

Douglas (1675–1742) advertised his "Course of Human and Comparative
Anatomy" at the end of his 1707 treatise on muscles. Unlike anatomy courses

directed toward surgeons, Douglas aimed toward a general audience and emphasized comparative anatomy, much like Duverney, and his syllabus included many demonstrations on animals. Cheselden (1688–1753), a surgeon, first advertised his course in 1711. While it occasionally mentioned surgical applications, it also emphasized comparative anatomy. In 1721, Cheselden advertised a joint course with the natural philosopher Francis Hauksbee, the younger, which explicitly excluded medical or surgical students.

Douglas and Cheselden lectured not in purpose-built anatomy halls, but in the back rooms of taverns, coffeehouses, or private homes. Yet the scene in even the most modest site for anatomy was filled with animal skeletons and at least one human skeleton as well as with prepared body parts, a dead body or two on the table, and various live and dead animals. Private courses could not compete for decoration with Surgeons' Hall, so wonderfully illustrated by William Hogarth in his "Fourth Stage of Cruelty" (1751). But the effects could be chilling enough.

Animals played a central role in this tableau. Although Douglas advertised his use of "fresh bodies" as a selling point, human bodies (often executed criminals, but also bodies stolen from graveyards) were hard to get, and most lecturers were lucky to have one or two per course. The "Benefit and Conveniency" of animal bodies, on the other hand, were obvious: they were easy to obtain and so fresh that they were often still alive.[29] Douglas and Cheselden viewed the animal body as a readily available exemplar of the human, a close if not exact copy. Like Duverney, they used animals for comparison and to show structures not easily seen in the human body. They provided multiple examples of divine planning and purpose. In addition, of course, animals could be opened while still alive, to show functions as well as structures, and could be experimented upon. Air-pumps were commonly used in demonstrations, and well-known seventeenth-century experiments such as the removal of a spleen were often reenacted.

Douglas, Cheselden, and other anatomical demonstrators took animals so much for granted that they mentioned nonhumans merely in passing. "The body" is indifferently animal or human. Dogs were most commonly employed, followed by rabbits, pigs, cats, and sheep. In this era when dogs were increasingly kept as pets, how did the anatomist's audience react to seeing them dissected, whining and writhing in the throes of death, their own death eerily reenacting the death of the nearby cadaver?[30] Although Cheselden makes no apology for using animals, Douglas sounds decidedly defensive in his treatise on muscles:

As for the Comparative Part of this Treatise, or the Interlacing the Descriptions of the Humane muscles with those of the Canine, that I presume needs no Apology. The many useful Discoveries drawn from the Dissection of Quadrupedes, the Knowledge of the true Structure of divers Parts of the Body, or the course of the Blood and Chyle, and of the Use and proper Action of the Parts that's chiefly owing to this sort of Dissection: These, I say, give a very warrantable Plea for insisting upon it, tho' it may be censur'd by the Vulgar.[31]

It is not entirely clear what Douglas is apologizing for—presuming animals are like humans, or using animals, or "this sort of Dissection" (i.e., vivisection). But this statement is remarkable simply for acknowledging the role of animals. Yet he does not mention cruelty, but the censorship of "the vulgar": the audience that does not understand science.

In the preface to his textbook on anatomy Cheselden declared, This Treatise being design'd for the Use of Those who study Anatomy for their Entertainment, or to qualify Themselves for the Knowledge of Physick or Surgery, and not for such as wou'd be critically knowing the most minute Parts; I have purposely omitted a great many nice, unnecessary Divisions, which are commonly made, and Descriptions of those small Vessels.[32]

The first use of anatomy was for entertainment, not for medicine. But Cheselden's statement is also disingenuous. To study the "minute parts" in dead bodies was difficult at any time, and decomposition quickly eliminated fine details. In addition, Cheselden used many animals to reveal structures and functions he could not reveal in the human body. His claim—that he will reveal the human body, but not too much—reveals the nature of his audience. The anatomist will not offend them by too much digging into a body becoming progressively more decayed. Even in animals, these most minute parts will not be examined, lest they offend the sensibilities of an increasingly sensitive audience. Cheselden's constant reference to teleology and the moral value of anatomy enforced the high tone he set. But even this minimalist anatomy would have the blood, smells, noise, and general atmosphere of an impolite science.

Animals in the moral theater of anatomy were instruments of a greater purpose. Their own moral standing was entirely dependent upon their role within the drama, and did not exist independently. Audiences experienced awe and admiration for the Creator and a greater apprehension of the imminence of death in the midst of life, and they very likely then examined the state of their own souls. Public anatomy served a function somewhere between reality TV and the passion play. It was a real-life drama with protagonists who carried widely known metaphorical labels.

Public anatomy declined in the eighteenth century, and largely disappeared by 1800. Many reasons can be given for this. While experimentation on animals continued throughout the eighteenth century, public anatomy became increasingly detached from research after 1700. As the research enterprise became more complex, it could not be sufficiently simplified for lay audiences, and the scientific value of public dissection therefore was increasingly dubious: these displays did not discover any new information, either from the corpse or from the animals, but simply showed what was known, and not all of that. Public display of animal experiments, even in scientific settings such as the Royal Society, declined precipitously after 1750. Among the upper classes, "sensibility" or sensitivity became more valued; violent spectacles such as public dissection were far too disturbing to those of sensitive nerves. As public approbation of them declined, they became accordingly less useful as either institutional or individual promotion. As medicine became more professionalized, demand increased for specialized anatomy lectures rather than the more general courses such as Cheselden's. Later entrepreneurial lecturers directed their advertisements toward medical students. Polite behavior divided the upper classes from the lower, thought to be of cruder, sturdier nerves that could withstand cruder entertainments. Although street performances that included animal combat continued to be popular throughout the eighteenth century, they were increasingly viewed as lower-class entertainments. By the end of the eighteenth century, public anatomy had lost its social, cultural, and moral functions.

A SHORT HISTORY OF CLASSIFICATION

By the end of the seventeenth century, concepts of classification had reached a crisis. The seemingly chaotic organization of cabinets and collections reflected a lack of consensus among classification schemes. The great influx of animals from the New World and other areas disrupted the old notion of a chain of being that was both full and complete, but there was little agreement about what might be a proper criterion for classification. The ideal, a "natural" system of classification that would display the order of nature, seemed increasingly out of reach. Although Aristotle had attempted to establish a natural system based on essential features and natural affinities, he also believed in a natural hierarchy that later taxonomists rejected. Various theories of plant classification multiplied during the seventeenth century, but the classification of animals lagged behind.

At the end of the seventeenth century, John Ray (1627–1705) attempted a natural classification of animals, but its complexity did not bode well for future endeavors. In 1735, the Swedish botanist Carl von Linné (Carolus Linnaeus, 1707–1778) described a rational classification of plants based on sexual parts in his *Systema naturae* (System of nature), which also presented a scheme for classifying animals, organizing them in six broad classes: quadrupeds, birds, amphibians, fish, insects, and worms. In the 1779 edition of *Systema Naturae*, he described nearly six thousand species of animals. His system was artificial, aimed at establishing order rather than reproducing nature's plan, and its use of the binomial nomenclature was widely adopted, as well as his hierarchical grouping that included Kingdom, Class, Order, Genus, Species, and Variety.[33]

Linné's system of classification was challenged by Georges-Louis Leclerc, comte de Buffon (1707–1788), whose forty-four-volume *Histoire naturelle* (1749–1788) was the most comprehensive and best-known work on natural history in the eighteenth century. Buffon argued that any system of classification was by definition arbitrary and artificial, and that reality resided in individuals, not in species. While he modified his views over the course of his life, adopting many Linnaean categories, Buffon is especially important for introducing the concept of time into the discussion of taxonomy, finding variability of species over time but constancy of form at higher taxonomic levels. Here he entered the cosmological debates that began with Descartes and continued through Newton and Leibniz.

As supervisor of the King's Garden and its menagerie, Buffon presided over a worldwide trade in plants and animals, and this knowledge is reflected in his *Histoire naturelle*. His collaborator Louis-Jean-Marie Daubenton (1716–1800) greatly assisted Buffon in his investigations into comparative anatomy, the backbone of the *Histoire naturelle*. In the first volume, Buffon offered a *Discourse on method* for natural history, based on direct observation. Buffon's emphasis on visual evidence is displayed in the lavish illustrations that graced the volumes; like Perrault's work, Buffon presented a "virtual menagerie," but one of universal breadth. Writing almost as a counter-Descartes, Buffon warns against making premature conclusions based on insufficient observation. Yet, he acknowledges, the abundance and diversity of nature is such that we cannot hope to comprehend it all. Following Perrault's *Mémoires*, he advocates a Baconian technique of observation and comparison of numerous individuals. The first truth he arrives at from this method is, he notes, "perhaps humiliating to humans: it is that we must classify ourselves as animals."[34] But Buffon goes on to state that any classification is in fact impossible; nature consists of individuals who differ in minute and imperceptible ways. Even plants, which are less complex than animals, have not been perfectly classified; there is always a group of "anomalies" that confound the taxonomist. Buffon condemns all current classification schemes as being artificial and incomplete, displaying "an error of metaphysics," what we might call a category mistake. The systems for classifying animals are even worse than those for plants.[35]

But what is his alternative? Buffon advocates a natural system based on observation of all characteristics of an organism. This does not, he points out, lead to a system as complete and complex as that of Linné, but it better reflects the truth of nature. Inevitably, Buffon's categories in 1749 were large and loose. But over the forty years of the *Histoire naturelle*, Buffon added a critical element to his system: the idea of time. Buffon came to see biological categories as temporally contingent, emphasizing the historical processes of nature, bringing "history" in our sense into natural history. The true explanation of present life forms lay in their history. In his 1778 work *Epoques de la nature* Buffon presented what one historian has called a "secular Genesis," a story of natural development over time that greatly extended the conventional time frame, allowing for development and diversification over time. While it would be an overstatement to call Buffon's narrative a theory of evolution, it set the groundwork for research in comparative anatomy, geology, and paleontology, which in turn provided the basis for Darwinian evolution. Buffon's King's Garden, which the French Revolution recreated as the Paris Museum of Natural History, was the site for much of the fundamental research into these areas.[36]

By the end of the eighteenth century, the distinction between natural history and natural philosophy had definitively broken down, as animals came to be studied from multiple perspectives. Animals lost much of their earlier symbolic meaning, but gained a history that grew progressively longer. In both laboratories and natural history museums animals were, more than ever, objects of scientific scrutiny.

CHAPTER SIX

Animality and Anthropology in Jean-Jacques Rousseau

JEAN-LUC GUICHET
Translated by Richard Byrne

During the eighteenth century, the question of animals acquired a new philosophical importance.[1] Stimulated by the challenge of the Cartesian "animal machine," animated by disputes about the souls of animals that had reached a crescendo during the last third of the previous century and continued among Enlightenment thinkers, engaged in by both empiricists and materialists, thinking about animals became an essential pivot in the new anthropology that sought to create a new definition of man by reducing the importance of the relationship to God and increasing the role of originary, primordial factors and empirical influences in this new definition.

The work of the empiricists was especially important. Locke reworked all of philosophy by reconsidering the value of sensation and perception; whereas the latter phenomena of consciousness had been undervalued and subject to suspicion, Locke brought these experiences to the forefront in his thought, and they became the origin and the very criteria of knowledge. From this standpoint, the animal was assigned a new closeness to man. This new closeness would be amplified within empiricist thought, not least in the radical sensationalism of Condillac, as well as within materialism which, as we see especially in both La Mettrie and Diderot, profited from the new thinking about animals. One answer—a very Cartesian but relatively synthetic tendency—was advanced from the middle of the century onward by Buffon, author of *L'Histoire naturelle* (1749–1789), one of the best-selling works of the Enlightenment. Rousseau, from a philosophical perspective, was also working on a much more effective synthesis that balanced Cartesian, empiricist, spiritualist, and materialist influences.

The importance of animals in the thought of Rousseau was first noticed by two well-known French scholars, one a specialist on Descartes (Henri Gouhier) and the other an authority on Rousseau (Pierre Burgelin). A brief exchange took place between the two men at a conference after Gouhier read a paper on the influence of Descartes on Rousseau's *Profession of Faith of a Savoyard Vicar*. Burgelin: "He [Rousseau] is always very concerned with the question of animals." Gouhier: "We must return to this question again."[2]

The question of the animal,[3] which neither Gouhier nor Burgelin really answered, appears to be of sincere interest to Rousseau; his is a diffuse but profound interest that goes to the very roots of his thinking. Rousseau's attraction to nature and living beings was both intellectual and emotional. He was convinced that it was impossible to understand man without taking as a starting point the constitutive relations with nature, consciousness, origins, history, all of which took him toward animals as if toward a decisive pole of interrogation, a questioning that often yielded important results. The animal was a key protagonist whom Rousseau's thought was destined to engage. Furthermore, whatever Rousseau sometimes said, the range of his reading and his own philosophical engagement is such that he was familiar with all those works in his period that discussed the animal and was anything but naive as to the problems and the debates associated with those works.

SENTIMENT AND THE ANIMAL SOUL

If, unlike Buffon, Rousseau was willing to grant that animals had a soul, it was because for him the spectrum of different kinds of truths was much greater than it was in the Cartesian tradition. Alongside purely rational truth derived from evidence and demonstration as well as empirical truth derived from the close interaction of the senses and understanding, there was a third category, that of "emotional truth" ("*vérité de sentiment*"). The latter category comes from the heart; it is not beyond the scope of reason, as in the work of Pascal, but cannot be totally transparent to reason either, without which it would be just a fleeting moment, a sort of vague and irrational feeling that anticipates the reason that will replace it. It is in fact of another order, from an independent source that gives access, in the same way as in Pascal, to the most essential and "vital" truths. However, it is not so much that reason and feelings stand in opposition in Rousseau's work. Rather, their close relationship means that they regulate one another and can only make sense and be relied upon within the context of that relationship. To take a moral example, if the heart naturally loves the good, then it is blind and susceptible to be fooled into thinking that it can recognize it; it must also possess reason in order to truly recognize the good. As Rousseau put it in the *Profession of Faith of a Savoyard Vicar,* in speaking of God: "Has he not given me conscience that I may love what is right, reason that I may perceive it, and freedom that I may choose it?"[4]

Reason, by the same token, left to itself and to its own arbitrary hypotheses without adequate foundations, creates merely abstract ideas and vanishes in its own vanity (with the double meaning of the term—both an unreality and a desire fueled by the emotions). Consequently, "it is not so much reasoning which we lack but the understanding of reasoning."[5] This understanding of reason may be external, in which case it is the external senses, or internal, in which case it is the internal sense, that of consciousness. Thus, the three types of access to truth—pure reason, empirical observation, and internal intuition—are perhaps less three distinct faculties (creating logical forms and critical reflection for reason; intuition of the "source," for the senses, divided itself into external and internal senses) of the activity of thinking, but must be indivisible if they are to function correctly.

More precisely, it is on the basis of our own experiences of knowledge that we judge by analogy those of animals. This is due to the fundamental importance of the truth of sentiment or feeling. It is because of the truth of sentiment that I can be certain of my own soul. Indeed, I am aware of myself, either on the basis of my will or even from simple sensations, as a subject of a spiritual nature. In the *Profession of Faith of a Savoyard Vicar,* it is the very act of feeling (*sentir*), a simple and elementary act, that implies the simplicity of its substratum and thus, given that matter is essentially divisable and composed of juxtaposed parts, its spirituality. A simple and ordinary feeling within me is enough for me to be aware of my own soul; it is not necessary to rise to the level of the more complex faculties of understanding and reason. It can only be within the framework of a relationship based on feelings, of emotional, personal, subjective, prelinguistic, and prerational ties, that the animal soul is likely to appear to me in its own right. The privileged and most undeniable element of this relationship is *pity,* an experience full of shared feeling and of confusion between my own feelings and those of the other living being, man or beast.

PITY

Pity makes no sense unless it supposes a deep and real analogy between one's self and the other self toward which pity is directed. Spontaneously aware of myself as a sentient being, I intuitively identify the same nature in the suffering being. Such pity is not deduced on the basis of a simple external analogy shaped by observation; it is an active empathy by which I sense within myself something exterior to myself, an essential identity despite the very different form that being might take. Sensation or sentiment (that is, an internalized moral feeling) of suffering is the crucible within which I test whether sensation within the other is deeply related to my own and thus whether, within this relationship, the being of the other is equal to my own.

> Emile, having thought little about sentient creatures, will be slow to discover what it means to suffer and die. Groans and cries will begin to stir his compassion, he will turn away his eyes at the sight of blood; the convulsions of a dying animal will cause him I know not what anguish before he knows the source of these impulses. ... So pity is born, the first relative sentiment which touches the human according to the order of nature. To become sensitive and compassionate, the child must know that he has fellow-creatures who suffer as he has suffered, who feel the pains he has felt, *and he must imagine that there are others who are capable of having these sensations as well.* Indeed, how can we let ourselves be stirred by pity unless we go beyond ourselves and *identify ourselves with the suffering animal, by leaving, so to speak, our own nature and taking on that of the animal* (my emphasis).[6]

THE LIMITS OF ANIMAL THOUGHT

Did Rousseau, who recognized thinking within animals, also believe that they had true understanding? This is the problem that both Locke and then Condillac had addressed following on from the work of Montaigne and Charron. It could seem likely that Rousseau, in his *Discourse on the Origin of Inequality* (1755), echoes their theories and abandons entirely the Cartesian animal machine hypothesis. It is true only to a certain point in spite of the Swiss philosopher's sympathy for the views of Locke and Condillac in the second of two crucial paragraphs from the first part of the book, which we cite at length.

> I see in all animals only an ingenious machine to which nature has given senses in order to keep itself in motion and protect itself ... against everything that is likely to destroy or disturb it. I see exactly the same things in the human machine, with this difference: that while nature alone activates everything in the operations of a beast, man participates in his own actions in his capacity as a free agent. The beast chooses or rejects by instinct, man by an act of free will, which means that the beast cannot deviate from the laws which are prescribed to it, even when it might be advantageous for it to do so, whereas a man often deviates from such rules to his own prejudice. This is why a pigeon would die of hunger beside a dish filled with

choice meats and a cat beside a pile of fruits or grain, even though either could very well nourish itself with the foods it disdains. ...

Every animal has ideas because it has senses; up to a certain point it even associates those ideas; and man differs from the beasts in this respect only in a matter of degree. Some philosophers have even asserted that there is more difference between one given man and another than there is between a given man and a given beast. Thus it is not his understanding which constitutes the specific distinction of man among all other animals, but his capacity as a free agent. Nature commands all animals, and the beast obeys. Man receives the same impulsion, but he recognizes himself as being free to acquiesce or resist; and it is above all in this consciousness of his freedom that the spirituality of his soul reveals itself, for physics explains in a certain way the mechanism of the senses and the formation of ideas, but in the power to will, or rather to choose, and in the feeling of that power, we see pure spiritual activity, of which the laws of mechanics can explain nothing.[7]

Understanding, etymologically, means the activity of comprehension. Most authors, despite great differences, agree that understanding is defined by three characteristics: (1) access to general ideas; (2) the capacity to connect ideas and the propositions behind them by an associative pathway, that is, reason; and finally (3) the reflexivity that makes it possible to reflect regularly on oneself and one's own functions and thus organize oneself according to certain methods, to correct oneself, and thus to progress. Moreover, these characteristics (generalization and abstraction, making logical connections, and establishing self-reflexivity) ensure a continuity of understanding oneself and one's autonomy in relation to both the senses and the external world. However, with regard first to general ideas, for Rousseau these could not be created by an animal since they absolutely presuppose language, of which animals are completely deprived. In this, Rousseau stands alongside almost all of the other writers of his period, all of whom agree on this point; even Locke shared this view despite all he credited animals with.

An exception would be Condillac, who argued in his *Treatise on Animals (1755)*, "Consequently, it [the instinct of beasts] makes no, *or almost no*, abstractions ... And because they make few abstractions, they have *few general ideas*" (my emphasis).[8]

But what about the categories of self-reflexivity and using logic? Locke certainly allows that a basic animal understanding exists. This is only on the basis of particular ideas and the logical links between them and only in a way closely associated with the circumstances of perception. Condillac, in advancing animal thought to the threshold of general ideas, granted it, accordingly, the capacity to reason and reflect, a capacity conceived not so much as a faculty of the animal existing independently of sensation or in innate fashion, as Locke had believed, but as a spontaneous, reflexive dimension of sensation, existing only in and through sensation. Thus the animal, in tentatively feeling its way by trial and error, starts to construct, from the outset, patterns of behavior that respond to its needs and are thus adapted to its environment. However, this process is soon halted by its very success because the limited environment the animal evolves in and the limited needs it satisfies dispenses the animal from searching further and reflecting.

Is this the same in Rousseau? Not at all. The *Discourse on Inequality* takes as an example the monkey that "without hesitating goes from one nut to another."[9] This animal, selected by Rousseau because it is among the most evolved and the closest to man, appears totally automated and governed by the double impulsion of its senses and the environment. If a particular memory comes to it, then it is a purely sensory experience, a passive and associative record of its sensations[10] and so is fundamentally different from a true memory that is made possible by true understanding. The "memory" of this monkey seems closer to what Buffon had called "reminiscence," but which he thought of as purely material, than to a true memory analogous to that of man which has a constitutive link to understanding. Furthermore, not only does the monkey produce no general ideas,[11] it does not combine any of the ideas it has within the framework of a logical schema. Animal thought is instead the interplay of particular ideas whose associations are not logical, reflective, and autonomous, but rather are governed by the fluctuating relationship between the conditions and needs of the physical body, past and present feelings, and stimuli from the animal's environment. In a word, the relationship between these ideas is biological rather than logical. The animal certainly has ideas, but they are not produced, reflected upon, and connected by understanding. It "combines"[12] them not in a free and logical way, but rather in a way entirely determined by the mechanisms of the senses and the passions, under the pull of external circumstances and according to correlations between present feelings and those it has experienced in the past. The words "without hesitating" in the description of the monkey demonstrates that, just as in Descartes and Buffon, there is an absence of reflexivity.

For Rousseau, there is no continuity and autonomy in the understanding of an animal that would allow it to follow its own norms and reflexively carve a path of logical necessity from one idea to the next. On the contrary, the thought of the animal is tossed about in an incessant to and fro between internal needs and feelings and external situations. Compared with the tenacity of human thought, working away in the seriousness of its interiority, the animal is affected by permanent distractions that combine with its thoughts to form ideas within the animal, rather than the animal forming the ideas itself. Thus, this monkey gives us the spectacle of a thought process that is always outside of itself without being free to take an interest in its own activities in themselves, of a thought process always on alert and on guard, permanently mobilized and always preoccupied by possible threats and the search for food. Here again, if we ignore for a moment the question of the soul, where the two certainly disagree, we see a close relationship between Rousseau's "monkey-machine," which is at the mercy of everything, including itself and its own thought, and the "dog-machine," in Buffon's *Natural History*.

THE STATE OF NATURE

For Rousseau, animals do not possess the essential characteristic of man—*perfectibility*—a characteristic already present within humans in the pure state of nature, where they behave at once as animals and already indeed as men. Thus, the fact that man in the state of nature learns how to optimize his physical resources and his senses, "since his body is the only tool savage man knows,"[13] and that, in this respect he is just like any other animal, does not mean that he is the same, since "savage men, dispersed among them [animals], *observe, imitate their industry and so rise* to the level of the Beasts' instinct."[14] To observe, to imitate (but not in a passive or mechanical way), to raise oneself up, there is in these actions something other than simple animality. Such actions demonstrate a capacity to leave the self, to go beyond the given that carries man further than animal learning that only consists in the narrowest possible adjustments of the body and its senses to the environment, and in a rigid conformity to milieu, in distinction to a reflective distance, which is characteristic of the human.

Perfectibility thus arises in the form of a polyvalency that the savage man acquires through imitation of other animals. Although this polyvalency applies in the first instance to the anatomical structure of man ("all things considered, the most advantageously organized of all"[15]), it is linked just as much to man's lack of a fixed and rigid instinct, the absence of which makes liberty possible. It is also the case, as this passage demonstrates, that as savage men are dispersed among the animals, they "observe and imitate their industry," which shows that the wild men are deliberate in their imitation. Take, for example, the diet of the savage man; to begin with he is a vegetarian and he subsists on fruits, nuts, and vegetables. He develops his diet to become an omnivore and occasionally a carnivore in a way that the pigeon and the cat of the *Discourse on Inequality* are incapable.[16] It is probable that this change in diet was the result of imitation of the predators and thus of man's perfectibility.

THE PONGOS

Original man, minimal man, reduced to the irrevocable core of his specificity (liberty and perfectibility) also contains within him a minimal animality (essentially self-love and pity) that unites him with the animals, without reducing him to this condition. Once again, perfectly an animal, but already man.

It is, however, impossible to observe this savage man since in all known cultures there is a separation between the pure original state of man and men already transformed by social relations, even if for some the balance between nature and culture is a source of happiness. However, between real savages and the ideal savage there is an intermediate figure, a real, living being that is at the same time an "ideal," in its close proximity to nature, but who may be man nonetheless: these are the creatures that were called *pongos*, in Rousseau's day. The term referred to the group of large anthropomorphic apes that today form the family *Pongidae*, a group that includes four species: *Pongo pygmaeus* (orangutans), *Gorilla gorilla* (gorillas), *Pan troglodytes* (chimpanzees), and *Pan paniscus* (bonobos). (See Figure 6.1.) During Rousseau's time no such distinctions were made, so these different varieties were taken to be one and the same, whether they lived in Africa (chimpanzees, gorillas) or in Indonesia (orang-outangs). Thus Rousseau cites the *Histoire des voyages*: "In the Kingdom of the Congo ... are found many of those big Animals *called Orang-Outangs in the East Indies*" (my emphasis).[17] On the shifting borders of animality, uncertain creatures appear; direct knowledge of these creatures has been blurred by testimonies and reporting. These mysterious textual creatures (described in frustratingly imprecise, prejudiced accounts totally unaware of the importance of their content) were dubious candidates for the category of the human, and Rousseau would examine their credentials very closely. This examination, which Rousseau puts in note J of the *Discourse on Inequality,* is extremely rigorous and highly scientific in both its spirit and its method, due as much to Rousseau's unprejudiced approach to the subject as to the criteria he used as well as to his critical engagement with his sources. The note is the practical application of the anthropological criteria that Rousseau sets out in the first part of the work, a first attempt to test the relevance of these criteria in relation to real things being examined and identified. It is, in a sense, like the photographic negative of the positive descriptions of human specificity. It is as if, below the principal text, where the savage man treads, walk the pongos; and both are tested by the same criteria of identification. Among the traditional criteria (morphology, intelligence, language) only one is central for Rousseau—perfectibility.

Rousseau examines criteria that justify the exclusion of these anthropomorphic beings from the category of the human, criteria that are only implicit in the work of the travel writers whose texts he examines. The physical criteria are manifestly insufficient as much because there is some resemblance between humans and *Pongidae*, as because of the obvious differences between humans.[18] There remain two other criteria that incline toward their exclusion: their stupidity and the absence of language. This latter absence can be

FIGURE 6.1: Pongo, or orangutan from Angola, given to Frederick Henry, Prince of Orange, Engraving in Abbé Antoine François Prévost d'Exiles, *Histoire générale des voyages*, vol. 5, Paris, 1748. Courtesy of the Division of Rare and Manuscript Collections, Cornell University Library.

confirmed among pongos without excluding the possibility of their humanity since the absence of language—central and decisive according to Descartes—is not relevant here for Rousseau since it would also exclude Rousseau's man-in-the-state-of-nature who is similarly lacking in language:

> weak reasons for those who know that, although the organ of speech is natural to man, speech itself is nevertheless not natural to him, and who recognize the extent to which his perfectibility may have raised Civil man above his original state.[19]

Rousseau argues moreover that we should judge behavior only by considering it in its entirety and that other actions of the pongos make it highly unlikely, for instance, that they are incapable of managing and maintaining a fire, as some of the travel writers claimed. "Really, it seems very strange that the Pongos, whose dexterity and strength are acknowledged, who know how to bury their dead and how to make themselves roofs out of branches, should not know how to push embers into a fire."[20] Staying true to the ideas expressed in the *Discourse*, the major criteria and the key to Rousseau's analysis is perfectibility. However, given the present state of observations of the pongos, it is impossible to decide their case. Rousseau therefore leaves open the question of their humanity and appears to be less concerned with deciding that issue than with raising doubts as to the certainties of the lines that delineate man from other creatures.

THE FREE AVIARY

The best possible relations with animals are most likely when they are tamed. In effect, that relationship makes it possible for Rousseau to act out, even if in a substitutive way, the synthesis of necessity and liberty that appears to define the ideal horizon of human relations. The animal, which receives attention in its own right in the work of Rousseau, thus acquires a symbolic meaning that places it, decisively, at the center of the debate about human values. This is exemplified in a particular episode in *La Nouvelle Héloïse*, a scene that takes place in Julie's garden (named the *Elysium*) and that can be called the "free aviary." An aviary without bars, where the ingenuity of Monsieur and Madame Wolmar has succeeded in attracting and retaining, without any constraint, an astonishing multitude of birds.[21]

The introduction of the hero of this epistolary novel, Saint-Preux, as well as the reader, into this magical place comprises a long letter within the novel as it becomes the setting for a carefully prepared scene. Rather than being a simple light-hearted relief that Rousseau introduces after a highly serious letter, or for that matter, a simple pretext for him to discuss his ideas about gardening, a whole process of sacralization, indicated even in the name *Elysium*, of this pastoral utopia shows that this setting is neither decorative nor anecdotal. Cut off and protected, accessible only to close friends, this setting has multiple echoes: the tradition of the sacred grove in Antiquity, the story of Ulysses' sojourn with Alcinous in Homer, the garden of Armida in Tasso's *Jerusalem Delivered*, and, more widely, all of the Biblical and medieval symbolism of this locus. Reserved for the initiated, it is in itself structured like a route of initiation, being revealed in several stages of which the free aviary is the apotheosis.

A temple of nature and of art, it is moreover a secret sanctuary of memory. A work interwoven with temporality, in its geography we discover the successive lures of nature that are in fact a history, that of the private life of Julie. On one hand, to the extent that Julie lives an exposed, social life, under the protective eye of her husband Wolmar, she is also living, in the same sacred space of her intimacy and truth, a different life oriented toward the past, driven by the perception of a memory that she at once reveals and conceals. The aviary expresses this in terms of the blissful throng of birds, whose happiness and freedom evoke her children and the prosperity of her household, a symbolic link that Julie herself confirms in words full of double meanings.

> [Wolmar] "The uninterrupted tranquillity they enjoy induces them to lay their eggs in this convenient place, where they want for nothing and where no one disturbs them. That is how the nation of the fathers [la patrie des pères] becomes that of the children, and how the populace thrives and multiplies."—"Ah," said Julie, "you no longer see anything! No one ever thinks beyond himself. But the inseparable mates, the zeal for domestic duties, paternal and maternal tenderness—you have missed all that. Two months ago you should have been here to give your eyes to the most charming spectacle and your heart to the sweetest sentiment of nature."[22]

There is a double symbolism in the free aviary episode because the orchard also contains captive fish whose lives were spared, just as was the case for Julie, but at the price of depriving the fish of their natural freedom, which is also the case for Julie. The heroine of the *Nouvelle Héloïse* makes this clear in a conversation with her husband. Saint-Preux: "I saw some fish. 'Ah, ah!' I said immediately, 'they are *prisoners* nevertheless.' 'Yes,' Wolmar said, 'They are *prisoners of war*, whose lives have been spared.' 'Without a doubt,' added his wife, 'some time ago, Fanchon stole from the kitchen some little perch which she brought here without my knowledge.'"[23] This is the last image that Saint-Preux carries with him when he leaves the Elysium, as though Julie's words are a troubling disavowal of such an apparently enchanting space.

Thus an ambivalent symbolism is attached to the Elysium, despite its perfectly elegant appearance. On the one hand it is a space of freedom, the most perfect symbol and triumph of Julie's "Elysian" ideal of union and peace, where man and the elements come together and lend their support to her aim of uniting all of the people who are precious to her, from her cousin and son to Lord Wolmar, and even including her former lover, Saint-Preux. On the other hand, the Elysium is at the same time intersected with the dark furtive shadows of her secret torments that tarnish the shine of this all-too-ideal harmony. This explains why the bottom of the garden, where all of the birds gather, which is the holiest of holy places, the sacred heart of this sacred space, which seems at once to be so near that one can see it and almost grasp it, is, at the same time, inaccessible, truly sacralized, in a word: separated. This pure image is surrounded at its base by a pool of reality, that of the pond of captive fish, which is its exact opposite and into which we can only tumble and drown if we are obstinate enough to try to ascend to the summit of unreality, which will be exactly what happens to Julie who eventually dies by falling into a lake at the end of the novel.

CONCLUSION

Throughout Rousseau's work, although there is no sustained and single discussion of animals, there is constant reference to them. In these discussions Rousseau takes into account all of the questions posed about animals during the Enlightenment. His work, far from simply contrasting man and animals, always thinks about them in terms of one another. By doing so, Rousseau offers at the core of the Enlightenment a balanced vision of their relationship, which he articulates according to a model of fundamental continuity between humans and animals, without, however, confusing them. This dual aim of forcefully connecting man and animal, while retaining a view of human specificity, is characteristic of the great mutations of thought that took place in relation to the question of animals during the eighteenth century; this in itself is characteristic of Rousseau's paradoxical centrality, in spite and because of his radical position within Enlightenment thought. We are still the heirs of these mutations, which were linked to a deep reconstruction of ethics and anthropology, a heritage that was strengthened in the following century with the help of the great Darwinian shift, which established the closeness of all living things based upon their common history.

CHAPTER SEVEN

Portraits of Animals, 1600–1800

MADELEINE PINAULT SØRENSEN
Translated by Janice C. Zinser

Continuing the sixteenth-century tradition, artists during the seventeenth and eighteenth centuries portrayed animals in various types of artwork, ranging from tapestry cartoons, to paintings, scientific illustrations, sculpture, and art objects. One very quickly notices diverse approaches, even by the same artist, making any synthesis problematic. There is no break with the previous century, nor will there be one with the following century. Whether surrounded by human characters or not, animals continue to be indispensable elements in mythological, religious, historical, or secular paintings. Consider, for example, the camels or dromedaries appearing in Biblical scenes, the ox and the ass in the life of Christ, the birds—swans and eagles—populating mythological scenes, or horses in historical or religious paintings. Moreover, especially in the seventeenth century, animals play a prominent role in emblems, allegories, symbols, fables, and metamorphoses.

Human interest in animals is even more in evidence with the influx of exotic animals brought back in great numbers aboard trading vessels. Expeditions, first to the Americas and the East, and later to Africa and the Pacific, introduced new species of animals that would have undoubtedly been deemed mythical during the previous centuries, but now became objects of study for scientists and artists. These animals were also objects of curiosity, kept in menageries or exhibited at European fairs where artists were able to draw and paint them.

Albert van Eckhout (1610–1665) and Frans Post (1612–1680) traveled with Prince Jan Mauritz de Nassau-Siegen to the Dutch colony Surinam, painting landscapes, people, and animals from this region.[1] In his cartoons[2] for the *Tenture des Nouvelles Indes* (New Indies Tapestry), François Desportes (1661–1743) copied the animals that Eckhout and Post had painted. Afterward, one observes depictions of exotic animals, such as the *Zebra*,[3] painted in a magnificent landscape by George Stubbs (1724–1806) after the live model brought from the Cape of Good Hope and housed in the royal menagerie at Buckingham Gate (See Figure 7.1) or the *Girafe*,[4] portrayed by an anonymous French artist around 1784.

There was an obvious public enthusiasm for all these strange and exotic animals that explains the popularity of the chameleon at the Royal Academy of Sciences in Paris and the one given to Madeleine de Scudéry by a friend,[5] which she turned into one of her salon's attractions and whose story she tells in her *Nouvelles Conversations de Morale*.[6] It later became the subject of a scientific study in the works of Claude Perrault.[7] Charles Le Brun (1619–1690), or one of his students, sketched it with remarkably lively eyes.[8] Pieter Boel (1622–1674) painted the chameleon in a curious monochrome rendering[9] that, although not drawn from life, expresses well the loneliness of this small

FIGURE 7.1: *A Zebra*, by Georges Stubbs, 1763, Oil on canvas, 103 × 127 cm. New Haven, Yale Center for British Art, Paul Mellon Collection.

creature. This taste for strange animals emerged in the work of other artists as well, especially the Dutch painter Marseus van Schrieck (1619–1678), who had a particular affinity for the reptilian world.

Animals were also prominent in still-life painting, which, for certain artists, began to take on monumental proportions,[10] or in the hunting scenes, so highly treasured by collectors and already very much in vogue during the previous century,[11] or in depictions of animal gatherings and combat between mammals and birds. Private collectors favored birds with strong colors such as parrots and cockatoos shown alone[12] or in the company of European or exotic birds in improbable gatherings and concerts, as well as in human portraits. Several Flemish and Dutch painters specialized in this genre of painting, considered a lesser art—as also in France—in relation to historical painting. Artists attempted to portray on their protagonists' faces expressions of hatred and fear found in hunting and animal combat scenes associated with the Baroque, as in the tempestuous *Chasses* (Hunting Scenes) of Pieter Paul Rubens (1577–1640).

MENAGERIES

Since Antiquity, rulers, princes, ecclesiastics, and private individuals have established menageries of varying size[13] in order to keep living animals, symbolizing their wealth and power. In menageries, as at fairs, one can see animals from all around the world. Menageries played an important role from an artistic perspective, allowing artists to study *ad vivum*, and accurately depict animals known previously only through often unreliable book illustrations. The role of menageries is emphasized by Jacques-Henri Bernardin de Saint-Pierre, when he writes in his *Mémoire sur la nécessité de joindre une Ménagerie au Jardin des Plantes de Paris* (Essay on the Necessity of Adding a Menagerie to the Botanical Garden in Paris): "The dead animal, however well prepared, is nothing more than a stuffed skin, a skeleton, an anatomy. Its major characteristic is lacking: the life that merits its inclusion in the animal kingdom."[14]

One of the most famous menageries was surely that of Louis XIV at Versailles. It was part of the politics of grandeur developed by the King. The animals kept there were mammals, large and small, and especially a host of birds of different sizes and color. All served as models for artists who came to draw from life, as did Pieter Boel,[15] who must be considered one of the greatest animal painters of the seventeenth century. We know nothing of his life. A painter "with talent," in other words, specializing in a very precise category, he served in the shadow of Charles Le Brun as the king's painter of animals.

His birth in Anvers, his apprenticeship under his father Jan Boel (1592–1640) and the animal painter Jan Fijt (1611–1661) and, according to certain sources of Frans Snyders, later in Genoa with Giovanni Benedetto Castiglione (1609–1664), prepared him to become an animal and still-life artist. His work at the Menagerie transformed his way of seeing animals. The starting point of this work was the creation of a group of studies for Le Brun that served as models for the *Maisons royales* (Royal Palaces) tapestry, which was woven at the Gobelins workshop.

Boel is undoubtedly the seventeenth-century artist who best understood and loved animals. For him, the Menagerie's inhabitants were no longer animals, but rather individuals whose personalities he sought to understand. Boel made hundreds of drawings in black chalk, white chalk, and a few strokes of pastel, quickly or more deliberately, depending on the temperament of the animal being sketched. Understanding animals better than anyone else, Boel does not attribute human feelings to them, but rather tries to capture what each one feels in its own way. In his drawings and sketches, we sense the warm and constant interest the artist felt for these captive animals, torn from their natural surroundings. Boel accords to each its own character as if it were being observed in the wild in its natural habitat. He is not an anatomist, but he has a unique ability to make us understand animals. We feel the deep folds in the elephant's skin, the short hair of the dromedary, as well as the delicate feet of the sultan's fowl, and the elegance of the Numidian crane, so pleasing to those who visited the Menagerie.

To draw these animals, Boel used various ruses, according to Claude Perrault[16] in his *Mémoires pour servir à l'histoire des animaux*. Concerning the elephant at Versailles, Perrault reports: "A painter wanted to draw it in an exceptional pose, with its trunk raised and its mouth open. To hold it in this pose, the painter's servant would throw fruit into its mouth, most often only pretending to throw it. The elephant grew indignant and, as if understanding that the painter's desire to portray it was the cause of this trick, instead of taking aim at the servant, it turned to the master, and shot forth from its trunk an abundance of water that ruined the paper on which the painter was sketching."[17] We can in fact identify the pose Perrault describes in one of Boel's drawings in which the animal's trunk is raised high in the air. Another quite dramatic drawing corresponding to Perrault's account shows the elephant turning abruptly and charging toward the artist. The animal gives the impression of being on the verge of leaping from the sheet of paper. (See Figure 7.2.)

Charles Le Brun used Boel's drawings for his own historical painting, his decors for the château at Versailles, and for the cupola of the château at Sceaux, where at least nineteen animal species were displayed. Boel's works were also copied up until the end of the eighteenth century by several other artists, such as François Desportes, the ornamental designer Claude Gillot

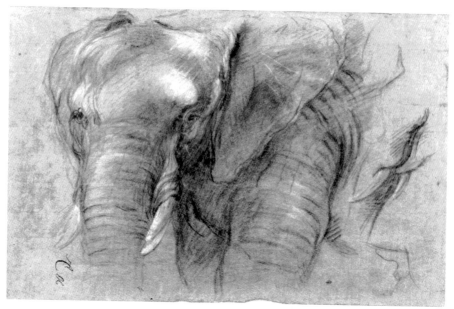

FIGURE 7.2: *An Elephant*, by Pieter Boel, ca. 1668–1674, Black chalk, heightened with white on gray paper, 29 × 44 cm. Paris, Musée du Louvre, Département des Arts graphiques. Courtesy of Musée du Louvre. Image © Musée du Louvre/Sebastian Straessle.

(1673–1722), Jean-Baptiste Oudry (1686–1755), and Jean Jacques Bachelier (1724–1806). The Menagerie animals and Boel's drawings also served as models for the king's painters, who executed paintings on vellum for the royal collection, which suggests these latter artists were not necessarily working from live models.

During the eighteenth century, the Menagerie at Versailles began its inexorable decline. A few artists came to work there: between 1739 and 1745, Oudry completed a set of ten canvases for a "natural history series" for the King's Garden, composed of a *Tiger*, a *Hyena Attacked by Two Mastiffs*, a *Leopard and Leopardess*, a *Barbary Sheep*, a *Gazelle*, a *Bustard and Guinea Fowl*, a *Tufted Crane*, a *Numidian Crane and Toucan*, a *Cassowary*, and a *Crane*, later purchased by Oudry's most fervent admirer: Prince Friedrich of Schwerin-Mecklenburg.[18] (See Figure 7.3.) The animals in these paintings are enhanced by being placed against sumptuous landscapes. At the Menagerie, Desportes drew a *Tiger*[19] that later served as the tapestry cartoon for the elephant in the *Nouvelles Indes* tapestry. Christophe Huet (1694–1759) also painted two birds named "Tocquands" (toucans) that he showed at the 1751 exhibition of the Academy of Saint-Luke.

FIGURE 7.3: *A Leopard*, by Jean-Baptiste Oudry, 1741, Oil on canvas, 131 × 160 cm. Schwerin, Staatliches Museum.

THE SCIENTIFIC STUDY OF ANIMALS

Once they died, animals from the Menagerie at Versailles were sent to Paris to the Royal Academy of Sciences, where, under the direction of Claude Perrault, they were dissected and studied. The Academicians, such as Philippe de La Hire (1640–1718), who has left us an extraordinary series of ostrich drawings,[20] described the animals in minute detail in an effort to understand their anatomy and its functions, not always a simple endeavor.

The artists collaborating with these scientists, Sebastien Leclerc (1637–1714) and later Philippe Simonneau (1685–1754), approached their subjects quite differently from the painters already mentioned. This difference in approach is clearly explained in the preface to the *Mémoires pour servir à l'histoire des animaux*, published by the Royal Academy of Sciences in Paris, where Perrault writes: "The key is not so much to portray well what one sees, but to see well what one wants to portray."[21] The illustrators working for the academy necessarily had to make choices in order for the reader to understand animal anatomy. The illustrators' approach contrasts therefore with that of the painters, who insisted on form, color, and the animal's nature.

FIGURE 7.4: *L'Effraie* (Owl), by Nicolas Robert, ca. 1670, Bodycolor on vellum, 41.2 × 31.4 cm. Paris, Bibliothèque centrale du Muséum national d'Histoire naturelle.

Naturalist artists created animal images, but not *portraits*. They participated in the establishment of the large-scale iconographic compendia such as those by the naturalist Ulisse Aldrovandi[22] and especially the collection of "Royal Vellum Paintings" that constitute the core holdings of the present-day collection of vellum painting at the National Museum of Natural History in Paris. The artists who worked for this collection were miniaturists, not necessarily working from live models, but rather from dead or stuffed specimens, from illustrations contained in the important naturalist works of Conrad Gesner and Ulisse Aldrovandi, or from Boel's drawings and sketches. In these vellums, so perfectly executed for the king, there is no life. The animals are generally portrayed standing, stiff, most often in profile, this pose being considered the best for displaying the individual characteristics of each specimen. The use of brilliant colors makes these vellum paintings very eye-catching, but they do not capture the mammals' lush fur nor the birds' light plumage. To create the illusion of their native habitats, the artist places them in stereotypical landscapes: an aquatic bird at the water's edge, surrounded by reeds and rushes; another bird found living in trees sits on a leafy branch. The gap between the naturalist painters and the artists is evident when one compares the vellums by Nicolas Robert (1614–1685) depicting an *Effraie* (Owl). (See Figure 7.4.) In one the miniaturist carries precision to the point of being unrealistic, in the other[23], he sees the animal as endowed with life nearer to an owl painted by Le Brun on the cupola of the *Pavillon de l'Aurore*.

The animals' expressions and behavior are not taken into consideration. The drawings or vellum paintings of the royal miniaturist painters and draftsmen associated with the Royal Academy of Sciences in Paris who strove for anatomical precision do not allow one to understand how the animal moves or uses its feet. On the other hand, a painter can depict the animal in motion and make it come alive. The sketches of Boel are far less detailed than the academic drawings, but they have the advantage of helping the viewer understand animal behavior. If we take, for example, the sketches of bears' paws, we can clearly see what Perrault describes in the *Mémoires,* specifically that the front paws are meant to "serve the main function of the hand which is to grasp" and are composed of four fingers joined together and a separable thumb, while the foot is meant to "make walking steadier" and is composed, as with the human foot, of a heel and five fingers.[24]

INTELLECTUAL INQUIRY

Animals also provided an opportunity for intellectual inquiry. They were called upon to justify conceptions about humankind and existence held by philosophers, doctors, and theologians, who often had conflicting ideas on these matters. René Descartes and his followers emphasized the idea of an "animal machine" made up of components called "organs." For the Cartesians, animals possess no intellect, no form of sensitivity, no capacity for affection, and therefore no soul. Theologians raised objections to this point of view as an intransigent one to say the least. An example of this opposing view can be seen in one of the illustrations of *La Chine*[25] by Father Athanasius Kircher. It shows a Chinese scholar in his study, standing before his writing desk. In the foreground there is a little monkey seated on the floor reading. (See Figure 7.5.) The decision to place a monkey in such a scene is not insignificant: Kircher clearly did not share Descartes' ideas, and sees in the monkey the possibility of thought. This engraving falls into the intellectual current opposing Cartesian ideas, shared by individuals of widely varying intellectual bent: the philosopher Pierre Gassendi; the poet Jean de La Fontaine, so expert at making animals speak in his *Fables;* Marguerite de La Sablière, La Fontaine's patroness; Madeleine de Scudéry; the moralist François de La Rochefoucauld, who composed his *Réflexions diverses* on human feeling and relationship to animals; the doctor Marin Cureau de La Chambre; and, in England, Thomas Hobbes. All of these thinkers stood in opposition to Descartes and convey in their work an image of animals who can think and feel and are close to humans in spite of

FIGURE 7.5: A Chinese Scribe Writing and Monkey Reading, Engraving in Athanasius Kircher, *China*, Amsterdam, 1670. Science, Industry & Business Library, The New York Public Library, Astor, Lenox and Tilden Foundations.

their differences. This concept of animals as being inseparable from humanity extends well back into our cultural past. Already a century before, we hear Michel de Montaigne reminding us of the *cousinage* ("cousinhood") between humans and animals.

Art theoreticians such as Roger de Piles or Claude III Nivelon also took an anti-Cartesian stance. Artists also rejected Descartes' theories. They were never indifferent to animals. Early on, artists recognized that animals are living beings, capable of feelings and reactions akin to those of humans. In the painting *The Monkey and the Cat*,[26] by Abraham Hondius (1630–1695), we see an illustration of the proverbial expression "to pull someone's chestnuts out of the fire." The monkey is attacking the cat who tries to take his chestnuts from the fire. Hondius adds a detail not in the fable: the monkey guides the cat's paw toward the fire, making him howl with pain. The howling animal, its maw open, is a frequently recurring theme; it is a dramatic touch invariably appreciated by viewers, undoubtedly because of a human fascination with suffering. The debate concerning the essential soul of animals, lasting throughout the seventeenth century, was continued in the following century by, among others: the Abbé Etienne Bonnot de Condillac, who outlined his theories in the *Traité des animaux*;[27] Georges Leclerc, Comte de Buffon, who composed a *Discours sur la nature des Animaux*, and who expounds on the character and sensitivity of animals throughout his *Histoire naturelle*; and the Abbé Claude Yvon, who devoted a long article in the *Encyclopédie* to the "Soul of Animals."[28] All of these intellectual debates had their repercussions in the thinking and work of artists of the period.

PHYSIOGNOMY

The inclination to see human traits in animals is a constant since Aristotle. This search has led philosophers, doctors, men of letters, and other inquiring minds to construct theories to study the relationship between humans and animals. During the seventeenth and eighteenth centuries, physiognomy (or "*physiognomonie*") enjoyed particular popularity within the Baroque movement in Paris during the first half of the seventeenth century and is closely associated with a predilection for portraiture. Physiognomy later became an artistic method that Charles Le Brun, First Royal Painter, presented in his *Conférence sur la physiognomonie de l'homme et ses rapports avec celle des animaux* (Lecture on the Physiognomy of Man and its Relation to that of Animals), delivered at the Royal Academy of Painting and Sculpture on March 28, 1671. The original text of this lecture is unfortunately lost, but there exists a partial copy by Nivelon[29] as well as drawings accompanying the text.[30] The drawings were executed using geometric lines laid out in triangles that account for every part of the human face and the animal's head. Today, the significance of these geometric constructions is unclear. The interplay of lines was probably meant to show the similar structure in eyes, ears, nose, mouth, and frontal orientation of the face. By these comparisons, Le Brun tried to demonstrate animal features in which "impressions of feelings" can be observed. From this, there stems a whole series of observations tending to emphasize characteristics common to both species. To execute his drawings, Le Brun used many sources: the illustrations from the basic work on physiognomy *(De Humana Physiognomia)*[31] by Giovanni Battista della Porta; the natural history books by Gesner and Aldrovandi; ancient busts and sculptures; and, above all, the drawings of Boel. Le Brun used Boel's designs first in drawings done in black chalk, where hesitations and second tries are evident; then in models done in pen and black ink, where he is essentially studying structural lines; in line drawings with no structure; and, finally, in very polished drawings in pen and ink, highlighted with black ink wash. (See Figures 7.6a and 7.6b.) With Le Brun, the life-like quality that characterized Boel's animals has disappeared; the animals are reduced to a head, full face, or in profile, and have become pedagogical models. The drawings of Le Brun show us figures of animals meant less to inform the viewer about animals than to gain a better understanding of humans. Le Brun's drawings convey the image of an animality close to humanity, just as certain portraits of humans that suggest a likeness with animals convey the image of a humanity close to animality. This fundamental concern will stretch into the following century.[32]

To demonstrate the relationship between animals and humans, Le Brun chose live animals kept at Versailles, whether large mammals (such as the lion, ox, camel, boar, or the bear), smaller animals (such as the cat, fox, wolf, or the monkey) or birds (the eagle, owl, parrot, or the crow). In his handwritten annotations, Le Brun lends human traits to these animals: the ox is "stupid," "fierce," "very fierce," or "sturdy"; the hare is "rather wild" than "fearful"; the lynx is full of "cruelty"; and the camel full of "stupidity" and "cleverness." These studies are completed by studies of animal eyes. In this respect, Le Brun follows the lead of scientists of the period who were studying the "seat of visual perception." In his *Essay des Merveilles de Nature et des plus nobles artifices* (Essay on the Wonders of Nature and the Noblest of Artifices),[33] Father Etienne Binet devoted the entirety of Chapter 12 to the eyes in relation to eloquence, that is to say, the manner of expressing one's thoughts and feelings. Accordingly, in the drawing of the two cats, Le Brun treats the eyes of each animal differently, those of one cat being stubborn and mistrusting, while the eyes of the other are stubborn and fierce. This concern with endowing animals with a human gaze is also illustrated in another drawing in which Le Brun gives human eyes, easily recognizable by their horizontality, to a horse and a lion.

FIGURE 7.6a: *Study of Eagles,* by Charles Le Brun, ca. 1671, Pen and brown ink, gray wash, 21.8 × 31.4 cm. Paris, Musée du Louvre, Département des Arts graphiques. Courtesy of Musée du Louvre.

FIGURE 7.6b: *Study of Eagle-Human,* by Charles Le Brun, ca. 1671, Pen and brown ink, gray wash, 22.3 × 31.6 cm. Paris, Musée du Louvre, Département des Arts graphiques. Courtesy of Musée du Louvre.

Somewhat forgotten at the beginning of the eighteenth century, physiognomy resurfaced in the second half of the century with the Groningen naturalist Pieter Camper; the Göttingen doctor Johann Friedrich Blumenbach; ideological doctors in France, such as Louis Moreau de La Sarthe, or the Zurich pastor Johann Kaspar Lavater. In the early nineteenth century, Louis-Marie-Joseph Morel d'Arleux and Dominique Vivant Denon used Le Brun's drawings in their *Dissertation sur le traité de Charles Le Brun concernant les rapports de la physionomie humaine avec celle des animaux* (Dissertation on the Treatise of Charles Le Brun Concerning the Relation of Human Physiognomy with that of Animals),[34] with plates engraved by Louis-Pierre Baltard (1764–1846) and André Legrand (unknown dates). This work appeared in English in the early nineteenth century.

Artists demonstrated in their works that animals have feelings and behaviors that are different from, but nonetheless close to, those of humans. The manner in which certain artists managed to make them come alive is also influencing the scientists. This is undoubtedly one of the reasons why scientists, when they needed illustrations for their works, no longer called on naturalist illustrators but on genuine artists, resulting in a shift from scientific illustration to genre painting. We can see this tendency clearly in comparing the illustrations done for Perrault with some of those done for Buffon's *Histoire naturelle*. The former are stiff since they are drawn from dead specimens and are always systematic in their presentation; the latter are much more life-like, forming small scenes adapted to each of the animals portrayed and allowing for a better appreciation of the animal's appearance and behavior.

BUFFON

The plates illustrating the *Histoire naturelle générale et particulière avec la description du Cabinet du Roi* (General and Detailed Natural History, with a Description of the Royal Collections)[35] of Buffon and Louis-Jean Marie Daubenton and their draftsmen, Buvée, the "American" (unknown dates) and Jacques de Sève (died 1788), were executed with this effect in mind. Buffon studied natural history, not from a general perspective, but in a manner taking only one point of view into consideration—the natural history of animals studied as *individuals* in different circumstances, in contrast to the system Carl Linnaeus proposed for the first time in the 1758 edition of his *Systema naturae*.

This manner of illustration, which is not original, was that adopted by earlier naturalists. The animals are still portrayed standing, most often in profile, but certain plates showing dissections, or the skeletons posed on a pedestal, are more scientific in nature. Less often, illustrations showing a live animal in the upper half and its skeleton in the lower half of the drawing are modeled on the illustrations in Perrault's *Mémoires*. Buffon's animals are portrayed from a variety of sources, not only from dead animals, dissected, stuffed, and stored in collections, preserved in alcohol, such as the Jaguar—which sometimes explains the liberty taken with reality—but also from earlier works of art, sculptures, paintings, engravings, and drawings, all of which material Buffon, Daubenton, Buvée, and de Sève used in their work since, in most instances, they did not have access to the animal they needed to describe and draw, nor had they ever seen them.

Buffon alludes several times to de Sève's own observations of animals that the draftsman had seen, and here it is clear that de Sève was a keen observer. He clearly does not have the same affection for animals as Boel, but he understands them very well. He was an especially gifted draftsman, probably trained more as a painter than as a naturalist illustrator. De Sève humanizes animals by lending them poses and expressions similar to those of humans or by portraying animals as humans like to see them. The squirrel, for example, a harmful animal but one loved by humans, is drawn with a great deal of tenderness. Each animal is studied as a portrait. Animals are set in a fanciful habitat, the American armadillo in "Incan" ruins, African animals in Egyptian ruins, or landscapes and northern animals in dense forests or open country.

The Elephant was drawn by de Sève after a small statue made in Naples in 1748 by the French sculptor Jacques François Joseph Saly (1717–1776),[36] who had observed the elephant, sent in 1742 by the Ottoman Sultan Mahmud I to Charles VII, King of the Two Sicilies, for his Naples Menagerie. (See Figure 7.7.) The terracotta is now lost, but is known from several drawings. Daubenton also worked from this small sculpture—36.45 cm in height—for his detailed description, where he included thirty-seven measurements of the small elephant, which he then multiplied by a factor of twelve to arrive at the actual height of the real elephant. Neither Buffon, Daubenton, nor de Sève had ever seen a real elephant.

De Sève twice copied Oudry's paintings, first to portray a hunting horse from the stables of Louis XV, its coat dappled with bay-brown spots, and then the *Rhinoceros*. This animal, a female named Klara, was shown in 1749 at the Saint-Germain fair, where Oudry painted her. The rhinoceros was engraved by Charpentier. Buffon perceived an error in Oudry's rendering: "Monsieur Oudry has made his rhinoceros' horn longer than that of the rhinoceros at the Saint-Germain fair that I saw and examined with a great deal of scrutiny. This feature is rendered more faithfully in Charpentier's print. Thus, it is from the latter print that we have drawn the horn of this figure, which in its other parts is drawn and reduced in size from Oudry's painting."[37] The painting was copied by de Sève, with a few changes required by the naturalist. Oudry's painting was never exhibited because of its large format, with the animal portrayed life-sized. A German artist at the time of the canvas' arrival at the home of the Prince von Schwerin-Mecklenbourg made a reduced-size copy.

De Sève delin.   C. Baquoy sculp.

FIGURE 7.7: *An Elephant*, Engraving by Charles Baquoy after drawing by Jacques de Sève, in Georges Leclerc de Buffon and Louis-Jean-Marie Daubenton, *L'Histoire naturelle et particulière avec la description du Cabinet du Roi*, vol. XI, Paris, 1764.

Klara herself then went to London, where she was drawn by George Edwards (1693–1773) and reproduced in his *Gleanings of Natural History, Exhibiting Figures of Quadrupeds, Birds, Insects, Plants, & c.*[38] Two years later Pietro Longhi (1702–1785) in Venice painted another rhinoceros.[39]

Again at the fair in Paris, a "jocko" (in fact, an orangutan) was exhibited in 1740, then in London, where it died. Its body was brought back to Paris in

wine spirits and thereafter stuffed and de Sève sketched it from its stuffed skin.
At the Saint-Laurent fair de Sève also drew a ferocious *Ouanderoo* (Lion-tailed
Macaque). A *Cape Hope Buffalo* and an *Asiatic Mouflon* were observed at the
Saint-Germain fair of 1774 and added to the *Supplement*.

Some drawings were done from life. The Royal Physician in Cayenne from
1735 to 1770, Jacques François Artur, sent back alive a three-toed sloth, only
known through some illustrations in natural history works but which had
never been seen alive in Paris. De Sève drew it in a pose that immediately allows
us to understand the animal's manner of climbing a tree. Buffon's figure was
most likely the model for Jean-Jacques Bachelier's painting, who represented the
animal in the company of a Baltimore oriole.[40] Bachelier also made a matching
painting entitled *Opossum and a Mynah Bird*.[41] These paintings by Buffon's
contemporaries would not have been completed without their strong interest in
natural history and without Buffon humanizing animals as much as he did.

We see a similar evolution in Holland in the eighteenth century, where
scientists and artists were working at the Menagerie of the Stathouder Guillaume V, on the Het Kleine Loo estate in Voorburg, near The Hague. The animals brought together there were more exotic than those at Versailles, due
to significant contributions from the prosperous West and East India Trading
Companies.[42] We know these animals through the paintings and drawings of
several artists, the most talented being Aert Schouman (1710–1792), author
of a great number of drawings of mammals and birds[43] that he places in landscapes recalling their natural environment, while at times fancifully departing
from reality.[44] (See Figure 7.8.) Once dead, the animals were sent for study to
Pieter Camper who sketched them and then to Arnout Vosmaer, Director of
the Natural History Collection of the Stathouder. Vosmaer chose from among
the drawings of Schouman and the other artists the best renderings for his
Regnum Animale.[45]

Some artists received commissions from scientists, and painted for them
real scientific portraits of animals. The Scottish doctor William Hunter commissioned Stubbs to execute a series of paintings of foreign animals that was
used for comparative anatomical study in the absence of living specimens.
These paintings, showing a *Pygmy Antelope*,[46] a *Nylghau of Bombay*, a *Cairy*,
and *The Duke of Richmond's First Bull Moose*,[47] were offered by the Gover-
nor of Quebec to the Duke of Richmond. (See Figure 7.9.) Hunter published a
description of this *Original from Quebec*. Stubbs painted the moose in accordance with the mode then prevalent, in profile, with a three-quarters view of
the head to highlight the snout. Since the young moose's antlers were not fully
grown, the artist included below, to the left, two antlers copied from another
animal. As Oudry had done before him, he surrounded the animal with a mysterious dark landscape that enhances its "between grey and brown" color, according to Hunter. Sir Joseph Banks asked Stubbs to paint a kangaroo, which

FIGURE 7.8: *A Blue Parrot*, by Aert Schouman, ca. 1760, Watercolor over black chalk, 37.2 × 24.9 cm. Paris, Collection Frits Lugt, Institut néerlandais. Courtesy of Collection Frits Lugt.

FIGURE 7.9: *The Duke of Richmond's First Bull Moose*, by George Stubbs, 1770, Oil on canvas, 61 × 70 cm. Glasgow, Hunterian Art Gallery. Image © Hunterian Museum and Art Gallery, University of Glasgow.

Stubbs did, using, according to some sources, a stuffed skin, or according to other sources, a drawing by Sydney Parkinson (1745–1771), one of the drafts-men from Captain James Cook's first voyage. Stubbs made several drawings of *Mouse Lemurs* belonging to the collector Marmaduke Tunstall.[48] For William's brother, John Hunter, Stubbs painted a *Rhinoceros*[49] and a *Yak or Tatar Ox*.

PORTRAITS OF ANIMALS

Influenced by Enlightenment philosophers and scientists, human behavior in respect to animals began to change and fell under the sway of sentimentality during the second half of the eighteenth century. Animals became compan-ions, friends, or confidants who shared the joys, sorrows, and dreams of their owners. Jean Hoüel (1735–1813) drew Jean-Jacques Rousseau in his retreat at Montmorency, in the company of his "well-loved" dog at his feet and his "old cat" Doyenne on his lap. In *Songe d'Amour* [50] by Jean-Honoré Fragonard (1732–1806), a young girl entrusts her secret to a tree trunk, with only her dog as a witness. In this kind of sentimental context, the loss of a cherished animal is experienced as so dramatic that with the end of the eighteenth century we see, both in England and France, miniature cenotaphs commemorating departed pets, following a tradition once practiced in ancient Rome. In this spirit Claude-Michel Clodion (1738–1814) sculpted *The Tomb of Ninette*[51] for the collector Pierre Jacques Onésyme Bergeret de Grancourt (1715–1785), in memory of the griffon dog of his second wife. (See Figure 7.10.) These works are not parodies of human tombstones, but rather an indication of the pronounced human sensibilities toward animals that resulted in the creation of dog cemeteries toward the end of the eighteenth century. To understand fully what animals meant to people, we would like to pause to consider what can be called "portraits" of animals, depicted alone or in the company of humans. In the seventeenth century, it is for the most part through portraits of humans that we encounter animal portraits; in the eighteenth century, the animal can become the sole subject of a work. Looking at these "portraits," one observes very quickly that they suggest an endless dialogue between humans and animals. Painters are interested in capturing the head, the gaze, and the gestures of animals. Certain artists are especially fond of emphasizing the ambiguous relationships existing between humans and animals that are an important preoccupation of seventeenth- and eighteenth-century thought. Artists execute these animal "portraits" in different ways, either in the context of official or private commissions, or in circumstances involving friends or family. This varying context explains the different forms of portraits as a function of the status of the animal, its owner, or the artist, who can be a painter, a scientific draftsman, or a sculptor. The typology of these animal portraits is difficult to characterize insofar as certain genres predate the seventeenth century, such as the equestrian portrait or the portrait of a man or woman with a dog. In the first half of the seventeenth century, true animal portraits, where animals are the main subject of the painting, are relatively scarce and often enigmatic.

The circumstances surrounding the execution of several seventeenth-century paintings considered to be among the most original are unknown. *Two Dogs in a Landscape*,[52] by Laurent de La Hyre (1606–1656), is an enigmatic painting that certain historians have understood as an illustration of the Flemish proverb, "*Daer twee honden knaegen aan been die draegen sich selden overeen*" ("Two dogs gnawing on the same bone are often at odds"). This interpretation is difficult to accept since La Hyre worked in a Parisian context, in an intellectual environment where proverbs were rarely heard. We would be more inclined to see this painting as a reference to political events, since the painting was made in a period of great turmoil in France, or as an allusion to a family episode of particular importance. The two dogs are not looking at the disputed lump of meat but at the viewer, as if seeking approval for their behavior. Jacques Thuillier sees this painting primarily as a "dog portrait."[53] The two animals, particularly the larger dog, with its muscles strained by the effort, are rendered in close detail.

FIGURE 7.10: *The Tomb of Ninette,* by Claude-Michel Clodion, ca. 1772–1773, Terracotta, 38 × 18 cm. Nancy, Musée historique lorrain. Photo © Gilbert Mangin.

Other animal portraits were associated with economic factors in Holland, for example, where artists portrayed the country's more attractive animals. Paulus Potter (1625–1654) paints an imposing *Bull*,[54] which has reminded some art historians of Pliny and the Greek painter Pausias. It does not seem appropriate to view this work as an emblem for the Butchers' Guild since it manifests no idealization of the model. On the contrary, realism is evident in all its aspects: the artist paints with precision the flies swarming around the head of the bull and around the cow lying at its side.[55] Fragonard continued this tradition in the eighteenth century with his *White Bull in Its Stable*,[56] as the only subject of the painting.

The social status of animals naturally depends on their different species, but within species there is a wide range in status. Examples can be found in horses and dogs,[57] both faithful companions of humans. During the seventeenth century horses and dogs were portrayed as symbols of power and wealth, standing alongside their owners and masters, or in equestrian portraits, as can be seen in the official portraits of Spanish royalty in the works of Diego da Silva Velázquez (1599–1660)[58] or in the work of Antoon Van Dyck (1599–1641), who executed several spectacular equestrian portraits of kings and other important aristocratic figures. Van Dyck painted two portraits of Charles I of England, the first on horseback[59] and the other, stunningly done, less ceremonial, showing the king standing in front of his horse in a posture that reveals considerable pride.[60] (See Figure 7.11.) The horse plays a prominent role in portraiture of the second half of the eighteenth century, especially in England where many aristocrats and members of the gentry commissioned portraits in which they appear with their faithful steeds. Sir Joshua Reynolds (1723–1792) continued the tradition of the aristocratic portrait of men with their horses, but he also painted *Lady Charles Spencer in Riding Habit*,[61] her hair windblown and a dreamy look on her face, with her gloved hand resting gently on her horse's muzzle. As Robert Rosenblum notes,[62] this is really a double portrait foreshadowing French portraits of the Romantic period. The love of the English for their horses is evident in the work of George Stubbs (1724–1806),[63] who captures successfully in his portraits this sometimes excessive love. In the *Portrait of Captain Samuel Sharpe Pocklington with His Wife Pleasance and His Sister Frances*,[64] Stubbs shows Pocklington standing in front of his horse at the center of the painting. Half kneeling, with another woman behind her, Mrs. Pocklington offers the horse her bridal bouquet. Here we have a portrait commemorating the Pocklington marriage, but where the horse is not overlooked! In contrast to this subject and its obvious sentimentality, Stubbs created a whole series of highly realistic individual portraits of superb race horses, showing his firm grasp of anatomy.[65] These are shown from the side, some with their owner on horseback—a member of the nobility or gentry, whether a man, often a well-known owner, or a woman—or with the trainer,

FIGURE 7.11: *King Charles I of England out Hunting*, by Antoon Van Dyck, ca. 1635, Oil on canvas, 266 × 207 cm. Paris, Musée du Louvre, Département des peintures.

jockey, or groom serving only as a foil for the horse. The artist used the same characteristics as those highlighted in human portraits to help distinguish each animal individually. The name of the horse and of the person presenting the horse is included in the title for each portrait. Thomas Pennant notes in respect to the magnificent *Lord Grosvenor's Arabian Stallion*[66] that Stubbs was "not less happy in representing animals in their stiller moments, than when agitated by their furious passions."[67] This manner of depicting horses leads to the tradition of portraying the "sporting life," still in vogue in our own era.

DOGS

The range of depictions of dogs is greater still. They are portrayed in public settings, such as hunt scenes, and in private settings, in portraits and genre painting. The theme of the hunt lent itself to the depiction of horses and dogs in different poses. It was popular among rulers and aristocrats, as can be observed in Oudry's paintings showing Louis XV in various hunting scenes. In the *Chasse en forêt de Saint-Germain*,[68] Oudry, who had the honor of participating in the royal hunt, chose to show *la curée*, the very moment when the dogs rush upon the body of the deer while the horses are held in check and the king and his retinue calmly consider the scene. The catalog for the Salon of 1750, where this painting was exhibited, pointed out that the horses and dogs were "exactly like Portraits," as were the participants in the hunt who have been identified. Stubbs shows the same moment in *The Grosvenor Hunt*,[69] painted for Richard, the first Earl of Grosvenor. The fact that these paintings have a decorative function does not exclude the possibility of the most realistic rendering of the animals.[70]

The king as hunter is a theme prevalent in the Middle Ages, subsequently recurring with regularity and with little variation. Velázquez painted several paintings with his subjects on foot, such as his portrait of Felipe IV, Don Ferdinando, and Baltasar Carlos depicted as hunters accompanied by their dogs.[71] King Carlos III is similarly shown as a hunter in different versions by Franceso y Goya y Lucientes (1746–1828).[72] The wish to preserve the image of dogs is exemplified in a series of portraits of the hunting dogs of Louis XIV and Louis XV, both avid hunters. François Desportes[73] was first commissioned to make such paintings, to be followed several years later by Jean-Baptiste Oudry.[74]

On the occasion of his entry into the Royal Academy of Painting and Sculpture in 1699, Desportes presented a self-portrait in hunting gear with two greyhounds, signifying his wealth.[75] He knew animals well and prepared for his final renderings by making sketches characterized by extreme freedom, showing hunting dogs in a variety of poses. The dogs no longer exist in anonymity but respond to the pet name painted on the canvas. Each portrait attempts to show each dog's special talents at the hunt. Oudry's approach is scarcely different from that of Desportes. He presents dogs that play a role, as in the theater, play-hunting rather than actually hunting. The dog's individual traits are highlighted, as in Oudry's portrait of three dogs,[76] where "Petite Fille" and "Charlotte" stop before a red partridge hidden in a clump of cornflowers and poppies, while "Gredinet," whom Louis XV called "my little Gredinet" and who is undoubtedly a bit more distracted, heads off in the opposite direction to pursue not game, but a peacock moth. The first painting in this series was devoted to the two female English greyhounds of Louis XV, *Misse* and *Turlu*,[77] each holding a place of honor in the king's chamber at Compiègne.

PETS

The pets most cherished by humans since Antiquity are dogs[78] and cats.[79] Humans have always had animals at their side, valued more or less, depending on the owner. Portraits of men, women, adolescents, children, or entire families in the company of dogs and cats have a long tradition. The affection existing between humans and other animals can already be felt in seventeenth-century portraits, and even more so in eighteenth-century paintings.

Dogs appear in family portraits such as the official portrait of *The Grand Dauphin Louis of Bourbon and His Family*[80] by Pierre Mignard (1612–1695) and the portrait by Van Dyck, *Philip, Fourth Count of Pembroke, and His Family.*[81] Van Dyck painted an entire series of portraits of aristocrats with their greyhounds, illustrating the haughty pride and casual attitude of their masters.[82] One of the most spectacular paintings is Van Dyck's *James Stuart, Duke of Lenox and Richmond.* (See Figure 7.12.) In the following century,

FIGURE 7.12: *James Stuart, Duke of Lenox and Richmond*, by Antoon Van Dyck, ca. 1634–1636, Oil on canvas, 215 × 128 cm. New York, The Metropolitan Museum of Art, Marquand Collection, Gift of Henry G. Marquand, 1889. Image © The Metropolitan Museum of Art.

Pompeo Girolamo Batoni (1708–87), an Italian portraitist popular throughout Europe, continued this tradition with his portraits of English lords on
their "Grand Tour" while living in Rome. Esteemed as symbols of power, large
guard dogs appear frequently in paintings from this period, an example being
the dog, perhaps painted by Velázquez, whose large size is underscored by the
presence of a dwarf at its side holding it by a leash.[83]

When the artist is free to depict the animal as he wishes, he reveals his personal attitude: Cornelius Vischer (1629–1658), a portrait engraver, gives himself free rein in drawing an adorable little *Spanish Dog*,[84] or "butterfly dog,"
wearing a collar with tiny bells, a true portrait of a beloved pet. A cheerful little
black-and-white spaniel appears in several drawings by Le Brun and Boel, as
well as in a painting by Nicasius Bernaerts,[85] another Flemish artist working
at the Gobelins, which leads us to think this little dog was from the painters'
circle of family and friends. This little dog was very fashionable throughout
Europe, as the portraits and genre scenes in which it appears[86] attest. It was
also associated with *fêtes galantes* scenes, such as those by Jean-Antoine Watteau,[87] and with the *Pastorales* of François Boucher (1703–1770).

Small dogs—King Charles spaniels, griffons, and pugs—appear more and
more frequently in all kinds of portraits. There is one type of self-portrait in
which artists often depicted themselves in a tender and complicit relationship with their favorite pet, be it a dog, cat, or monkey. In his *Self Portrait*[88]
William Hogarth (1697–1764) portrayed himself with Trump, his second
pug, who was his daily companion and occasional model. (See Figure 7.13.)
Hogarth's first dog, named Pugg, died in 1730, and his third dog, Crab, appeared after 1750. Trump earns a place of honor: he poses front stage, sitting
beside a stack of three books by Great Britain's greatest authors—William
Shakespeare, Jonathan Swift, and John Milton—upon which rests the oval
self-portrait of the artist. To the side is the palette with the celebrated "S-line"
Hogarth used in developing his artistic theories. In this representation of his
dog, we understand the important place the animal occupied in the life of his
master. Although Hogarth dearly loved his pug Trump, he used him in satirical
fashion in an episode of his series *The Life of a Scoundrel*.[89] To the righthand
side of the *Married to the Old Heiress* scene, Hogarth paints a couple of pugs
parodying the unsavory scene of the scoundrel's marriage in the Marylebone
Church located in London's outskirts. The groom is represented by Trump,
whereas the other dog, sightless in one eye, symbolizes the bride who is also
half-blind.

Companion dogs were also linked to femininity and children. Their popularity continued to increase throughout the eighteenth century. Madame de
Pompadour commissioned a portrait of herself by François Boucher in the
company of "Mimi" and "Inès" who are also found in portraits by Bachelier and Huet. In the official portrait of the *Duchess of Alba*,[90] Goya painted

FIGURE 7.13: *The Painter and His Pug*, by William Hogarth, 1745, Oil on canvas, 90 × 70 cm. London, Tate Gallery.

a white bichon, matching the color of the dress of his model; on its rear left leg, the bichon sports a red ribbon identical in color to the belt and ribbons worn by the Duchess. This is also the case of the pug belonging to the *Marquise de Pontejos*,[91] where the dog's collar is adorned with bells, and a bow matches the belt of his mistress.

FIGURE 7.14: *Madame Abington Dressed as "Miss Prue" in Congreve's "Love for Love,"* by Sir Joshua Reynolds, 1771, Oil on canvas, 77 × 64 cm. New Haven, Yale Center for British Art, Paul Mellon Collection.

The presence—albeit discreet—of the seated griffon dog, half obscured by the back of the chair, in Reynolds's *Madame Abington Dressed as "Miss Prue,"*[92] emphasizes the fact that the animal is party to every instant in the life of its mistress. (See Figure 7.14.) Elsewhere, *Nelly O'Brien,*[93] a courtesan, also posed for Reynolds, with her griffon dog on her lap, burrowing into her dress and lace cape. (See Figure 7.15.) In the Reynolds portrait of *Georgiana, Countess Spencer with Lady Georgiana Spencer,*[94] the griffon dog to the left raises its paw toward the pair, as if to join this scene of motherly affection. This kind of portrait recurs in the works of artists far less known, attesting to the popularity of these portraits among a wide range of clients.

In contrast to these charming portraits, there is the case of a portrait[95] painted by Reynolds of *George Augustus Selwyn* (1719–1791), undoubtedly

FIGURE 7.15: *Nelly O'Brien*, by Sir Joshua Reynolds, ca. 1762–1764, Oil on canvas, 126 × 100 cm. London, Wallace Collection. © By kind permission of the Trustees of the Wallace Collection, London.

a quite unpleasant social climber in the service of Lord March, who is depicted with his pug Râton. Wearing a foul expression, the dog occupies the center of the painting. A similar unsavory aura can be found in a drawing by Dominique Vivant Denon (1747–1825), who portrays the revolutionary Georges Couthon.[96] The subject of this painting had a bloody reputation as an instigator of the Terror, facts known by any reader of history books at the time. Couthon is represented, however, as one of his contemporaries noted, sentimentally petting his little dog.

Dogs are also the subject of actual portraits wherein they are the sole focus. In the portrait of the basset hound *Pehr*,[97] Oudry conveys all the affection that the dog's master, Count Carl Gustav Tessin (1695–1770), held for this dog, whom he called "admirable." This work, presented at the Salon of 1740, met with enormous success because it translated so well the feelings anyone can

ARTISTIC REPRESENTATION

have toward a pet animal. The dog, full of confidence, is shown beneath the hanging carcasses of a young rabbit and a pheasant, a rifle off to one side, undoubtedly recalling the animal's talents as a hunting dog.

The portrait of *Diane,* the beautiful white Italian greyhound[98] belonging to Bergeret de Grancourt, painted by François-André Vincent (1746–1816), is much more sophisticated. (See Figure 7.16.) Exhibited at the Salon of 1777, the painting shows the dog striking a refined pose, treated as if it were a portrait on display, with its luxurious cushion bordered in gold cording and its fabric draped in heavy folds. Bachelier as well painted a black *King Charles,*[99] lying on a stool upholstered in a superb yellow damask.

English artists specialized in this genre. Thomas Gainsborough (1727–1788) produced an exceptionally elegant portrait of a *Pomeranian Bitch and Puppy.*[100] As he had done with horses, Stubbs also painted a series of dogs, rendered realistically and without sentimentality, but where we sense the character of each of his models. Among them, a somewhat pouting *White Poodle*[101] and a charming *Spanish Dog* belonging to the portraitist Richard Cosway, who, like Louis XV's dog *Gredinet,* is pursuing a butterfly.[102] Stubbs also painted the

FIGURE 7.16: *Portrait of Diane, Monsieur Bergeret de Grancourt's Greyhound,* by François-André Vincent, 1774, Oil on canvas, 61 × 73 cm. Besançon, Musée des Beaux-Arts et d'Archéologie. © Besançon, Musée des Beaux-Arts et d'Archéologie.

Prince of Wales's dogs *Fino*,[103] a black-and-white Spitz dog, and *Tiny*, a chestnut spaniel, and several *Foxhounds*.

Children also have their dogs, and their relationship is the focus of many paintings replete with emotion. One of the sons of Charles I rests a hand on the head of his dog, who looks up at him affectionately in a portrait by Van Dyck.[104] In the portrait of *Prince Felipe Próspero*,[105] son of King Felipe IV and of Mariana of Austria, Velázquez is embarrassed as he paints a stiff and sad little prince; in contrast, he paints with abandon when producing a magnificent portrait of a little white dog, its head resting on the arms of a chair, looking at the painter with animated eyes.

Portraits showing a child and a dog were very popular in the eighteenth century. Robert Rosenblum sees in both Greuze and Reynolds precursors of "pre-Freudian ideas that arose in the nineteenth century about the child, seen as a kind of earthly angel who was practically interchangeable with kittens, puppies and bunnies."[106] Jean-Baptiste Greuze (1725–1805) painted a *Young Child Playing with Her Dog*[107] that is a double portrait, one of the child, most probably the third daughter of the artist, Louise Gabrielle, and the other of the "minor breed," a spaniel frightened by the artist's unexpected appearance in the child's room when she should have been asleep. Displayed at the Salon of 1769, this work met with considerable success,[108] compensating for the poor reception accorded the artist's *Septimus Severus*,[109] the work he had executed on the occasion of his admission into the Royal Academy of Painting and Sculpture. A few years later, in the same vein, Reynolds painted *Miss Jane Bowles*[110] embracing her spaniel, and shortly thereafter, a charming portrait of *Charles, Count of Dalkeith*[111] in the company of his black spaniel, petting a small owl that he points toward with his left index finger. The scene takes place in a lush summer landscape. For the pendant to this painting, representing Charles's sister, Reynolds chose a winter landscape in which we see a terrier gazing at the warmly bundled girl and a robin hopping about in the snow. Every one of these paintings highlights the love children have for their pets.

CATS

In the seventeenth century cats are represented by numerous European artists. In a canvas by Pietro Paolini (1603–1681), representing an unidentified writer,[112] a cat appears as the writer's silent little companion, poised on his shoulder. The writer leans his head on his hand and holds his pen as he rereads what he has just written. The cat seemingly occupies an increasingly important place during the following century. Artists chose cats as subjects of a significant number of drawings, including single animals and groups with several figures. Among the best known were those of Watteau and Gainsborough. In the eighteenth century, the cat became the ideal companion of women, as can be seen in the drawings of Louis Carrogis known also as Carmontelle (1717–1806) who portrays, among other aristocratic women of the period, *The Countess of Ségur and Her Grandson*.[113] (See Figure 7.17.) When we see this enormous cat sitting on the lap of this aged lady, who is looking at her grandson through a lorgnette, we can imagine that the animal is better treated than the intimidated little boy standing quite erect, in front of his grandmother, who is undoubtedly lecturing him. As is the case with dogs, cats were portrayed realistically. Bachelier twice painted a magnificent *White Angora Cat* in a garden, in one case gazing at a butterfly,[114] in another looking at a bird it is eager to catch.[115] The artist renders perfectly the cat's soft fluffy fur, its beautiful feathery tail

FIGURE 7.17: *Portrait of Philippe-Angélique de Froissy, Comtesse de Ségur, Holding Her Cat, and Her Grandson Joseph-Alexandre Vicomte de Ségur,* by Louis Carrogis called Carmontelle, ca. 1760–1762 Watercolor over black chalk, 26.6 × 16.9 cm. Versailles, Musée national du château. © Photo RMN–Daniel Arnaudet / Jean Schormans.

gracefully raised, and especially the extremely avid gaze directed toward the coveted other creature.

MONKEYS

Small monkeys were in vogue as pets as early as the sixteenth century nearly all over Europe. Artists depicted them in various poses,[116] most often aping humans by wearing hats, playing, holding baby monkeys by the paw, after the model offered in the paintings of David Teniers the younger (1610–1690), who specialized in the genre he called *Singeries* (Monkey Business) that continued into the eighteenth century in the works of Watteau and Chardin.[117] The artist Christophe Huet painted monkeys as part of the decoration of two monkey rooms (*la Grande et la Petite Singerie*) at the château in Chantilly, and at the Hôtel Rohan in Paris. This genre became quite popular, continuing throughout the nineteenth century. The fate of these animals, at once playthings and prisoners, is exemplified in de Sève's illustration for Buffon's *Histoire naturelle* of the sad-looking *Sai à gorge blanche* (White-faced Capuchin),[118] wearing a chain that has no doubt caused him to break the china cup at his feet. This allusive manner of depicting a chained animal is nothing new; it appears already in the drawings of Pisanello (1395–1455), in the work of Paolo Veronese (1528–1588), and in the work of Flemish and Dutch painters—Hendrik Goltzius (1558–1617)[119] and Peter Bruegel the Elder,[120] for example, in whose work some historians have read symbolic meanings.

Each individual had his favorite animal. Frans Hals (1580–1666) painted three children playing with a goat pulling a cart.[121] A century later, the portraitist François Hubert-Drouais (1727–1775) painted the portrait of Charles-Philippe de France, Count of Artois, the future Charles X in the company of his sister Madame Clothilde, future queen of Sardinia,[122] seen riding on a white goat. Drouais's execution is more elegant than that of Hals, but the spirit is the same in both paintings; the pleasures of childhood are highlighted, as in the case of Bachelier's huge canvas *Les Amusements de l'Enfance*.[123] Donkeys, rabbits, and birds are seen in this kind of painting. Hals executed a rapid, energetic portrait of the old woman, *Malle Babli*,[124] depicted holding a beer mug and sporting an owl on her shoulder, a symbol of insanity and stupidity. Madame de Pompadour commissioned Bachelier to paint her birds, and she ordered Oudry to portray her *Chinese Golden Pheasant*.[125]

SHOW ANIMALS

Some works, however, do not focus on animals themselves but rather on the way their masters treat them. The life of certain animals is particularly harsh.

They are without rights. Anyone can kill his animal if he so desires. History recalls the Great Cat Massacre that took place on Rue Saint-Séverin in Paris, near the print shop of Jacques Vincent, on a day of collective madness.[126] Hogarth shows in his portrait of the *Grey Children*[127] (the future Count of Stamford and his sister Lady Maria Grey) the extent to which children can be malicious to animals. The young boy holds the little dog by its rear paws and shakes it, a diversion that certainly pleases the child, for it is this "amusement" that the artist depicts in the painting.

Such show animals, trained dogs or dancing bears, were featured in shows at fairs. Young Savoyards (often chimneysweeps) went from town to town carrying marmots in boxes and showing them for a few coins. They were featured in the seventeenth century in the work of David Teniers and continued to appear into the eighteenth century. Watteau uses them as a subject in several drawings and in a canvas[128] showing a young Savoyard in full face, with his marmot. On the surface, the scene is realistic, but behind this are sexually implicit messages relating to women. The marmot is easily tamed, can dance to oboe music, standing upright as Watteau shows in his painting.[129] Another subject appearing in eighteenth-century painting is the *serinette*, a mechanical musical instrument, a kind of small drum-shaped organ cranked steadily to train canaries to sing featured in several works by Chardin.[130] A young woman serving as a model, comfortably seated, holds in her lap a *serinette*. The canaries were quite highly valued, as the funerary memorials sculpted in their honor by Clodion[131] and Jean-Antoine Houdon (1741–1828) attest.

A number of paintings show animals who have become portraits of their masters. Dogs must be intelligent or they suffer the fate of Pouf, the dog Madame d'Épinay sent back whence it came, because of its meager intelligence. The spaniel becomes a pianist[132] in the work of Philip Reinagle (1749–1833). (See Figure 7.18.) Seated on a piano stool, its paws resting on the keyboard, the dog gazes quite confidently at the spectator. On the piano we see the score for "God Save the King." Laurence Lubin proposes that we regard this as a reference to young musical prodigies, such as William Crotch, who, at the age of two, played this patriotic song on the piano. Reinagle's dog is clever and, moreover, he belongs to a master who wants him to resemble a well-educated human, with a taste for the fine arts. Still, dogs can suffer from the whims of their masters. The well-groomed Havanese poodle, by Bachelier, who sits up and begs,[133] has become the toy of his master; the tuft of hair on its head is tied back with a pink ribbon, its nails are trimmed, and another unfurled ribbon hides the dog's penis. The dog's gaze is somewhat pathetic, making us think that it feels ridiculous. (See Figure 7.19.) The name of the person who commissioned this disturbing painting is unknown.

FIGURE 7.18: *Portrait of an Extraordinary Musical Dog,* by Philip Reinagle, before 1805, Oil on canvas, 72 × 93 cm. Richmond, Virginia Museum of Fine Arts, The Paul Mellon Collection. Photo Ron Jennings © Virginia Museum of Fine Arts.

FIGURE 7.19: *A Dog of the Havanese Breed,* by Jean Jacques Bachelier, 1768, Oil on canvas, 70 × 91 cm. Durham, Bowes Museum; Barnard Castle. Photo Syd Neville © Bowes Museum; Barnard Castle.

HUMANITY

Le Brun shows in his drawings for the *Physiognomonie* that many animals can easily be compared to humans. Some have emphasized that animals' structure and temperament bring them undoubtedly closer to humanity. The relationships between human and simian traits are the subject of nine drawings by Le Brun. In one, the artist presents three different monkey-like profiles for the man seen face on, but with scarcely any changes in respect to the portrait of the monkey drawn on a separate page. The large primates, shown at fairs and kept in menageries, were of particular interest to scientists who studied them in relation to humans and to philosophers such as Jean-Jacques Rousseau who reflected on the filiation of monkeys and humans. A strange anonymous painting shows the *Genealogical Tree of Monkeys*[134] painted after the illustrations in Buffon. The monkeys closest to humans are placed at the bottom. This illustrates the relationship between humans and monkeys that Buffon emphasized throughout the *Histoire naturelle* and that still speaks to us today. Moreover, in granting monkeys a genealogical tree, the painter situated them close to humanity.

The association of monkeys and humans led to the desire to "educate" monkeys and give them human manners. This is the lesson of Tethart Philip Christian Haag (1737–1812) in a drawing of the orangutan given to Guillaume V of Orange, which is depicted eating with a spoon and fork,[135] a strictly human habit. The orangutan, a female, is also shown standing up to pick a piece of fruit,[136] as would a human. Aert Shouman also extended the analogy between humans and animals. In his imaginary depiction[137] of the Menagerie of Guillaume V, where the artist brings together animals in a clearing, he shows an *American Black Spider Monkey* up in a tree, bearing a resemblance to a human.[138] This image is so striking that it will later be used by one of the draftsmen of the French naturalist Pierre-Joseph Buch'oz (1731–1807), Guillaume de Favannes,[139] who continued to accentuate the human aspect of monkeys.

The boundaries between humanity and animality are blurred when an artist depicts the animal in a human posture and, moreover, moved by human sentiment. Nicolas Maréchal (1753–1803), painted in the Republican An VII (1798 or 1799), for the collection at the National Museum of Natural History in Paris, an incredible figure of a Barbary Macaque[140] peering contentedly at itself in a mirror, wondering: "Am I the fairest?" To highlight the connection with the human attitude of the ape, behind the mirror the artist has placed a powder box, a hairpin, and a comb—objects symbolizing human vanity. The artist even goes so far as to inscribe on his work *"nosce te ipsum"* ("know thyself"). (See Figure 7.20.)

FIGURE 7.20: *A Macaque*, by Nicolas Maréchal, 1793, Bodycolor on vellum, 41.2 × 31.4 cm. Paris, Bibliothèque centrale du Muséum national d'Histoire naturelle.

HUMAN FEELINGS

The majority of painters capably render what animals feel and what we humans call feelings to such a degree that artists had recourse to the same methods for painting animals that they did for human portraits. The entire range of human feelings recurs in these animals: love, hatred, fear, anguish. or joy.

During a period when mothers were encouraged by doctors to nurse their infants, Oudry gives us an example of maternal love in animals. In his *Hunting Dog Nursing Her Young*,[141] dating from 1752 and displayed at the Salon of 1753, Oudry shows a white- and ginger-colored dog, housed in a stable, nursing three of her puppies, while three others sleep at her side, having drunk their fill. (See Figure 2.6.) This tranquil image is reinforced by the surrounding half shadow and the beam of sunlight illuminating only the animals. The painting, whose subject brought it great success, was purchased by the Baron d'Holbach, a collaborator on the *Encyclopédie*.[142] The same mood characterizes the vellum painted for the collection of the museum by Nicolas Maréchal, representing *La Lionne et ses petits nés à la Ménagerie*.[143] This work celebrates the first birth of lions in captivity, at least in France, which explains the caption painted on the cage wall, reminding us that the scene takes place at the Menagerie. The lioness is stretched out on straw in her cage in the company of her three young cubs. Everything comes together in this work to touch the viewer with an image of maternal love, but we will later understand that it carries another message.

In contrast, animals are also capable of hatred, of defending their turf with unequaled aggression, and of ferociously attacking animals of their own species as well as others, either in hunt scenes or in animal fight scenes that were ever popular in the eighteenth century. This is evident in two paintings by Bachelier, *The Polish Bear Attacked by Dogs* and its pendant painting *The African Lion Struggling with Bulldogs*.[144] Violence among animals is a common theme for artists, for it can also reference human violence, as we have seen with *Two Dogs in a Landscape* by La Hyre.

Artists undoubtedly considered wild species to be the best vehicles for conveying the feelings animal can experience. One example among many others is Oudry's *Study of a Leopard*.[145] (See Figure 7.3.) The subject of this painting is defined in a note sent by Oudry to Schwerin in 1750 as an "angry male tiger" (like all of his contemporaries, Oudry uses "tiger" to signify leopard) and that of its pendant as a "tigress in a tranquil pose." Oudry plays more on the contrast in expression and less on the distinction between male and female animals.

George Stubbs produced several works portraying a lion furiously attacking a horse, a theme already seen in classical Antiquity,[146] but he turns to this subject with such force and life that certain historians have seen a connection with Edmund Burke's *Inquiry into the Origin of Our Ideas on the Sublime and*

Beautiful.[147] Specifically, Stubbs painted versions of *A Horse Frightened by a Lion*,[148] *A Horse Attacked by a Lion*,[149] and *A Horse Devoured by a Lion*.[150] These same subjects rendered in enamel painted on Wedgwood bisque were very popular. Expressing hatred and horror, these depictions heavily influenced nineteenth-century English and French artists.

Still, the lion is capable of love toward other animals. Georges Toscan, the first librarian of the Museum of Natural History in Paris, relates in *La Décade philosophique*[151] a love story between a lion, named Woira, and her cage-mate dog, who were reared together and who adored one another. Brought from Senegal to the Versailles Menagerie, they were then transferred during the Revolution to the Botanical Garden, where the dog died of a severe case of mange. Woira lived on, disconsolate. Nicolas Maréchal, during the Republican An II (1793–1794), produced a beautiful drawing[152] in which the lion can be seen embracing the dog who whispers in her ear. Jean Hoüel devoted a volume of twenty plates, entitled *L'Histoire naturelle des deux Éléphants*,[153] to the two elephants named Hans and Parkie belonging to the Dutch Stathouder. The animals were brought to the Menagerie at the Museum of Natural History as war trophies. Hoüel shows that the customs and manners of pachyderms are not so removed from those of humans. We see the elephants drinking, eating, bathing, embracing for the first time, and attempting to reproduce, and we see the baby elephant being born and how it nurses. There are plates showing how best to draw elephants. Hans died in 1801; Parkie survived her mate by several years, but experienced great sorrow. Hoüel's work can be seen as the synthesis of all earlier approaches to animal representation during the seventeenth and eighteenth centuries. It is a book addressing both the physical and moral aspects of animals in which Hoüel also decries the "vile prison" where the two elephants were kept, devoting a plate to the subject.

THE PRISONER

The imprisoned animal is a theme common to several artists. The menagerie entailed animals' loss of freedom, and many people of the period were oblivious to the fact that animals could suffer from this lack of freedom. At the Menagerie in Versailles, the proximity between the animals was such that some were killed by others, inspiring constant fear in many of the animals. Boel's drawings of the civet shows anguish in the eyes of the animal. Living conditions for these animals, most often pent up in small cages, were precarious and far from the nearly idyllic depictions by Melchior Hondecoeter (1636–1695) of the menagerie of William III of Orange[154] and by Schouman of that of Guillaume V.

There are many drawings of captive lions. They serve as artists' models. The drawings of Albrecht Dürer (1471–1528), Rembrandt Harmensz van Rijn

(1606–1669), and of Le Brun were engraved, along with his own drawings, by Bernard Picart (1673–1733) in his *Recueil des Lions dessinez d'après nature par divers maîtres* (Collection of Lions Drawn from Nature by Various Masters).[155] We see the lion also in religious scenes, with Saint Jerome, for example, and in hunting scenes. For Rubens, the lion remains, in the Baroque spirit, a wild and raging animal, cruel and victorious, roaring and leaping. For Le Brun the lion remains foremost the King of the Animals with features inspired from ancient masks. Later, Stubbs ignores that the lion was prisoner and renders the animal leaping vigorously.[156]

Rembrandt and Boel take entirely different approaches to this subject. Both portray the imprisoned animal, but conceal the cage bars. The King of the Animals is then no longer king but a poor captive lying on the ground whose image contrasts with that of the fabled triumphant lion. Rembrandt drew the lion *nae't leven* ("from nature") at least nineteen times,[157] undoubtedly at a fair or in one of the stables owned by the West India Trading Company in Amsterdam. For the most part Rembrandt draws the animal lying down, as if resting. There is a striking difference in one drawing between the animal's overall posture and its frontal gaze, seemingly fixed on imaginary prey.[158] (See Figure 7.21.) Boel devoted a series of drawings to the lion in which he conveys the animal's loneliness by means of a sad or furious gaze, making us forget its

FIGURE 7.21: *A Lion,* by Rembrandt Harmensz van Rijn, ca. 1650, Pen and brown ink, brown wash, 13.8 × 20.7 cm. Paris, Musée du Louvre, Département des Arts graphiques. Courtesy of Musée du Louvre.

ferocity. Boel too focuses on the recumbent lion, emphasizing every detail to show off each part of the animal. In both cases, the lion is not resigned to being a captive: we can sense it is about to leap forward. Perhaps without intending to do so, these two artists drew attention to the fate of the animal prisoner.

In the vellum painting portraying *La Lionne et ses petits nés à la Ménagerie*, Maréchal presented not only a portrayal of maternal love, but also the image of a captive mother, confined to a stable whose metal bars are partially obscured by reeds. The lioness turns her head toward a blue sky symbolizing freedom. This work is contemporaneous with the Revolution that was supposed to bring liberty to the people. The purpose of the menagerie was to serve natural history, according to its first director, Bernard-Germain-Étienne de La Ville, Count of Lacépède, who published an essay in the *Décade Philosophique* in 1795, entitled *"Quelques idées concernant les établissements appelés Ménageries"* (Ideas Concerning the Institutions Called Menageries), where animals "free to move about in more or less large enclosures will rid a free people of images of constraint and slavery."[159] The image of the imprisoned lioness somehow becomes an image of calm servitude and public happiness.

If this image was intended to reassure, there were other animal figures in the last quarter of the eighteenth century that, on the contrary, were no longer faithful companions but rather products of the blackest dreams symbolizing inherited human fears and anxieties. Goya, the Swiss Henri Fuseli (1741–1825), and the Englishman William Blake (1757–1827) populate some of their darkest works with goats, laughing donkeys, and monstrous snakes that are far from realistically or scientifically portrayed, directly heralding Romanticism and certain fantastic works of the nineteenth century. Friendly and realistic animal portraits, however, continued to predominate throughout the eighteenth century.

NOTES

Introduction

I owe a special debt of gratitude to Brigitte Resl, for her extraordinary generosity in helping me edit this volume. Kathryn Hoffmann, Twyla Meding, Henry Phillips, Larry Riggs, and Amy Wygant offered many valuable comments and suggestions when I read an early version of the first chapter at the Society for Seventeenth-Century French Studies conference at Oxford University in July of 2006. Madeleine Pinault Sørensen personally showed me many exquisite paintings and drawings of animals in the Louvre, while Bent Sørensen helped with images and much thoughtful advice. My original interest in the subject of animals grew out of collaboration with Jennifer Ham, whose ideas, advice, and support are the inspiration for all of my work. Watching Francesca compete with her horses is always a lesson in human and animal grace and beauty.

1. Jean-Jacques Rousseau, *Oeuvres complètes* (Paris: Gallimard, 1959), vol. I, p. 1089.
2. Jacques Derrida, "The Animal That Therefore I Am," *Critical Inquiry* 28, no. 2 (Winter 2002): 369–418, at p. 418.
3. I would like to thank Tristan Palmer for first bringing to my attention Wright of Derby's *Bird in the Air Pump.*
4. Immanuel Kant, "What Is Enlightenment," in *Basic Writings of Kant*, ed. Allen W. Wood (New York: Modern Library, 2001), pp. 135–141.
5. James Ferguson, cited in Judy Egerton, *Wright of Derby* (New York: Metropolitan Museum of Art, 1990), p. 19.
6. See James Armstrong's description of J. J. Audubon's asphyxiation of an eagle in "Audubon's Ornithological Biography and the Question of 'Other Minds,'" in *Animal Acts: Configuring the Human in Western History,* ed. Jennifer Ham and Matthew Senior (New York: Routledge, 1997), pp. 103–125, pp. 108–109.
7. John Cottingham, Robert Stoothoff, and Dugald Murdoch, trans., *The Philosophical Writings of Descartes*, Principles of Philosophy (Cambridge, UK: Cambridge University Press, 1984), vol. I, p. 207.

8. John Locke, *An Essay Concerning Human Understanding* (Amherst, NY: Prometheus, 1995), p. 433.

9. See Krzysztof Pomian, "Vision and Cognition," in *Picturing Science, Producing Art,* ed. Caroline Jones and Peter Galison (New York: Routledge, 1998), pp. 211–231.

10. René Descartes, *Le Monde, L'Homme,* ed. Annie Bitbol-Hespériès (Paris: Seuil, 1996), p. 9.

11. See "Discourse Two: Refraction," in *Optics,* Cottingham, Stoothoff, and Murdoch, *Descartes: Selected Philosophical Writings* (Cambridge: Cambridge University Press, 1998) pp. 156–164.

12. See William Schupbach, "A Select Iconography of Animal Experiment," in *Vivisection in Historical Perspective,* ed. Nicolas Rupke (New York: Routledge, 1989).

13. Jacques-Henri Bernardin de Saint-Pierre, *Oeuvres Complètes,* 12 vols. (Paris: Méquignon-Marvis, 1818), vol. 5, p. 105.

14. Rousseau, *Oeuvres complètes,* vol. IV, p. 159. See Chapter 6 of the present volume for the importance of Rousseau in Enlightenment thinking about animals; see also Jean-Luc Guichet, *Rousseau, l'animal et l'homme: L'animalité dans l'horizon anthropologique des Lumières* (Paris: Cerf, 2006), for an authoritative account of animality in the writings of Descartes, Condillac, Bayle, Diderot, La Mettrie, and others. On animals during the early modern period, see Leonora Cohen Rosenfield, *From Beast-Machine to Man-Machine: The Theme of Animal Soul in French Letters from Descartes to La Mettrie* (New York: Oxford University Press, 1940); Keith Thomas, *Man and the Natural World* (New York: Oxford University Press, 1983); Thierry Gontier, *De l'homme à l'animal: Montaigne et Descartes ou les paradoxes de la philosophie moderne sur la nature des animaux* (Paris: Vrin, 2000); Donna Landry, *The Invention of the Countryside: Hunting, Walking, and Ecology in English Literature 1671–1831* (New York: Palgrave, 2001); Bruce Boehrer, *Shakespeare among the Animals: Nature and Society in the Drama of Early Modern England* (New York: Palgrave, 2002); Anita Guerrini, "The Ethics of Animal Experimentation in Seventeenth-Century England," *Journal of the History of Ideas* 50, no. 3 (1989): 391–407, and *Experimenting with Humans and Animals: From Galen to Animal Rights* (Baltimore: Johns Hopkins University Press, 2003); Peter Harrison, "Reading Vital Signs: Animals and the Experimental Philosophy," in *Renaissance Beasts: Of Animals, Humans, and Other Wonderful Creatures,* ed. Erica Fudge (Urbana: University of Illinois Press, 2004), pp. 186–207; Frank Palmeri, ed., *Humans and Other Animals in Eighteenth-Century British Culture: Representation, Hybridity, Ethics* (Burlington VT: Aldershot, 2006); Erica Fudge, *Perceiving Animals: Humans and Beasts in Early Modern English Culture* (Urbana: University of Illinois Press, 2002), and *Brutal Reasoning: Animals, Rationality, and Humanity in Early Modern England* (Ithaca, NY: Cornell University Press, 2006); Louise Robbins, *Elephant Slaves and Pampered Parrots: Exotic Animals in Eighteenth-Century France* (Baltimore: Johns Hopkins University Press, 2002). Robbins's *Elephant Slaves* and Fudge's *Brutal Reasoning* contain extensive annotated bibliographies.

15. Michel Foucault, *Les mots et les choses: Une Archéologie des sciences humaines* (Paris: Gallimard, 1966), p. 29 (my translation).

16. Ibid., p. 32.

17. Ibid., p. 31.

18. Ibid., p. 29.

19. Ibid., p. 18.

20. I have commented on Foucault's interpretation of *Las Meninas* in two previous essays: "The Ménagerie and the Labyrinthe: Animals at Versailles, 1662–1792," in Fudge, *Renaissance Beasts*, pp. 208–232, and "Seeing the Versailles Ménagerie," *Papers in French Seventeenth-Century Literature* 30, no. 59 (2003): 351–363.

21. Derrida, "The Animal That Therefore I Am."

22. Ibid., pp. 372, 381.

23. Ibid., p. 381.

24. Ibid.

25. Ibid., p. 402.

26. Ibid., p. 409.

27. Ibid.

28. Ibid., p. 416.

29. Ibid., p. 409.

30. W. J. T. Mitchell, "Illusion: Looking at Animals Looking," in *Picture Theory: Essays on Verbal and Visual Representation* (Chicago: University of Chicago Press, 1994), pp. 329–344.

31. Marc Fumaroli, ed., *La Fontaine: Fables* (Paris: La Pochotéque, 1985), Bk. VI, pp. xvii, 359.

32. Charles Perrault, "Little Red Riding Hood," in *The Classic Fairy Tales*, ed. Maria Tatar (New York: Norton, 1999), p. 13, slightly modified.

33. See Chapter 1 of the present volume for further discussion of Descartes' denial of language to animals.

34. Walter Friedlaender, *Caravaggio Studies* (Princeton, NJ: Princeton University Press, 1955), p. 7.

35. Ibid., p. 9.

36. *The HarperCollins Study Bible: New Revised Standard Version*, ed. Wayne Meeks (New York: HarperCollins, 1993), p. 2263.

37. Rousseau, *Deuxième Promenade*, in *Oeuvres complètes*, vol. I, pp. 1002–1010, 1005.

38. Michel Foucault, *Histoire de la folie à l'âge classique* (Paris: Gallimard, 1972), p. 165 (my translation).

39. "L'Hospital Général pour le Renfermement des Pauvres de Paris," cited in Maximilien Vessier, *La Pitié-Salpêtrière: quatre siècles d'histoire et d'histoires* (Paris: Hôpital de la Pitié-Salpêtrière, 1999), p. 57.

40. Ibid.

41. Foucault, *Folie*, p. 176.

42. Ibid., p. 124.

43. Ibid., p. 165. For an excellent discussion of animality in Foucault, see Clare Palmer, "Madness and Animality in Michel Foucault's *Madness and Civilization*," in *Animal Philosophy: Ethics and Identity,* ed. Peter Atterton and Matthew Calarco (New York: Continuum, 2004), pp. 72–84; see also Saïd Chebili, *Figures de l'animalité dans l'oeuvre de Michel Foucault* (Paris: L'Harmattan, 1999).

44. Foucault, *Folie*, p. 165.

45. Ibid., p. 167.

46. Ibid., p. 168.

47. "In France, until the Revolution, a walk to Bicêtre to watch the spectacle of the great lunatics (*des grands insensés*) remained a common Sunday pastime of the Right Bank bourgeoisie." Foucault, *Folie*, p. 161.

48. Ibid., p. 163.

49. Cited in ibid., p. 172.

50. On the history of the Ménagerie, see Gustave Loisel, *Histoire des ménageries de l'antiquité à nos jours,* 3 vols. (Paris: Doin et fils, 1912); Alfred Marie and Jeanne Marie, *Versailles au temps de Louis XIV* (Paris: Imprimerie Nationale, 1976); Gérard Mabille, "La Ménagerie de Versailles," *Gazette des Beaux-Arts* 116 (1974): 5–36; Iriye Masumi, "Le Vau's Ménagerie and the Rise of the Animalier: Enclosing, Dissecting, and Representing the Animal in Early Modern France" (PhD diss., University of Michigan, 1994); Chandra Mukerji, *Territorial Ambitions and the Gardens of Versailles* (Cambridge, UK: Cambridge University Press, 1997); Eric Baratay and Elisabeth Hardouin-Fugier, *Zoos: Histoire des jardins zoologiques en occident, XVIe–XXe siècle* (Paris: La Découverte, 1998), pp. 62–96; Robbins, *Elephant Slaves and Pampered Parrots*; Senior, "The Ménagerie" and "Seeing the Versailles Ménagerie."

51. Foucault, *Folie,* p. 203.

52. On Boel and other *animaliers* who observed animals at Versailles, see Madeleine Pinault Sørensen, *Sur le vif: dessins d'animaux de Pieter Boel* (Paris: Réunion des musées nationaux, 2001) and "Les animaux du roi: De Pieter Boel aux dessinateurs de l'Académie royale des Sciences," in *L'animal au XVIIe siècle, Actes de la 1ère journée d'études du Centre de recherches sur le XVIIe siècle,* ed. Charles Mazouer (Tübingen, Germany: Gunter Narr, 2003), pp. 159–183; Elisabeth Foucart Walter, *Pieter Boel (1622–1674): peintre des animaux de Louis XIV* (Paris: Réunion des musées nationaux, 2001). Other important studies of animals and the visual that are relevant to the period 1600–1800 are Madeleine Pinault Sørensen, *The Painter as Naturalist: From Dürer to Redouté* (Paris: Flammarion, 1991); Sarah R. Cohen, "Chardin's Fur: Painting, Materialism, and the Question of the Animal Soul," *Eighteenth-Century Studies* 38, no. 1 (2004): 39–61; and Nathaniel Wolloch, *Subjugated Animals: Animals and Anthropocentrism in Early Modern European Culture* (Amherst, NY: Humanity Books, 2006).

53. On the idea of animals at Versailles as courtiers, see Aurélia Gaillard, "Bestiaire réel, bestiaire enchanté: les animaux à Versailles sous Louis XIV," in Mazouer, *L'animal au XVIIe siècle,* pp. 185–198, at p. 191.

54. Louise Robbins argues convincingly that this liberation scene did not actually take place, but was a myth created by Paul Huot, a royalist sympathizer who was trying to discredit the Jacobins: see *Elephant Slaves,* p. 214.

55. Mary Abbe, "Doug Argue: Big Picture," *Art News,* January 1995, p. 95.

56. Doug Argue, "Lecture," http://www.dougargue.com/lecture/lectue_weismann.html.

57. Ibid.

58. Herman, a character in Isaac Bashevis Singer's "The Letter Writer," declares that "for the animals it is an eternal Treblinka"; cited by Charles Patterson, *Eternal Treblinka: Our Treatment of Animals and the Holocaust* (New York: Lantern Books, 2002), p. 3.

Chapter 1

1. Seamus Heaney, *Beowulf: A New Verse Translation* (London: W. W. Norton, 2000), verse 2820.

2. Ibid., verse 799.

3. H. A. Guerber, *Myths of Northern Lands* (New York: American Book Company, 1895), p. 27.

4. Jan Bremmer, *The Early Greek Concept of the Soul* (Princeton, NJ: Princeton University Press, 1983), p. 126.

5. Homer, *The Iliad,* trans. Robert Fagles (New York: Penguin, 1990), 3.46–49.

6. Ibid., 4.542–544.

7. Voltaire, *Dictionnaire Philosophique* (Paris: Garnier Flammarion, 1964), p. 26.

8. For a complete discussion of these terms, see Erwin Rohde, *Psyche: The Cult of Souls and the Belief in Immortality among the Greeks* (London: Routledge and Keagan Paul, 1950); Bremmer, *Concept of the Soul.*

9. Homer, *The Odyssey,* trans. E. V. Rieu (New York: Penguin, 1991), 14.426.

10. Ibid., 11.220.

11. Ibid., 11.403.

12. Bremmer, *Concept of the Soul,* p. 54.

13. Homer, *Iliad,* 9.646.

14. Ibid., 9.237.

15. Ibid., 4.524–528.

16. Ibid., 4.545–548.

17. Ibid., 5.151–159.

18. Plato, *Timaeus and Crito,* trans. Desmond Lee (London: Penguin, 1977), bk. 39, p. 101.

19. Ibid.

20. Ibid., p. 102.

21. Ibid., bk, 49, p. 123.

22. Ibid.

23. Ibid.

24. Aristotle, *De Anima,* trans. Hugh Lawson-Tancred (London: Penguin Books, 1986), p. 157.

25. Ibid., p. 158.

26. Ibid.

27. Ibid., p. 161.

28. Ibid., p. 210.

29. Ibid., p. 203.

30. Ibid.

31. Ibid.

32. Ibid., p. 163.

33. Jonathan Barnes, ed., *The Complete Works of Aristotle: The Revised Oxford Translation, Volume One* (Princeton, NJ: Princeton University Press, 1984), *Metaphysics* 981b 25–35.

34. Barnes, Aristotle, *Generation of Animals,* 731 30–45.

35. "In the case of growth, soul also clearly functions as a formal cause, taking the part, it has been suggested, of DNA in modern biology." Hugh Lawson-Tancred, in notes to his translation of Aristotle, *De Anima,* p. 164.

36. Aristotle, *De Anima,* p. 165.

37. Thomas Aquinas, *Summa Theologica, Tertia Partis, Supplementum,* cited in Roger French, *Dissection and Vivisection in the European Renaissance* (Aldershot, UK: Ashgate, 1999), p. 9.

38. *The HarperCollins Study Bible: New Revised Standard Version,* ed. Wayne Meeks (New York: HarperCollins, 1993), p. 47.

39. "Soul: Jewish Concept," *The Encyclopedia of Religion*, ed. Mircea Eliade (New York: Macmillan, 1987), p. 450.

40. "While Descartes was a corpuscularist, he was not an atomist, since he set no lower limit of divisibility on the corpuscles whose existence he assumed." Thomas Steele Hall, trans., René Descartes, *Treatise on Man* (Cambridge, MA: Harvard University Press, 1972), p. 5, 11n.

41. René Descartes, *Le Monde, L'Homme*, ed. Annie Bitbol-Hespériès (Paris: Seuil, 1996), p. 11. All citations from *Le Monde* are from this edition, my translations. Passages from *L'Homme*, sometimes slightly modified, are from Hall's translation of the *Treatise on Man* cited in the preceding note; for the *Discourse on Method*, I have used, with minor changes, John Cottingham, Robert Stoothoff, Dugald Murdoch, trans., *The Philosophical Writings of Descartes*, 3 vols. (Cambridge, UK: Cambridge University Press, 1984).

42. "Our soul is united with a body; the proof of this is that the soul moves the body and experiences sense impressions by means of it; that is what is meant by saying that it is the *form*. By an unwarranted extension of this experience to nature as a whole, we attribute to exterior bodies internal principles of movement analogous to our soul: *substantial forms*; and properties analogous to our sensations (hot, cold, hard, etc): *real qualities*. By actually distinguishing the soul from the body, [Cartesian] metaphysics eliminates the confused ideas of form and qualities, leaving physical objects with only extension and movement, the proper objects of true physics." Etienne Gilson, "Commentaire Historique," in *Discours de la méthode*, ed. Etienne Gilson (Paris: Vrin, 1962), p. 384.

43. Descartes, *Discourse*, p. 134.

44. Descartes, *L'Homme*, p. 13.

45. Descartes, *Discourse*, p. 134.

46. Descartes, *L'Homme*, p. 119.

47. Ibid., p. 126.

48. Descartes was familiar with animated statues in the royal gardens at St. Germain-en-Laye as well as the work of Salomon de Caus, whose *Les Raisons des forces mouvantes* (1615) contained plans for an animated statue of Neptune very similar to what Descartes describes; see Bitbol-Hespériès, p. 177, and J. Baltrusaitis, *Anamorphoses* (Paris: Flammarion, 1984).

49. Descartes, *L'Homme*, p 120.

50. Qtd. in Bitbol-Hespériès, p. 198.

51. Qtd. in ibid., p. 195.

52. Descartes, *L'Homme*, p. 168.

53. Ibid.

54. Ibid., p. 155.

55. Qtd. in Bitbol-Hespériès, p. 200.

56. Descartes, *L'Homme*, p. 146.

57. René Descartes, *La Dioptrique, Oeuvres et lettres*, ed. André Bridoux (Paris: Gallimard, 1953), p. 201.

58. Karl Marx, *Capital, Volume 1*, trans. Ben Fowkes (New York: Penguin, 1990), p. 209; see also Georg Lukács, "Reification and the Consciousness of the Proletariat," in *History and Class Consciousness* (New York: Merlin, 1967), pp. 87–111, and "Reification," in *Dictionary of Marxist Thought*, ed. Tom Bottomore (London: Blackwell, 1983), pp. 463–465.

59. Marx, *Capital*, p. 1054.

60. See Dennis Des Chene, *Spirits and Clocks: Machine and Organism in Descartes* (Ithaca, NY: Cornell University Press, 2001), for a detailed discussion of the actual machines that influenced Descartes' anatomy.

61. Descartes, *L'Homme*, p. 167.

62. Descartes, *Discourse*, p. 92.

63. Ibid.

64. Ibid., p. 93.

65. Letter to the Marquis of Newcastle, November, 23, 1646, *Oeuvres et lettres*, p. 1252.

66. Descartes, *Discourse*, p. 66.

67. Ibid.

68. Ibid., p. 92.

69. Ibid., p. 93.

70. Ibid., p. 17.

71. Summary of Cordemoy's ideas in Leonora Cohen Rosenfield, *From Beast-Machine to Man-Machine: The Theme of Animal Soul in French Letters from Descartes to La Mettrie* (New York: Octagon, 1968), p. 39. On animal language in the early modern period, see my "'When the Beasts Spoke': Animal Speech and Classical Reason in Descartes and La Fontaine," in *Animal Acts: Configuring the Human in Western History*, ed. Jennifer Ham and Matthew Senior (New York: Routledge, 1997), pp. 61–84; R. W. Serjeantson, "The Passions and Animal Language, 1540–1700," *Journal of the History of Ideas* 62, no. 3 (2001): 425–444; Brian Cummings, "Pliny's Literate Elephant and the Idea of Animal Language in Renaissance Thought," in *Renaissance Beasts: Of Animals, Humans, and Other Wonderful Creatures*, ed. Erica Fudge (Urbana: University of Illinois Press, 2004), pp. 164–185.

72. Géraud de Cordemoy, *Discours physique de la parole*, qtd. in Rosenfield, *From Beast-Machine to Man-Machine*, p. 214.

73. Descartes, *Discourse*, p. 141.

74. Ibid., p. 95.

75. On the animal soul controversy, see Rosenfield, *From Beast-Machine to Man-Machine*; Henri Busson and Ferdinand Gohin, *Jean de La Fontaine, Discours à Mme de la Sablière* (Geneva: Droz, 1967); Keith Thomas, *Man and the Natural World* (New York: Oxford University Press, 1983), pp. 137–142; Peter Harrison, "Descartes on Animals," *Philosophical Quarterly* 42 (1992): 219–227 and "Animal Souls, Metempsychosis, and Theodicy in Seventeenth-Century English Thought," *Journal of the History of Philosophy* 31, no. 4 (1993): 519–544; Luc Ferry and Claudine Germé, *Des Animaux et des hommes: Anthologie des textes remarquables, écrits sur le sujet, du XVe siècle à nos jours* (Paris: Livre de poche, 1994), pp. 7–156; Jean-Luc Guichet, *Rousseau, l'animal et l'homme: L'animalité dans l'horizon anthropologique des Lumières* (Paris: Cerf, 2006), pp. 39–73.

76. Harrison, "Animal Souls," pp. 538–544.

77. Rosenfield, *From Beast-Machine to Man-Machine*, p. 46.

78. Letter to Mersenne, June 11, 1640, *Oeuvres de Descartes*, 11 vols., ed. Charles Adam and Paul Tannery (Paris: Leopold Cerf, 1897–1909), vol. III, p. 85.

79. Descartes, *Oeuvres et lettres, Sixième Réponses*, p. 531.

80. Bayle, qtd. in Rosenfield, *From Beast-Machine to Man-Machine*, p. 125.

81. John Locke, *An Essay Concerning Human Understanding* (Amherst, NY: Prometheus, 1995), p. 60.

82. Ibid., p. 105.

83. Voltaire, *Dictionnaire*, p. 26.

Chapter 2

1. *La venerie de Iacques du Fouilloux* (Paris: Pierre Billaine, 1635), chap. 1. All translations from the French are mine, unless otherwise noted. Du Fouilloux's work was
   translated into English, German, and Italian; see the introduction to Jacques du
   Fouilloux, *La Vénerie et L'Adolescence*, ed. Gunnar Tilander, series *Cynegetica*
   XVI (Stockholm: Almqvist and Wiksell, 1967); and François Remigereau, ed.,
   *Jacques du Fouilloux et son traité de "La vénerie"; étude biographique et biblio-
   graphique* (Paris: Les Belles Lettres, 1952).

2. Du Fouilloux writes that after seeking out both ancient and modern explanations
   of the origin of *chiens courants*, he has deemed Joannes Monumetensis' account
   (most likely Geoffrey of Monmouth's *Historia Regum Britanniae*) the most complete. Monmouth gives a much more coherent account of the legend of Brutus and
   his journey to Britain; it differs from the account in *La vénerie*, most important in
   that Monmouth never mentions canines at all.

3. This genealogy, if not entirely believable, is a way of designating France as the in-
   heritor of the cultural legacy of Antiquity by connecting its divine-right monarchy
   to this orphaned Trojan prince.

4. Some of Du Fouilloux's information belies a Renaissance-era concept of biology,
   such as his admonition to carefully select the first dog to mate with a young
   bitch, since every litter she produces for the rest of her life will contain one puppy
   from the first dog.

5. A *limier* is a hound "trained to sniff out prey without making any noise that might
   scare it away," according to Tilander (*La Vénerie*, Glossary, p. 259) and "a large
   dog that the hunter uses to find the beast, and then to chase it when he wants to
   hunt it," according to the 1694 Académie Française dictionary. They lead the pack
   during the chase and are considered the most valuable dogs.

6. *La venerie*, chap. 36.

7. It is the deer's ability to scheme and plot to deceive hounds and hunters by the ruses
   that Jean de La Fontaine cites as a proof of animal intelligence in his *Discours à
   Madame de la Sablière* about the souls of animals.

8. *La venerie*, chap. 44.

9. Charles Bergman, *Orion's Legacy: A Cultural History of Man as Hunter* (New
   York: Dutton, 1996), pp. 145–148.

10. *La venerie*, chaps. 37 and 38, respectively.

11. Remigereau, *Jacques du Fouilloux*, p. 46.

12. Bergman, *Orion's Legacy*, pp. 142–143.

13. Remigereau, *Jacques du Fouilloux*, p. 56.

14. From the journal of Jean Héroard, governor-physician to the dauphin Louis,
    cited in Daniel Fabre, "Une enfance de roi," *Ethnologie Française* 21 (1991):
    392–414.

15. Ibid., p. 41.

16. Fabre notes that this freeing of birds—perhaps based on the Provençal custom
    of letting birds fly around the figure of the Christ child at Midnight Mass—was

retained after Louis XIII as part of the coronation ceremony (up through Charles X) and that the subsequent allegorical meaning assigned was that it represented the pardoning of prisoners: ibid., p. 42.

17. Pluvinel's text was published posthumously, first in 1623 as *Le maneige royal*, then with improvements to the text in 1625 as *L'Instruction du Roy en l'exercice de monter à cheval*. Citations in this chapter refer to the 1666 edition (Amsterdam: Jean Schipper).

18. Pluvinel, *L'Instruction du Roy*, p. 3.

19. Ibid.

20. *Les Nopces de Pelée et de Thetis, Comedie Italienne en Musique, entre-meslée d'un Ballet sur le mesme sujet, dansé par sa Majesté* (Paris: Robert Ballard, 1654), p. 6.

21. For more about Python and the iconography of the *Fronde*, see Robert Berger, "Tourists during the Reign of the Sun King: Access to the Louvre and Versailles and the Anatomy of Guidebooks and Other Printed Aids," in *Paris, Center of Artistic Enlightenment* (University Park: Pennsylvania State University Press, 1988); and *In the Garden of the Sun King: Studies on the Park of Versailles under Louis XIV* (Washington, DC: Dumbarton Oaks Research Library and Collection, 1985).

22. Charlotte Elizabeth, Duchesse d'Orléans, *Fragments of Original Letters, of Madame Charlotte Elizabeth of Bavaria, Duchess of Orleans; Written from the Year 1715 to 1720, to His Serene Highness Anthony Ulric, Duke of B- W-; and to Her Royal Highness Carolina, Princess of Wales. Translated from the French. In two volumes* (London, 1790), vol. 1, pp. 66–67 (December 14, 1719).

23. For analysis of the importance of this book of devises for the crafting of the royal image, see Marianne Grivel and Marc Fumaroli, eds., *Devises pour les tapisseries du roi* (Paris: Herscher, 1988), and also Claire Goldstein, "Building the Grand Siècle: The Context of Literary Ttransformations from Vaux-le-Vicomte to Versailles (1656–1715)" (PhD diss., University of Pennsylvania, 2000).

24. Grivel and Fumaroli, *Devises pour les tapisseries du roi*, p. 37.

25. Sculpted by Jacques Houzeau, cast in bronze by the Kellers, ca. 1687.

26. Béatrix Saule, *Versailles triomphant: une journée de Louis XIV* (Paris: Flammarion, 1996), p. 116.

27. Philippe Salvadori, *La chasse sous l'Ancien Régime* (Paris: Fayard, 1996), p. 198.

28. Charles Perrault, *Contes* (Paris: GF Flammarion 1991), p. 268.

29. Ibid., pp. 268–269.

30. Ibid., p. 271.

31. Ibid., p.190.

32. Ibid., p. 192.

33. Ibid., p. 195.

34. Ibid., pp. 194–195.

35. Ibid.

36. The hunter coming upon a beautiful shepherdess and instantly falling in love is a common pastoral trope. This is also the main plot in Du Fouilloux's poem "L'Adolescence." For Du Fouilloux, however, the hunter who becomes the prey "wounded by love" is not just metaphorical; after seeing the shepherdess, the hunter is attacked by dogs because he is clad in a wolfskin suit.

37. Perrault, *Contes*, pp. 197–198.

38. Ibid., p. 200.

39. Ibid., p. 201.

40. Ibid., p. 204.

41. Jean-Baptiste Poquelin de Molière, *Oeuvres complètes de Molière*, ed. Robert Jouanny (Paris: Garnier Frères, 1962), vol. 2, Act 1, Scene 1, lines 69–74, p. 584.

42. Ibid., Act 2, Scene 1, p. 594.

43. Perrault, *Contes*, p. 263.

44. Keith Thomas, *Man and the Natural World* (New York: Oxford University Press, 1983), p. 41.

45. Salvadori, *La chasse sous l'Ancien Régime*, p. 239.

46. Edmond Jean-François Barbier, *Chronique de la Régence et du règne de Louis XV, ou journal de Barbier* (Paris: Charpentier, 1858), pp. 211–212 (April 8, 1722).

47. Ibid.

48. Garry Marvin, "Wild Killing," in *Killing Animals*, ed., Animal Studies Group (Urbana: University of Illinois Press, 2006), p. 25.

49. The 1694 edition of the *Dictionnaire de l'Académie Française* lists this expression in the entry for *moineau*.

50. Thomas, *Man and the Natural World*, p. 150.

51. Michel de Montaigne, "De la cruauté," in *Essais*, 3 vols. (Paris: GF Flammarion, 1972), vol. 2, pp. 91–104. See Erica Fudge's analysis of this essay, "Two Ethics: Killing Animals in the Past and the Present," in Animal Studies Group, ed., *Killing Animals*, pp. 99–119.

52. Ibid., p. 102.

53. Ibid.

54. *Encyclopédie*, vol. 3, p. 224. ARTFL Project, www.lib.uchicago.edu/efts/ARTFL/projects/encyc/.

55. Ibid.

56. Hal Opperman, *J.-B. Oudry* (Paris: Réunion des musées nationaux, 1982), p. 204.

57. Louis Gougenot, *Lettre sur la peinture, sculpture, et architecture*. Qtd. in Opperman, *Oudry*, p. 204.

58. Hal Opperman, *J.-B. Oudry, 1686–1755* (Fort Worth, TX: Kimbell Art Museum, 1983), p. 184.

59. Masumi Iriye, "Le Vau's Menagerie and the Rise of the Animalier: Enclosing, Dissecting, and Representing Animals in Early Modern France" (PhD diss., University of Michigan, 1994), p. 189.

60. *La Chasse aux bêtes puantes et féroces* (Paris: Imprimerie de la Liberté, 1789), pp. 5–7.

61. Ibid., p. 11.

Chapter 3

1. Harriet Ritvo, *The Animal Estate: The English and Other Creatures in the Victorian Age* (Cambridge, MA: Harvard University Press, 1987), p. 3.

2. Ibid., p. 2.

3. Ibid., p. 3.

4. Donna Haraway, *The Companion Species Manifesto: Dogs, People, and Significant Otherness* (Chicago: Prickly Paradigm Press, 2003), p. 49.

5. Keith Thomas, *Man and the Natural World* (New York: Oxford University Press, 1983), p. 301.
6. Ibid., pp. 288–300.
7. Ibid., p. 98.
8. Ritvo, *Animal Estate*, pp. 45–81.
9. Karen L. Raber, "'Reasonable Creatures': William Cavendish and the Art of Dressage," in *Renaissance Culture and the Everyday*, ed. Patricia Fumerton and Simon Hunt (Philadelphia: University of Pennsylvania Press, 1999), pp. 42–66.
10. Donna Landry, "The Bloody-Shouldered Arabian and Early Modern English Culture," *Criticism* 46, no. 1 (2004): 41–69, at p. 42.
11. Gervase Markham, *Markham's Faithful Farrier*, 1631, pp. 12–13.
12. Ibid., p. 13.
13. Ibid., p. 15.
14. Gail Kern Paster, "Melancholy Cats, Lugged Bears, and Early Modern Cosmology: Reading Shakespeare's Psychological Materialism across the Species Barrier," in *Reading the Early Modern Passions: Essays in the Cultural History of Emotion*, ed. Gail Kern Paster, Katherine Rowe, and Mary Floyd-Wilson (Philadelphia: University of Pennsylvania Press, 2004), pp. 113–129, at 117–118.
15. Ibid., p. 119.
16. John Goodridge, *Rural Life in Eighteenth-Century English Poetry* (Cambridge, UK: Cambridge University Press, 1995), p. 99; Mark Overton, *Agricultural Revolution in England: The Transformation of the Agrarian Economy, 1500–1850* (Cambridge, UK: Cambridge University Press, 1996), pp. 198ff. Floating fields involved running a shallow river of water over a field, which protected it through winter freezes. See also Leonard Cantor, *The Changing English Countryside, 1400–1700* (New York: Routledge, 1987), pp. 48–49.
17. Thomas Bewick, *General History of Quadrupeds*, 1790; repr., 1804, p. 50.
18. Goodridge, *Rural Life*, p. 101.
19. Qtd. in Thomas, *Man and the Natural World*, p. 26.
20. Overton, *Agricultural Revolution*, pp. 114–115.
21. Ritvo, *Animal Estate*. On increases in cattle and farm animal size, see also Joan Thirsk, ed., *The Agrarian History of England and Wales*, vol. V, *1640–1750* (Cambridge, UK: Cambridge University Press, 1985), pp. 10–11.
22. "The second feature of the pet was that it was given an individual personal name. ... Dogs, horses, and other domestic animals who were adjuncts to human society (metonymical humans, as Claude Levi-Strauss calls them) had also long been given names. But their names were only semi-human and emphasized their social distance." Thomas, *Man and the Natural World*, p. 113.
23. Qtd. in Robert C. Allen, *Enclosure and the Yeoman* (Oxford, UK: Clarendon, 1992), p. 111.
24. George Cooke, *The Compleat English Farmer*, 1771, p. 30.
25. *The Husbandman's Magazine*, London, 1718, p. 15.
26. John Mills, *A Treatise on Cattle*, 1795, p. 15.
27. George Culley, *Observations on Livestock*, 1786; repr., 1804, p. 17.
28. Ibid., p. 43.
29. Thomas, *Man and the Natural World*, p. 67.
30. Ibid., p. 33.
31. Jessica Riskin, "The Defecating Duck, or The Ambiguous Origins of Artificial Life," *Critical Inquiry* 29 (Summer 2003): 599–633, at p. 606.

32. Ibid., p. 633.

33. Timothy Reis, "Calculating Humans: Mathematics, War, and the Colonial Calculus," in *Arts of Calculation: Numerical Thought in Early Modern Europe*, ed.
David Glimp and Michelle R. Warren (New York: Palgrave, 2004), pp. 137–164,
at p. 151.

34. Ibid., p. 156.

35. Patricia Cahill, "Killing by Computation: Military Mathematics, the Elizabethan
Social Body, and Marlowe's *Tamburlaine*," in Glimp and Warren, *Arts of Calculation*, pp. 165–186, at. p. 172.

36. Carolyn Merchant, *The Death of Nature: Women, Ecology and the Scientific
Revolution* (San Francisco: Harper & Row, 1980); repr., 1989, p. 169.

37. Bewick, *General History*, p. 326.

38. Merchant, *Death of Nature*, p. 1.

39. Thomas, *Man and the Natural World*, p. 117.

40. Ibid., p. 110.

41. Alexander Pope, *Rape of the Lock, The Poems of Alexander Pope*, ed. John Butt
(London: Methuen, 1965), pp. 281–282.

42. Jodi L. Wyett, "The Lap of Luxury: Lapdogs, Literature and Social Meaning in the
'Long' Eighteenth Century," *Literature Interpretation Theory* 10 (2001): 275–301,
at p. 275.

43. Shakespeare dedicated both *Venus and Adonis* and *Lucrece* to the earl; but at least
a dozen other works were offered for his attention and possible patronage over
the years. The earl has been proposed as the W. H. of the sonnets, making him the
rather narcissistic young aristocrat of the first 126. Unlikely, but if true, it would
be compatible with a dedication like John Clapham's in 1592 of his *Narcissus*
(Akrigg speculates that as secretary to Burghley, Clapham was making a pointed
criticism of Southampton's self-love and effeminacy: G.P.V. Akrigg, *Shakespeare
and the Earl of Southampton* [Cambridge, MA: Harvard University Press, 1978],
pp. 33–34). The earl's patronage relations have also provided fodder for critics
interested in his sexuality. On the whole Akrigg believes Wriothesley's later association with Spanish renegade Antonio Perez left him "surrounded by a vague
aura of homosexuality" (ibid., p. 38). Wriothesley's appearance probably contributes to this titillated response by early biographers. Rowse describes the Hilliard miniature of the earl as emphasizing feminine characteristics, "the sensitive
curve of lip and nostril, the fine arched eyebrows … the long curling tresses" (A. L.
Rowse, *Shakespeare's Southampton: Patron of Virginia* [New York: Harper &
Row, 1965], pp. 60–61), although Rowse finds the expression on the earl's face
quite masculine ("an ambivalent type" [ibid., p. 61]). We know next to nothing
concrete about the earl's sexuality except that he married Elizabeth Verney on the
sly and was punished for it by Elizabeth, but had a reasonably happy marriage
nonetheless.

44. Edward Topsell, *The Historie of Foure-Footed Beastes*, London, 1607, p. 106.

45. Ibid., p. 104.

46. Ibid., 105.

47. Ibid., p. 105.

48. Akrigg, *Shakespeare*; Rowse, *Shakespeare's Southampton*.

49. Erica Fudge, *Perceiving Animals: Humans and Beasts in Early Modern English
Culture* (New York: Macmillan, 2000), p. 13.

50. Roy Strong, *Van Dyck: Charles I on Horseback* (London: Allen Lane for the Penguin Press, 1972); Raber, "'Reasonable Creatures'"; Landry, "Bloody-Shouldered Arabian."

51. Katherine MacDonogh, *Reigning Cats and Dogs: A History of Pets at Court since the Renaissance* (New York: St. Martin's Press, 1999), p. 98.

52. See Chapter 7 in this volume for further discussion of the importance of the pet in art during this period.

53. Ronald Paulson, *Popular and Polite Art in the Age of Hogarth and Fielding* (Notre Dame, IN: University of Notre Dame Press, 1979), p. 62.

54. Judy Egerton, *George Stubbs 1724–1806* (London: Tate Gallery Publishing, 1984), p. 60.

55. Raber, "'Reasonable Creatures'"; Landry, "Bloody-Shouldered Arabian."

56. To bolster the case for a deliberate decision to leave the painting as is, it is worth noting that Stubbs uses the abstract background in other works.

57. Hogarth's work, as noted, offers a similar replacement of the human with the dog. Not only did Hogarth remain "unashamed, even proud, of the doggish quotient in himself" (Paulson, *Popular and Polite Art*, p. 56), but he was quite willing to have the dogs in his satirical art supplant him, or other human characters. Unlike horses, however, dogs remain more marginal overall; as Paulson observes, dogs often figure at the root of some disruption to order in Hogarth's images (ibid., p. 61).

58. Landry, "Bloody-Shouldered Arabian," p. 59.

59. Pope, "Bounce to Fop," *Poems of Alexander Pope*, pp. 823–826.

60. William Cowper, "The Retired Cat," *The Poetical Works of William Cowper*, ed. H. S. Mildford (Oxford, UK: Oxford University Press, 1926), p. 407.

61. The fact of the pet in the poem is erased in most critical discussions of it, which reduce Selima to a code for all women; while these are not incorrect readings, they do not allow the poem to participate in a broader array of semiotic fields, one of which should be the material and ideological history of pets. See Stephen Greenblat, ed., *The Norton Anthology of English LIterature*, vol. 1 (New York: W.W. Norton, 2005), p. 2865.

62. David Perkins, "Cowper's Hares," *Eighteenth-Century Life* 20, no. 2 (1996): 57–69. Cowper also wrote an "Epitaph on a Free but Tame Redbreast," in honor of a friend's lost bird, as well as "On a Goldfinch Starved to Death in His Cage," and a set of poems representing a dialog with his dog Beau, among other animal poems.

63. Byron, "Inscription on the Monument of a Newfoundland Dog," *The Poetical Works of Lord Byron* (Boston: James R. Osgood and Co., 1874), vol. 1, pp. 221–222.

64. Kathleen Kete, *The Beast in the Boudoir: Petkeeping in Nineteenth-Century Paris* (Berkeley: University of California Press, 1994), p. 2.

65. Fudge, *Perceiving Animals*, p. 136.

66. Thomas, *Man and the Natural World*, p. 94.

67. Ibid.

68. Ibid., p. 118.

69. Ibid., p. 119.

70. Haraway, *Companion Species Manifesto*, p. 37.

71. Ibid., p. 33.

72. Marjorie Garber, "Heavy Petting," in *Human, All Too Human*, ed. Diana Fuss (New York: Routledge, 1996), pp. 11–36, at p. 28.

73. Ibid.

74. Kete, *Beast in the Boudoir*, p. 37.

75. Alan Beck and Aaron Katcher, eds., *Between Pets and People: The Importance of Animal Companionship* (New York: G. P. Putnam's Sons, 1983), pp. 121–123.

76. See, for example, Anthony L. Podberscek, Elizabeth S. Paul, and James A. Serpell, eds., *Companion Animals and Us: Exploring the Relationships between People and Pets* (Cambridge, UK: Cambridge University Press, 2000); Phil Arkow, ed., *The Loving Bond: Companion Animals in the Helping Professions* (Saratoga, CA: R&E Publishers, 1987); Beck and Katcher, *Between Pets and People*.

77. See Haraway on distributed evolution: Haraway, *Companion Species Manifesto*, p. 28. An excellent example of reciprocal education between animals and humans is found in *Keri Brandt* ("A language of their own: An Interactivist Approach to Human-Horse Communication," Society and Animals 12:4 (2004) 299–316); there is no real reason to believe that the experiences of horses and riders learning a new mutual "language" through bodily signs and gestures is very different from the experiences of the best and most successful trainers of past eras, reflected in the language and attitudes of figures such as, for instance, William Cavendish or Thomas Bedingfield—but the interpretive framework has changed, and the way the communication process is now coded socially and culturally makes it possible to emphasize the horse's degree of participation in the construction of a shared nonverbal language.

78. I use the term *dwelling* here in the Heideggerian sense as well as for its usual connotations; see Heidegger's "Building, Dwelling, Thinking," in Martin Heidegger, *Poetry, Language, Thought*, ed. and trans. Albert Hofstadtler (New York: Harper and Row, 1971), pp. 145–161.

Chapter 4

1. This is not to be confused with other efforts to unite countries into "Britain," that is, the union of the English and Scottish parliaments in 1707 and the "Union" of 1801, endeavoring to join Great Britain and Ireland.

2. See Chapter 3 in the present volume for a discussion of the development of cattle as a source of meat during the early modern period.

3. C. J. Sisson, "The Red Bull Company and the Importunate Widow," *Shakespeare Survey* 7 (1954): 57–68, at p. 60.

4. Ibid., p. 66.

5. Bridewell Court Minute Books, Guildhall Library, MS33011/4, 1597/8–1604, fols. 327v–332r. Duncan Salkeld gives a good account of the case in "Literary Traces in Bridewell and Bethlem, 1602–1624," *Review of English Studies*, n.s., 56, no. 225 (June 2005): 379–385. See also Eva Griffith, "Christopher Beeston, His Property and Properties," in *A Handbook on Early Modern Theatre*, ed. Richard Dutton (Oxford, UK: Oxford University Press, 2007). Extracts may also be found in *English Professional Theatre, 1530–1660*, ed. Glynne Wickham, Herbert Berry, and William Ingram (Cambridge, UK: Cambridge University Press, 2000), p. 175.

6. John Cordy Jeaffreson, ed., *Middlesex County Records* (Old Series), 4 vols. (London: Middlesex County Records Society, 1886–1892; repr., London: Greater London Council, 1972), vol. II, p. 170.

7. Ibid., p. 170. See also William Le Hardy, ed., *Middlesex Sessions Records* (New Series), 4 vols. (London: Guildhall, 1935–1941), vol. IV, p. 37.

8. Ibid., p. 273.

9. William J. Pinks, *The History of Clerkenwell*, 2nd ed., ed. by Edward J. Wood (London: Charles Herbert, 1881), p. 294.

10. Today it is a "dead meat" market—but this was only so since 1868. Prior to this time, until 1855 when it was moved to Copenhagen Fields, it had been a livestock and horse market. See Alec Forshaw and Theo Bergstrom, *Smithfield: Past and Present* (London: Robert Hale, 1990), pp. 77–79.

11. Ibid., p. 20.

12. Ibid., p. 21. The market was granted a charter in 1327 (ibid., p. 20).

13. John Richardson, *The Annals of London* (London: Cassell & Co., 2000), p. 56.

14. Philip E. Jones, *The Butchers of London: A History of the Worshipful Company of Butchers of the City of London* (London: Secker and Warburg, 1976), p. 99. See also Pinks, *History of Clerkenwell*, p. 294, for both fourteenth-century customs charged for road repair and a mid-sixteenth-century act concerning payments deducted from rents.

15. See also Joan Thirsk, ed., *The Agrarian History of England and Wales*, vol. IV, *1500–1640* (Cambridge, UK: Cambridge University Press, 1967), p. 542, on farmers in England reluctant to sell their produce at the far-distant capital.

16. *Letter Book K*, p. 220; Jones, *Butchers of London*, p. 99.

17. *Calendar of Plea and Memoranda Rolls, 1364–81*, p. 94; *Letter Book G*, p. 288; *Letter Book H*, pp. 301, 372; *Close Rolls, 1369–1374*, pp. 31, 178; *1385–1389*, p. 304; *Journal of the Common Council* 8, fol. 28v. See also Jones, *Butchers of London*, p. 10.

18. Forshaw and Bergstrom, *Smithfield*, p. 20.

19. Pinks, *History of Clerkenwell*, pp. 296–304.

20. Ibid., pp. 444–446. See also Bernard Rudden, *The New River: A Legal History* (Oxford, UK: Clarendon, 1985), pp. 7–26 and *History of the New River* [no author cited], Thames Water [n.d.].

21. See answers to interrogatories 2 and 33 in the case of "Worth v. Baskervile," NA C24/500/9. For more on Greene see Herbert Berry, "Thomas Greene," *Dictionary of National Biography* (Oxford, UK: Oxford University Press, 2004), vol. 23, pp. 583–584.

22. Jones, *Butchers of London*, pp. 100–101.

23. Derek Keene, "Metropolitan Values: Migration, Mobility and Cultural Norms, London 1100–1700," in *The Development of Standard English, 1300–1800*, ed. L. Wright (Cambridge, UK: Cambridge University Press, 2000), pp. 93–114, at p. 109.

24. See Thirsk, *Agrarian History*, p. 539, for evidence of London purchasers traveling to the Midlands to buy livestock.

25. Ibid., pp. 509 and 512, for further examples of relationships between London purchasers and the traders beyond London's jurisdiction.

26. Ibid., p. 560, concerning inns as marts and those that catered to drovers.

27. See Figure 4.1. For a complete survey of the "Agas" map see Adrian Prockter and Robert Taylor, *The A to Z of Elizabethan London* (Lympne Castle, Kent, UK: Harry Margary, in association with the Guildhall Library, 1979).

28. Pinks, *History of Clerkenwell*, pp. 95–101.

29. Katie Whitaker, *Mad Madge: Margaret Cavendish, Duchess of Newcastle, Royalist, Writer and Romantic* (London: Chatto and Windus, 2002), pp. 83 and 291.

30. Published in French at Antwerp in 1658; republished in English in London, 1667, with emendations (Pinks, *History of Clerkenwell*, p. 97). See also Whitaker, *Mad Madge*, p. 208. For further discussion of the training methods of William Cavendish and others, see Karen Raber and Treva J. Tucker, eds., *The Culture of the Horse: Status, Discipline, and Identity in the Early Modern World* (New York: Palgrave, 2005).

31. See William Joseph Tighe, "The Gentlemen Pensioners in Elizabethan Politics and Government" (PhD diss., University of Cambridge, 1983), pp. 72, 323.

32. See Neville Williams, "The Master of the Royal Tents and His Records," in *Prisca Munimenta: Studies in Archival and Administrative History Presented to Dr. A. E. Hollaender*, ed. Felicity Ranger (London: University of London Press, 1973), pp. 162–168.

33. The inventory of the goods of this residence includes, among the ordinary items of a Tudor home, a "Cast of Counters" and "one payer of golde Wayghtes" plus "j almynak." The inventory, dated 1585, is likely to have been part of notes made in relation to the accession of a minor to the title. Bedingfeld papers, Oxbrugh Hall, Norfolk (privately owned). I am grateful to the present Henry Bedingfeld at Oxbrugh and his family for allowing me to look at these documents. For further comment on Thomas Bedingfeld and his knowledge of horsemanship, see Kate van Orden, "From *Gens d'armes* to *Gentilhommes*: Dressage, Civility and the *Ballet à Cheval*," in Raber and Tucker, *Culture of the Horse*, pp. 197–222, at pp. 202–203.

34. M. C. Bradbrook, *John Webster: Citizen and Dramatist* (London: Weidenfeld and Nicolson, 1980), p. 11 and David Gunby, "John Webster," *New Dictionary of National Biography*. Webster's plays performed at the Red Bull include *The White Devil*, first produced there ca. 1611–1612 and published in 1612 and the controversial *Keep the Widow Waking*—lost but based on a notorious case of its time. His involvement in a trade may explain the sporadic nature of Webster's playwriting.

35. Ipswich Suffolk Record Office, uncatalogued Seckford Papers, GB431:10, 255, Box 1, bundle [ca. 1826].

36. See Barbara Ravelhofer, "'Beasts of Recreacion': Henslowe's White Bears," *English Literary Renaissance* 32, no. 2 (Spring 2002): 287–323, and Teresa Grant, "White Bears in *Mucedorus*, *The Winter's Tale*, and *Oberon, The Fairy Prince*," *Notes & Queries* 246, n.s., 48, no. 3 (September 2001): 311–313, for observations on bears performing entertainments with humans.

37. Eva Griffith, "Banks, William [Richard] (*fl.* 1591–1637)," *New Dictionary of National Biography*. See also the discussion of Morocco the Intelligent Horse in Erica Fudge, *Brutal Reasoning: Animals, Rationality, and Humanity in Early Modern England* (Ithaca, NY: Cornell University Press, 2006), pp. 123–146.

38. Thomas Bastard, *Chrestoleros*, London, 1598, p. 62.

39. See Herbert Berry, "The Four Inns," in Wickham, Ingram, and Berry, *English Professional Theatre*, pp. 295–305.

40. Ben Jonson, *Bartholomew Fair*, ed. G. R. Hibbard (London: Ernest Benn, 1977), p. 8.

41. Ibid., p. 9.

42. William Shakespeare, *Cymbeline*, The Arden Shakespeare, ed. J. M. Nosworthy (London: Methuen, 1955), p. 175.

43. Thomas Heywood, *The Dramatic Works of Thomas Heywood now first collected with illustrative notes and a memoir of the author in six volumes*, ed. Shepherd [?] (London: John Pearson, 1874), vol. V, p. 168.

44. See Berry, "Thomas Greene"; however, the baboon comparison is also questioned. See Matthew Steggle, "'Greene's Baboone': Thomas Greene, Ape Impersonator?," *Theatre Notebook* 60 (2006): 72–75.

45. A letter from the Privy Council written in 1570 adjured prominent religious figures to see that a copy of Foxe was put into every parish throughout the nation. See Thomas S. Freeman, "Providence and Prescription: The Account of Elizabeth in Foxe's 'Book of Martyrs,'" in *The Myth of Elizabeth*, ed. Susan Doran and Thomas S. Freeman (Basingstoke, UK: Palgrave Macmillan, 2003), pp. 27–55, at p. 46.

46. John Foxe, *Actes and Monuments of these latter and perillous dayes ...* (London: John Day, 1563). Curiously paginated, Sir Henry's part of the story in Foxe is to be found on pages 1713 (I) to 1716.

47. Both parts of the play are found in *The Dramatic Works of Thomas Heywood*, I, 189–351. The particular scene is found on pp. 229–230.

48. See George F. Reynolds, "*Mucedorus*, Most Popular Elizabethan Play?," in *Studies in the English Renaissance Drama*, ed. Josephine W. Bennett, Oscar Cargill, and Vernon Hall Jr. (London: Peter Owen & Vision Press, 1959), pp. 248–268.

49. See Ben Jonson, *Ben Jonson*, 11 vols., ed. C. H. Herford, P. Simpson, and E. Simpson (Oxford, UK: Clarendon, 1925–1963), vol. 7, pp. 337–356, at p. 351. For the Tudor-Stuart period at the Tower of London menagerie, see Daniel Hahn, *The Tower Menagerie: The Amazing True Story of the Royal Collection of Wild Beasts* (London: Pocket Books, 2004), chap. 4, pp. 85–115.

50. Part II of the play was published in 1606, 1609, 1623, and 1633.

51. Heywood, *The Silver Age, Dramatic Works*, III, p. 122.

52. Ibid., pp. 135, 139, 140, and 152, respectively.

53. Ibid., pp. 154–155.

54. Heywood, *The Brazen Age, Dramatic Works*, III, pp. 165–256, pp. 175–176.

55. Ibid., p. 217.

56. James Wright, *Historia Histrionica: An Historical Account of the English Stage, Shewing the Ancient Use, Improvement, and Perfection, of Dramatick Representations in This Nation*, London, 1699, B3r.

57. Thomas Tomkis, *Albumazar*, London, 1615, C1r.

58. Heywood, *Brazen Age*, pp. 255–256.

59. See Forshaw and Bergstrom, *Smithfield*, pp. 34–35, and Jones, *Butchers of London*, p. 97.

60. William le Hardy, *Middlesex Sessions Records*, IV, p. 37.

61. Ibid., I, p. xxiii.

62. See A. Daly Briscoe, *A Tudor Worthy: Thomas Seckford of Woodbridge* (Ipswich, UK: East Anglian Magazine, 1979), pp. 85–86.

Chapter 5

1. Phillip Sloan, "Natural History, 1670–1802," in *Companion to the History of Modern Science*, ed. R. C. Olby et al. (London: Routledge, 1990), pp. 295–313, at pp. 296–297.

2. Robert Boyle, *General Heads for the Natural History of a Country, Great or Small; Drawn out for the use of Travellers and Navigators* (London: for John Taylor and S. Helford, 1692).

3. William Harvey, *The Anatomical Exercises of William Harvey*, ed. Geoffrey Keynes (1928; repr., New York: Dover, 1995).

4. William Harvey, *Anatomical Lectures*, ed. and trans. Gweneth Whitteridge (Edinburgh: E. and S. Livingstone, 1964).

5. William Harvey, *Disputations Touching the Generation of Animals*, ed. and trans. Gweneth Whitteridge (Oxford, UK: Blackwell, 1981).

6. J. A. Smith and K. M. Boyd, eds., *Lives in the Balance* (Oxford, UK: Oxford University Press, 1991), p. 300.

7. René Descartes, *Discourse on Method*, trans. F. E. Sutcliffe (Harmondsworth, UK: Penguin, 1968).

8. Ibid., Discourse 5. Eighteenth-century makers of automata seemed to attempt to prove Descartes correct: see Jessica Riskin, "The Defecating Duck, or The Ambiguous Origins of Artificial Life," *Critical Inquiry* 29 (Summer 2003): 599–633.

9. There is much controversy about Descartes' views; see, for example, John Cottingham, "'A Brute to the Brutes?' Descartes' Treatment of Animals," *Philosophy* 53 (1978): 551–559.

10. Richard Lower, "The Method Observed in Transfusing the Blood out of One Animal into Another," *Philosophical Transactions* 2 (1666): 353–358.

11. Edmund King to Robert Boyle, November 25, 1667, in Boyle, *Works*, ed. T. Birch, London, 1772, vol. 6, pp. 646–647.

12. Jean-Jacques Peumery, *Les origines de la transfusion sanguine* (Amsterdam: Israel, 1975); A. D. Farr, "The First Human Blood Transfusion," *Medical History* 24 (1980): 143–162.

13. *The Correspondence of Marcello Malpighi*, 5 vols., ed. and trans. H. B. Adelmann (Ithaca, NY: Cornell University Press, 1975), vol. 1, passim.

14. F. J. Cole, *A History of Comparative Anatomy* (1949; repr., New York: Dover, 1975).

15. Claude Perrault, comp., *Mémoires pour servir à l'histoire naturelle des animaux*, 2 vols. (Paris: Imprimerie Royale, 1671–1676).

16. Robert Boyle, *Some Considerations Touching the Usefulness of Experimental Natural Philosophy*, 2nd ed. (Oxford, UK: R. Davis, 1671).

17. Robert Boyle, "New Pneumatical Experiments about Respiration," *Philosophical Transactions* 5 (1670): 2044.

18. Carlo Fracassati, "An Account of Some Experiments of Injecting Liquors into the Veins of Animals," *Philosophical Transactions* 2 (1667): 490.

19. Nicolas Fontaine, *Mémoires pour servir a l'histoire de Port-Royal*, (Cologne, 1738), vol. 2, pp. 52–53, qtd. in Leonora Cohen Rosenfield, *From Beast-Machine to Man-Machine: The Theme of Animal Soul in French Letters from Descartes to La Mettrie* (New York: Oxford University Press, 1940; repr., New York: Octagon, 1968), p. 54.

20. Niels Stensen to Thomas Bartholin, 1661, qtd. in Frederik Ruysch, *Dilucidatio valvularum in vasis lymphaticis et lacteis*, 1665, ed. A. M. Luyendijk-Elshout (Nieuwkoop, the Netherlands: B. de Graaf, 1964), Introduction, p. 36.

21. Junius (pseudonym), "The Air-Pump," *Gentleman's Magazine* 10 (April 1740): 194.

22. Abraham Trembley, *Mémoires pour servir à l'histoire d'un genre de polypes d'eau douce* (Leiden, Holland: J. & H. Verbeek, 1744); Albrecht von Haller, *A Treatise on the Sensible and Irritable Parts of Animals* (London: J. Nourse, 1755).

23. Simon Schaffer, "Natural Philosophy and Public Spectacle," *History of Science* 21 (1983): 1–46.

24. Alexander Monro primus, "The History of Anatomy," 1739, MS 166, Medical Library, University of Otago, Dunedin, New Zealand, ff. I–IV.

25. René Girard, *Violence and the Sacred*, trans. Patrick Gregory (Baltimore: Johns Hopkins University Press, 1977), pp. 10–11.

26. Ibid.

27. J.-G. Duverney, *Lettre á Monsieur ***. Contenant plusieurs nouvelles observations sur l'osteologie* (Paris: Laurent d'Houry, 1689), p. 9.

28. J.-G. Duverney, *Oeuvres anatomiques*, 2 vols. (Paris: C. A. Jombert, 1761), vol. 2, p. 2.

29. James Douglas, *Myographiae Comparatae Specimen, or A Comparative Description of All the Muscles in a Man and in a Quadruped* (London: G. Strachan, 1707), p. viii.

30. On the rise of pet keeping, see Keith Thomas, *Man and the Natural World* (New York: Oxford University Press, 1983).

31. Douglas, *Myographiae*, pp. vi–vii.

32. William Cheselden, *The Anatomy of the Humane Body* (London: N. Cliff and D. Jackson, 1713), p. 109.

33. For further discussion of these points, see Paul Lawrence Farber, *Finding Order in Nature* (Baltimore: Johns Hopkins University Press, 2000); Sloan, "Natural History."

34. Georges-Louis Leclerc, Comte de Buffon, *Histoire naturelle générale et particulière: avec la Description du Cabinet du Roy. Tome première* (Paris: Imprimerie Royale, 1749), p. 12. My translation.

35. Ibid., p. 20.

36. Farber, *Finding Order in Nature*, p. 20; Sloan, "Natural History," pp. 304–306.

Chapter 6

1. The present chapter is based on a selection of passages from Jean-Luc Guichet, *Rousseau, l'animal et l'homme: L'animalité dans l'horizon anthropologique des Lumières* (Paris: Cerf, 2006); the editor gratefully acknowledges permission to publish these passages, granted by Les Editions du Cerf, Paris.

2. *Annales Jean-Jacques Rousseau*, vol. 35, 1959–1962, p. 155; this discussion followed Gouhier's paper, "Ce que le vicaire doit à Descartes" ("What the Vicar Owes to Descartes").

3. Let us immediately clarify an important point of vocabulary. Rousseau was working during a pivotal moment when the sense of the French word *animal*—whose primitive meaning had been all living things—had begun to differentiate itself and converge with the word *bête* (beast) but with its etymology remaining very different; the result is that the two meanings of the term *animal* are found in his work, sometimes used with a precise meaning and sometimes a meaning more analogous to our contemporary usage. The same is true in Buffon's work, compared, for example, with Condillac, who uses the stricter and more classical meaning. It is important to note that throughout his work Rousseau prefers the word *animal* (which emphasizes the unity of humans and other beings) over the word *bête* (which is part of a logic of separation).

4. Jean Jacques Rousseau, *Émile*, trans. Barbara Foxley (London: Everyman's Library, 1963), p. 257.

5. Jean Jacques Rousseau, *Lettres morales*, [third letter], in *Œuvres complètes*, vol. IV (Paris: Gallimard, 1969), p. 1095.

6. Rousseau, *Émile,* pp. 183–184 (my emphasis).

7. Jean Jacques Rousseau, *A Discourse on Inequality,* trans. Maurice Cranston (New York: Penguin Books, 1984), p. 87.

8. Etienne Bonnot de Condillac, *Traité des animaux* (Paris: Vrin, 1987), p. 494 (my emphasis). The apparently careful terms "very few" and "few general ideas" mean a great deal in fact since, while allowing that the animal only has some general ideas, these concessions bring the animal to the verge of human understanding in stretching the links between understanding and the immediately sensible.

9. Rousseau, *Discourse on Inequality,* p. 95.

10. "The sight of one of these nuts recalls to his memory the sensations he received from the other": ibid., p. 95.

11. "Are we to think that he has the general idea of this sort of fruit and compares its archetype with these two particulars? Surely not": ibid.

12. "Up to a point it even combines its ideas": ibid., p. 87.

13. Ibid., p. 82.

14. Ibid. (my emphasis).

15. Ibid.

16. Ibid., p. 87.

17. Ibid., Note J, p. 155 (my emphasis).

18. So much so that the famous phrase of Montaigne and Charron is found to be pertinent here, at least in relation to physical characteristics: "one finds in the description of these supposed monsters striking conformities with the human species, *and smaller differences than might be pointed to between one human being and another*" (my emphasis), ibid., p. 156.

19. Ibid.

20. Ibid., p. 157.

21. *Julie, or The New Héloise,* part IV, letter XI from Saint-Preux to Lord Bomston: see Jean Jacques Rousseau, *La Nouvelle Héloise,* trans. Judith H. McDowell (University Park: Pennsylvania State University Press, 1968).

22. Ibid., p. 309.

23. Ibid., p. 310 (my emphasis).

Chapter 7

1. Nationalmuset, Copenhagen; and Musée du Louvre, Paris.

2. Salons of 1738 and 1739. Musée du Louvre, Paris.

3. 1763. Yale Center for British Art, Paul Mellon Collection, New Haven.

4. Muséum national d'histoire naturelle, Paris.

5. Nathalie Grande, "Une vedette des salons: le caméléon," in *L'animal au XVIIe siècle: Actes de la 1ère journée d'études du Centre de recherches sur le XVIIe siècle européen (1600–1700) (Université Michel de Montaigne-Bordeaux III),* ed. Charles Mazouer (Tubingen: Narr, 2003), pp. 89–102.

6. Madeleine de Scudéry, *Nouvelles conversations de morale* (Paris: Veuve de Sébastien Marbe-Cramoisy, 1688), vol. 2, pp. 496–539.

7. Claude Perraut, *Description anatomique d'un caméléon, d'un casoar, d'un dromadaire, d'un ours et d'une gazelle* (Paris: F. Léonard, 1669), with a drawing by Sébastien Leclerc (1637–1714), engraved by Abraham Bosse (1604–1676).

8. Musée du Louvre, Paris.

9. Musée du Louvre, Paris.

10. See, for example, the *Marchés* of Frans Snyders (1579–1657) or the *Animaux et ustensiles*, also called the *Départ de Jacob pour la Mésopotamie* of Boel. Musée du Louvre, Paris.

11. See the cartoons of Barend Van Orley (1488–1541) for the twelve *Mois* in the set of tapestries *Les Chasses de Maximilien*, ca. 1525. Musée du Louvre, Paris.

12. Snyders, *Les Perroquets*. Musée des Beaux-Arts, Grenoble.

13. Gustave Loisel, *Histoire de la Ménagerie de l'antiquité à nos jours,* 3 vols. (Paris: Doin et fils, 1912).

14. Jacques-Henri Bernardin de Saint-Pierre, "Mémoire sur la nécessité de joindre une ménagerie au Jardin des plantes de Paris," in *Oeuvres de Jacques-Henri Bernardin de Saint Pierre,* 12 vols., ed. L. Aimé-Martin (Paris: Armand-Aubrée, 1834), vol. 11, p. 403.

15. Painted sketches: Musée du Louvre, Paris; Elisabeth Foucart Walter, *Pieter Boel 1622–1674. Peintre de Louis XIV. Le fond des études peintes des Gobelins. Les dossiers du Musée du Louvre* (Paris: Réunion des musées nationaux, 2001); Drawings, Musée du Louvre, Paris; Madeleine Pinault Sørensen, *Sur le vif. Dessins d'animaux de Pieter Boel (1622–1674)* (Paris: Réunion des musées nationaux and Franco Maria Ricci, 2001).

16. Antoine Picon, "Vers une histoire naturelle des animaux," in *Claude Perrault, 1613–1688 ou la curiosité d'un classique* (Paris: Picard, 1988), pp. 53–74.

17. Published in *Mémoires de l'Académie royale des sciences depuis 1666* (Paris: La Compagnie des Libraires, 1734), vol. 3, pt. 3, pp. 119–120.

18. Exhibition *Collection des ducs de Mecklembourg-Schwerin, Animaux d'Oudry*, Fontainebleau, Musée national du Château et Versailles, Musée national des Châteaux de Versailles et de Trianon, 2003–2004. Catalog by Vincent Droguet, Xavier Salmon, and Danièle Véron-Denise.

19. Musée du Louvre, Paris; Manufacture nationale de porcelaine, Sèvres.

20. Bibliothèque de l'Institut de France, Paris.

21. Claude Perrault, *Mémoires pour servir à l'histoire des animaux* (Paris: Imprimerie Royale, 1676), p. 20.

22. Biblioteca Universitaria di Bologna, Bologna.

23. Bibliothèque centrale du Muséum national d'Histoire naturelle, Paris, Vélins.

24. Perrault, *Description anatomique*, pp. 85–89.

25. *La Chine d'Athanase Kirchere de la Compagnie de Jesus …*, traduit par F. S. Dalquié (Amsterdam: J. Jansson et les héritiers de E. Weyerstraet, 1670).

26. Cleveland Museum of Art, Cleveland.

27. Abbé de Condillac, *Traité des animaux* (Paris: Vrin, 1987).

28. Claude Yvon, "L'âme des bêtes," in *L'Encyclopédie, ou Dictionnaire raisonné des sciences, des arts et des métiers,* 35 vols. (Paris and Neuchâtel, 1751–1780), vol. 1, pp. 343–353.

29. Also through the texts of Henri Testelin (1616–1695) and Etienne Picart (1632–1721).

30. Musée du Louvre, Paris; Jennifer Montagu, *The Expression of the Passions: The Origin and Influence of Charles Le Brun's Conference sur l'expression générale et particulière* (New Haven and London: Yale University Press, 1994); Madeleine Pinault Sørensen, "La Physiognomonie," in *Musée du Louvre, Département des Arts graphiques, Inventaire général des dessins, École française, Charles Le Brun (1619–1690),* 2 vols. (Paris: Réunion des musées nationaux, 2000), vol. 2, pp. 571–650.

31. Giovanni Battista della Porta, *De humana physiognomia* (Vice AEquensis: Josephum Cacchium, 1586).

32. Jean-Luc Guichet, *Rousseau, l'animal et l'homme. L'animalité dans l'horizon anthropologique des Lumières* (Paris: Cerf, 2006).

33. Etienne Binet, *Essay des Merveilles de Nature et des plus nobles artifices* (Rouen: Osmont, 1621).

34. Madeleine Pinault Sørensen, ed., *De la physionomie humaine et animale: dessins de Charles Le Brun gravés pour la Chalcographie du musée Napoléon en 1806* (Paris: Réunion des musées nationaux, 2000).

35. Paris: Imprimerie Royale, 1749–1767. There are fifteen volumes for mammals; and nine volumes on birds are published between 1770 and 1783. The *Supplément* includes seven volumes published between 1774 and 1789. Thierry Hoquet, *Buffon illustré, les gravures de l'Histoire naturelle (1749–1767)* (Paris: Publications scientifiques du Muséum national d'Histoire naturelle, 2007).

36. Bent Sørensen, "L'éléphant de Jacques François Joseph Saly," *Gazette des Beaux-Arts* (October 1995): 139–148.

37. Buffon, Georges-Louis, comte de, *Histoire naturelle, générale et particulière*, 31 vols. (Paris: Imprimerie Royale, 1749–1789), vol. 23, p. 171.

38. George Edwards, *Gleanings of Natural History*, 3 vols. (London, 1758–1764). On the rhinoceros: Tim H. Clarke, *The Rhinoceros from Dürer to Stubbs 1515–1799* (London and New York: Sotheby's, 1986).

39. 1751. Ca'Rezzonico, Venice.

40. Private collection, Switzerland.

41. Private collection, Switzerland.

42. *Een vorstelijke dierentuin De menagerie van Willem V / Le zoo du prince. La ménagerie du stathouder Guillaume V*, under the direction of B. C. Sliggers and A. A. Wertheim (Amsterdam: Walburg Instituut, 1994).

43. Set of bird drawings, Collection Frits Lugt, Paris; Exhibition *La volière imaginaire, Aquarelles d'oiseaux par Aert Schouman (1710–1792)*, Fondation Custodia, Collection Frits Lugt, Paris, 1982. Brochure by Meile D. Haga.

44. The artist also sketched from stuffed specimens.

45. Arnout Vosmaer, *Regnum Animale*, Amsterdam, 1766–1804.

46. In reality a Blackbuck. 1770–1778. Hunterian Art Gallery, Glasgow.

47. 1770. Hunterian Art Gallery, Glasgow.

48. 1773. British Museum, London.

49. 1790 or 1791. Private collection.

50. 1780. Musée du Louvre, Paris.

51. Musée historique lorrain, Nancy, and a private collection, Paris; also probably another terracotta at the Musée Cognac-Jay, Paris.

52. 1632. Musée Saint-Vaast, Arras.

53. Pierre Rosenberg and Jacques Thuillier, *Laurent de La Hyre 1606–1656, L'Homme et l'oeuvre* (Geneva and Grenoble: Skira, 1988), p. 75.

54. 1647. Mauritshuis, The Hague. We can also mention his *Cheval pie* (Pied horse), 1652. Musée du Louvre, Paris.

55. The figure and sheep to the right were added when the artist enlarged his painting.

56. Before 1785. Musée du Louvre, Paris.

57. Patricia de Fougerolle, Katherine MacDonald, and Marie-Christine Prestat, *Vies de Chiens*, Exposition Catalog, Hôtel Guénégaud, Paris, 2000–2001 (Paris: Alain de Gourcuff, 2000).

58. *Phillip IV*, *Prince Baltasar Carlos*, 1635, and the *Duke of Olivares*, 1634. The Prado, Madrid.

59. 1635–1636. National Gallery, London.

60. Ca. 1635. Musée du Louvre, Paris.

61. Ca. 1775. Private collection.

62. Robert Rosenblum, "L'emprunt ne saurait guère être traité de plagiat: Reynolds et le contexte international," Exhibition *Sir Joshua Reynolds 1723–1792*, Galeries nationales du Grand Palais, Paris, 1985; Royal Academy of Arts, London, 1985–1986 (Paris: Editions de la Réunion des musées nationaux, 1985), p. 80. In 1766, Sir Reynolds painted a superb *Portrait of Lady Spencer* very affectionately holding her black spaniel in her arms; Goodwood House, The Trustees of Goodwood House.

63. Exhibition *Stubbs and the Horse*, Kimbell Art Museum, Fort Worth, 2004–2005. Catalog by Malcolm Warner, Robin Blake, Lance Mayer, and Gay Myers.

64. 1769. National Gallery of Art, Washington.

65. Stubbs published *The Anatomy of the Horse*, with 24 plates, in London in 1766; Malcolm Cormack, "Stubbs and Science," in *Fearful Symmetry, George Stubbs, Painter of the English Enlightenment* (New York: Hall and Knight, 2000), pp. 37–84.

66. 1766–1770. Kimbell Art Museum, Fort Worth.

67. Thomas Pennant, *British Zoology* (London: Printed for Benjamin White, 1768–1770), vol. 4, pp. 42–44, cited in Exhibition catalog *Stubbs and the Horse*, Kimbell Art Museum, Fort Worth, 2004–2005, no. 49.

68. 1730. Musée des Augustins, Toulouse. See Chapter 2 for a detailed description of the curée, the highly ritualized killing of the deer.

69. 1762. His Grace the Duke of Westminster, London.

70. Animal paintings can be intended for interior decoration, for tapestry cartoons, for decorated lintels or fireplace screens.

71. All three works were completed in 1635. The Prado, Madrid.

72. The Prado, Madrid.

73. Musée du Louvre, Paris.

74. Musée du Louvre, Paris; held also at the Musée national du Château, Fontaine-bleau, and at the Musée national du Château, Compiègne.

75. 1699. Musée du Louvre, Paris.

76. 1727. Musée national du Château Fontainebleau.

77. 1725. Musée national du Château Fontainebleau.

78. Robert Rosenblum, *The Dog in Art from Rococo to Post-Modernism* (New York: Abrams, 1988); and Erika Billeter, *Hunde und ihre Maler zwischen Tizians Aristokraten und Picassos Gauklern* (Bern: Benteli, 2005).

79. Elisabeth Foucart Walter and Pierre Rosenberg, *The Painted Cat: The Cat in Western Painting from the Fifteenth to the Twentieth Century* (New York: Rizzoli, 1988). See Chapter 3 for further discussion of the emergence of the pet in early modern Europe.

80. 1687. Musée national du Château de Versailles et de Trianon, Versailles.

81. Lord Pembroke, Wilton House.

82. *James Stuart, Duke of Lennox and Richmond*, 1635–1636. Metropolitan Museum of Art, New York.

83. Ca. 1680. The Prado, Madrid.

84. Rijksmuseum, Rijksprentenkabinet, Amsterdam; Collection Frits Lugt, Paris.

85. Musée du Louvre, Paris.

86. Pieter de Hooch (1629–1684), *La Buveuse*, 1658. Musée du Louvre, Paris.

87. Watteau also copied dogs painted by Rubens in the Galerie de Marie de Medicis; Musée du Louvre, Paris.

88. 1745. Tate Gallery, London.

89. John Soane's Museum, London.

90. 1795. Collection of the Dukes of Alba, Madrid.

91. 1786. National Gallery of Art, Washington.

92. "Miss Prue" is a poorly reared country girl in *Love for Love* by William Congreve (1670–1729), which explains the posture of the model. 1771. Yale Center for British Art, Paul Mellon Collection, New Haven.

93. 1760–1762. Wallace Collection, London.

94. Collection of Count Spencer, Althorp.

95. 1764–1765. Collection of the Count of Rosebery, Dalmeny House.

96. Metropolitan Museum of Art, New York.

97. 1740. Nationalmuseum, Stockholm.

98. 1774. Musée des Beaux-Arts et d'Archéologie, Besançon. The size of the painting, by its width, corresponds to the height prevalently used for human portraits.

99. 1759. Private collection, Paris.

100. Tate Gallery, London.

101. Ca. 1780. Paul Mellon Collection, Upperville, Virginia.

102. 1775. Private collection.

103. 1791? Her Majesty the Queen. Fino is also portrayed in *The Prince of Wales' Phaeton*, 1793. Her Majesty the Queen.

104. Galerie Sabauda, Turino.

105. 1659. Kunsthistorisches Museum, Vienna.

106. Exhibition *Sir Joshua Reynolds 1723–1792*, op. cit., p. 70.

107. 1767. Private collection, England; Exhibition *Jean-Baptiste Greuze, 1725–1805*, Wadsworth Atheneum, Hartford; The California Palace of the Legion of Honor, San Francisco; and Musée des Beaux-Arts, Dijon, 1976–1977, no. 55; Emma Barker, *Greuze and the Painting of Sentiment* (Cambridge, UK: Cambridge University Press, 2005), p. 104, illus. 22.

108. See the critiques of the *Salons* by Denis Diderot and Catherine-Elie Fréron.

109. Musée du Louvre, Paris.

110. 1775. Wallace Collection, London.

111. 1777. Collection of the Duke of Buccleuch and Queensbury K. T., Bowhill.

112. Former Guinigi Collection, Lucques.

113. Musée national du Château et de Tre'anon, Versailles.

114. Musée Lambinet, Versailles.

115. 1760. Private collection, Paris.

116. Bernard Marret, *Les Singeries dans la peinture. Portraits de l'artiste en singe* (Paris: Somogy, 2001).

117. Ca. 1726; *Le Singe antiquaire*, Musée du Louvre, Paris; and the pair of paintings *Le Singe peintre* and *Le Singe antiquaire*, Musée des Beaux-Arts, Chartres.

118. Buffon, *Histoire naturelle*, vol. 15, 1767, pl. 9.

119. *Deux singes*; Staatliche Museen, Preussicher Kulturbesitz, Gemäldegalerie, Berlin.

120. Rijksmuseum, Rijksprentenkabinet, Amsterdam.

121. Musées Royaux des Beaux-Arts, Brussels.

122. 1762. Musée du Louvre, Paris.

123. Musée de Picardie, Amiens.

124. Ca. 1629–1630. Staatliche Museen, Berlin.

125. 1753. Private collection.

126. Robert Darnton, *The Great Cat Massacre* (New York: Basic Books, 1984), chap. 2.

127. 1740. Washington University, Saint Louis (Missouri).

128. 1716. The Hermitage, Saint Petersburg.

129. David Posner, "An Aspect of Watteau: 'Peintre de la réalité,'" in *Études d'art français offertes à Charles Sterling*, ed. Albert Châtelet and Nicole Reynau (Paris: Presses Universitaires de France, 1975), pp. 279–286.

130. For example, in a private collection, Paris.

131. Musée national de la Renaissance, Écouen.

132. Virginia Museum of the Fine Arts, Paul Mellon Collection, Richmond; Laurence Lubin, "Philip Reinagle's 'Extraordinary Musical Dog,'" *Music in Art International, Journal for Music Iconography* 22 (1998): 157–173, at p. 169.

133. Bowes Museum, Barnard Castle, Durham.

134. Musée Buffon, Montbard.

135. Artis Bibliothek, Amsterdam.

136. Het Loo, Appeldorn.

137. The animals were actually kept in a cage.

138. 1784. Drawing: Collection Frits Lugt, Paris; canvas: Royal Collections, The Hague.

139. Bibliothèque centrale du Muséum national d'histoire naturelle, Paris.

140. Bibliothèque centrale du Muséum national d'histoire naturelle, Paris.

141. 1752. Musée de la chasse et de la nature, Paris; copy Musée des beaux-arts, Narbonne.

142. Diderot mentioned this work a few years later in his Salon of 1767.

143. Bibliothèque centrale du Muséum d'histoire naturelle, Paris.

144. Salon of 1757; both in the Musée de Picardie, Amiens.

145. Staatliches Museum, Schwerin.

146. Marble. Museo di Capitole, Rome. Numerous copies exist.

147. 1756. London.

148. 1763. Private collection; and 1770. Walker Art Gallery, Liverpool.

149. 1762. Yale Center for British Art, Paul Mellon Collection, New Haven (with a pendant painting entitled *Lion Attacking a Stag*); 1765; ca. 1768–1769. Same collection; 1770. Yale University Art Gallery, New Haven.

150. 1763. Tate Gallery, London.

151. Georges Toscan, *Histoire du lion de la Ménagerie du Muséum national d'Histoire naturelle et de son chien* (Paris: Cuchet, 1795), pp. 193–199.

152. Salon du Dessin, 2006, Paris; the drawing is anonymously engraved.

153. Jean Hoüel, *Histoire naturelle des deux éléphans, mâle et femelle, du Muséum de Paris, venus de Hollande en France en l'an VI* (Paris: l'auteur, 1803).

154. Mauritshuis, The Hague.

155. 1729. Amsterdam.

156. 1770. Philadelphia Museum of Art and a private collection, Philadelphia.

157. Most probably, these drawings were part of a book or album mentioned in Rembrandt's 1656 inventory. Peter Schatborn, "Bessten nae't level," *De Kroniek van hat Rembrandthuis* 29 (1977): 3–32.

158. Musée du Louvre, Paris. Exhibition *Rembrandt dessinateur, Chefs-d'œuvre des collections en France*, Paris, Musée du Louvre, 2006–2007, no. 40, by Carel van Tuyll van Serooskerken.

159. Bernard-Germain-Étienne Lacépède, "Quelques idées concernant les établissements appelés Ménageries," in *La Décade Philosophique* (20 Frimaire, Year IV), vol. VII, pp. 449–462, at p. 459.

BIBLIOGRAPHY

Abbe, Mary. "Doug Argue: Big Picture." *Art News,* January 1995, p. 95.

Akrigg, G. P. V. *Shakespeare and the Earl of Southampton.* Cambridge, MA: Harvard University Press, 1978.

Allen, Robert C. *Enclosure and the Yeoman.* Oxford, UK: Clarendon, 1992.

Anon. "La Chasse aux bêtes puantes et féroces." Paris: Imprimerie de la Liberté, 1789.

[Anon.]. *History of the New River.* London? Thames Water [n.d.].

Aristotle. *De Anima.* Translated by Hugh Lawson-Tancred. London: Penguin Books, 1986.

Arkow, Phil, ed. *The Loving Bond: Companion Animals in the Helping Professions.* Saratoga, CA: R&E Publishers, 1987.

Armstrong, James. "Audubon's Ornithological Biography and the Question of 'Other Minds.'" In *Animal Acts: Configuring the Human in Western History,* edited by Jennifer Ham and Matthew Senior, pp. 103–125. New York: Routledge, 1997.

Baltrusaitis, J. *Anamorphoses.* Paris: Flammarion, 1984.

Baratay, Eric, and Elisabeth Hardouin-Fugier. *Zoo: A History of Zoological Gardens in the West.* London: Reaktion, 2002.

Baratay, Eric, and Elisabeth Hardouin-Fugier. *Zoos: Histoire des jardins zoologiques en occident, XVIe–XXe siècle.* Paris: La Découverte, 1998.

Barbier, Edmond Jean-François. *Chronique de la Régence et du règne de Louis XV, ou journal de Barbier.* Paris: Charpentier, 1858.

Barker, Emma. *Greuze and the Painting of Sentiment.* Cambridge, UK: Cambridge University Press, 2005.

Barnes, Jonathan, ed. *The Complete Works of Aristotle: The Revised Oxford Translation, Volume One.* Princeton, NJ: Princeton University Press, 1984.

Barrett, Robert. *The Perfect and Experienced Farrier.* 1660.

Bastard, Thomas. *Chrestoleros.* London, 1598.

Beck, Alan, and Aaron Katcher, eds. *Between Pets and People: The Importance of Animal Companionship.* New York: G. P. Putnam's Sons, 1983.

Berger, Robert. *In the Garden of the Sun King: Studies on the Park of Versailles under Louis XIV.* Washington, DC: Dumbarton Oaks Research Library and Collection, 1985.

Berger, Robert. "Tourists during the Reign of the Sun King: Access to the Louvre and Versailles and the Anatomy of Guidebooks and Other Printed Aids." In *Paris, Center of Artistic Enlightenment*. University Park: Pennsylvania State University Press, 1988.

Bergman, Charles. *Orion's Legacy: A Cultural History of Man as Hunter*. New York: Dutton, 1996.

Bernardin de Saint Pierre, Jacques-Henri. "Mémoire sur la nécessité de joindre une ménagerie au Jardin des plantes de Paris." In *Oeuvres de Jacques-Henri Bernardin de Saint Pierre*, edited by L. Aimé-Martin. 12 vols. Paris: Armand-Aubrée, 1834.

Bernardin de Saint Pierre, Jacques-Henri. *Oeuvres Complètes*. 12 vols. Paris: Méquignon-Marvis, 1818.

Bewick, Thomas. *General History of Quadrupeds*. 1790. Reprint, 1804.

Billeter, Erika. *Hunde und ihre Maler zwischen Tizians Aristokraten und Picassos Gauklern*. Bern: Benteli, 2005.

Binet, Etienne. *Essay des Merveilles de Nature et des plus nobles artifices*. Rouen: Osmont, 1621.

Boehrer, Bruce. *Shakespeare among the Animals: Nature and Society in the Drama of Early Modern England*. New York: Palgave, 2002.

Boyle, Robert. *General Heads for the Natural History of a Country, Great or Small; Drawn out for the Use of Travellers and Navigators*. London: John Taylor and S. Helford, 1692.

Boyle, Robert. "New Pneumatical Experiments about Respiration." *Philosophical Transactions* 5 (1670): 2044.

Boyle, Robert. *Some Considerations Touching the Usefulness* of *Experimental Natural Philosophy*. 2nd ed. Oxford, UK: R. Davis, 1671.

Boyle, Robert. *Works*. Edited by T. Birch. London, 1772.

Bradbrook, M. C. *John Webster: Citizen and Dramatist*. London: Weidenfeld and Nicolson, 1980.

Brandt, Keri. "A Language of Their Own: An Interactivist Approach to Human-Horse Communication." *Society and Animals* 12, no. 4 (2004): 299–316.

Bremmer, Jan. *The Early Greek Concept of the Soul*. Princeton, NJ: Princeton University Press, 1983.

Briscoe, A. Daly. *A Tudor Worthy: Thomas Seckford of Woodbridge*. Ipswich, UK: East Anglian Magazine, 1979.

Buffon, Georges-Louis Leclerq, comte de. *Histoire naturelle générale et particulière: avec la description du Cabinet du Roi*. 31 vols. Paris: Imprimerie Royale, 1749–1789.

Busson, Henri, and Ferdinand Gohin. *Jean de La Fontaine, Discours à Mme de la Sablière*. Geneva: Droz, 1967.

Byron, Lord. "Inscription on the Monument of a Newfoundland Dog." *The Poetical Works of Lord Byron*, vol. 1, pp. 221–222. Boston: James R. Osgood and Co., 1874.

Cahill, Patricia. "Killing by Computation: Military Mathematics, the Elizabethan Social Body, and Marlowe's *Tamburlaine*." In *Arts of Calculation: Numerical Thought in Early Modern Europe*, edited by David Glimp and Michelle R. Warren, pp. 165–186. New York: Palgrave, 2004.

Cantor, Leonard. *The Changing English Countryside, 1400–1700*. New York: Routledge, 1987.

Chebili, Saïd. *Figures de l'animalité dans l'oeuvre de Michel Foucault*. Paris: L'Harmattan, 1999.

Chene, Dennis Des. *Spirits and Clocks: Machine and Organism in Descartes*. Ithaca, NY: Cornell University Press, 2001.

Cheselden, William. *The Anatomy of the Humane Body*. London: N. Cliff and D. Jackson, 1713.

La Chine d'Athanase Kirchere de la Compagnie de Jesus ... Traduit par F. S. Dalquié. Amsterdam: J. Jansson et les héritiers de E. Weyerstraet, 1670.

Clarke, Tim H. *The Rhinoceros from Dürer to Stubbs 1515–1799*. London and New York: Sotheby's, 1986.

Cohen, Sarah R. "Chardin's Fur: Painting, Materialism, and the Question of the Animal Soul." *Eighteenth-Century Studies* 38, no. 1 (2004): 39–61.

Cole, F. J. *A History of Comparative Anatomy*. 1949. Reprint, New York: Dover, 1975.

Condillac, Etienne Bonnot de. *Traité des animaux*. Paris: Vrin, 1987.

Cooke, George. *The Compleat English Farmer*. 1771.

Cormack, Malcolm. "Stubbs and Science." In *Fearful Symmetry, George Stubbs, Painter of the English Enlightenment*, pp. 37–84. New York: Hall and Knight, 2000.

The Correspondence of Marcello Malpighi. 5 vols. Edited and translated by H. B. Adelmann. 5 vols. Ithaca, NY: Cornell University Press, 1975.

Cottingham, John. "'A Brute to the Brutes?' Descartes' Treatment of Animals." *Philosophy* 53 (1978): 551–559.

Cottingham, John, Robert Stoothoff, and Dugald Murdoch, trans. *The Philosophical Writings of Descartes*. Principles of Philosophy. Cambridge, UK: Cambridge University Press, 1984.

Cowper, William. "The Retired Cat." *The Poetical Works of William Cowper*. Edited by H. S. Mildford, p. 407. Oxford, UK: Oxford University Press, 1926.

Culley, George. *Observations on Livestock*. 1786. Reprint, 1804.

Cummings, Brian. "Pliny's Literate Elephant and the Idea of Animal Language in Renaissance Thought." In *Renaissance Beasts: Of Animals, Humans, and Other Wonderful Creatures*, edited by Erica Fudge, pp. 164–185. Urbana: University of Illinois Press, 2004.

Darnton, Robert. *The Great Cat Massacre*. New York: Basic Books, 1984.

Derrida, Jacques. "The Animal That Therefore I Am." *Critical Inquiry* 28, no. 2 (Winter 2002): 369–418.

Descartes, René. *Discourse on Method*. Translated by F. E. Sutcliffe. Harmondsworth, UK: Penguin, 1968.

Descartes, René. *La Dioptrique, Oeuvres et lettres*. Edited by André Bridoux. Paris: Gallimard, 1953.

Descartes, René. *Le Monde, L'Homme*. Edited by Annie Bitbol-Hespériès. Paris: Seuil, 1996.

Descartes, René. *Oeuvres de Descartes*. 11 vols. Edited by Charles Adam and Paul Tannery. Paris: Leopold Cerf, 1897–1909.

Devises pour les tapisseries du roi. Edited by Marianne Grivel and Marc Fumaroli. Paris: Herscher, 1988.

Douglas, James. *Myographiae Comparatae Specimen, or A Comparative Description of All the Muscles in a Man and in a Quadruped*. London: G. Strachan, 1707.

Du Fouilloux, Jacques. *La venerie de Iacques du Fouilloux, suivi de L'Adolescence de l'auteur*. Paris: Pierre Billaine, 1635.

Du Fouilloux, Jacques. *La Vénerie et L'Adolescence*. Edited by Gunnar Tilander. Series Cynegetica XVI. Stockholm: Almqvist and Wiksell, 1967.

Duverney, J.-G. *Lettre á Monsieur* ***. *Contenant plusieurs nouvelles observations sur l'osteologie*. Paris: Laurent d'Houry, 1689.

Duverney, J.-G. *Oeuvres anatomiques*. 2 vols. Paris: C. A. Jombert, 1761.

Edwards, George. *Gleanings of Natural History*. 3 vols. London, 1758–1764.

Een vorstelijke dierentuin De menagerie van Willem V / Le zoo du prince. La ménagerie du stathouder Guillaume V. Under the direction of B. C. Sliggers and A. A. Wertheim. Amsterdam: Walburg Instituut, 1994.

Egerton, Judy. *George Stubbs 1724–1806*. London: Tate Gallery Publishing, 1984.

Egerton, Judy. *Wright of Derby*. New York: Metropolitan Museum of Art, 1990.

The Encyclopedia of Religion. Edited by Mircea Eliade. New York: Macmillan, 1987.

Encyclopédie. ARTFL Project. www.lib.uchicago.edu/efts/ARTFL/projects/encyc/.

Encyclopédie, ou, Dictionnaire raisonné des sciences, des arts et des métiers. Edited by Diderot and D'Alembert. Paris: Briasson, 1751–1765.

Fabre, Daniel. "Une enfance de roi." *Ethnologie Française* 21 (1991): 392–414.

Farber, Paul Lawrence. *Finding Order in Nature*. Baltimore: Johns Hopkins University Press, 2000.

Farr, A. D. "The First Human Blood Transfusion." *Medical History* 24 (1980): 143–162.

Ferry, Luc, and Claudine Germé. *Des Animaux et des hommes: Anthologie des textes remarquables, écrits sur le sujet, du XVe siècle à nos jours*. Paris: Livre de poche, 1994.

Forshaw, Alec, and Theo Bergstrom. *Smithfield: Past and Present*. London: Robert Hale, 1990.

Foucart Walter, Elisabeth. *Pieter Boel 1622–1674. Peintre de Louis XIV. Le fond des études peintes des Gobelins. Les dossiers du Musée du Louvre*. Paris: Réunion des musées nationaux, 2001.

Foucart Walter, Elisabeth, and Pierre Rosenberg. *The Painted Cat: The Cat in Western Painting from the Fifteenth to the Twentieth Century*. New York: Rizzoli, 1988.

Foucault, Michel. *Histoire de la folie à l'âge classique*. Paris: Gallimard, 1972.

Foucault, Michel. *Les mots et les choses: Une Archéologie des sciences humaines*. Paris: Gallimard, 1966.

Fougerolle, Patricia de, Katherine MacDonald, and Marie-Christine Prestat. *Vies de Chiens*. Exposition Catalog, Hôtel Guénégaud, Paris, 2000–2001, Paris: Alain de Gourcuff, 2000.

Foxe, John. *Actes and Monuments of these latter and perillous dayes* ... London: John Day, 1563.

Fracassati, Carlo. "An Account of Some Experiments of Injecting Liquors into the Veins of Animals." *Philosophical Transactions* 2 (1667): 490.

Freeman, Thomas S. "Providence and Prescription: The Account of Elizabeth in Foxe's 'Book of Martyrs.'" In *The Myth of Elizabeth*, edited by Susan Doran and Thomas S. Freeman. Basingstoke, UK: Palgrave Macmillan, 2003.

French, Roger. *Dissection and Vivisection in the European Renaissance*. Aldershot, UK: Ashgate, 1999.

Friedlaender, Walter. *Caravaggio Studies*. Princeton, NJ: Princeton University Press, 1955.

Fudge, Erica. *Brutal Reasoning: Animals, Rationality, and Humanity in Early Modern England*. Ithaca, NY: Cornell University Press, 2006.

Fudge, Erica. *Perceiving Animals: Humans and Beasts in Early Modern English Culture*. New York: Macmillan, 2000; Urbana: University of Illinois Press, 2002.

Fudge, Erica. "Two Ethics: Killing Animals in the Past and the Present." In *Killing Animals*, Animal Studies Group, pp. 99–119. Urbana: University of Illinois Press, 2006.

Fumaroli, Marc, ed. *La Fontaine: Fables*. Paris: La Pochotéque, 1985.

Gaillard, Aurélia. "Bestiaire réel, bestiaire enchanté: les animaux à Versailles sous Louis XIV." In *L'animal au XVIIe siècle, Actes de la 1ère journée d'études du Centre de recherches sur le XVIIe siècle*, edited by Charles Mazouer, pp. 185–198. Tübingen, Germany: Gunter Narr, 2003.

Garber, Marjorie. "Heavy Petting." In *Human, All Too Human*, edited by Diana Fuss, pp. 11–36. New York: Routledge, 1996.

Girard, René. *Violence and the Sacred*. Translated by Patrick Gregory. Baltimore: Johns Hopkins University Press, 1977.

Goldstein, Claire. "Building the Grand Siècle: The Context of Literary Transformations from Vaux-le-Vicomte to Versailles (1656–1715)." PhD diss., University of Pennsylvania, 2000.

Gontier, Thierry. *De l'homme à l'animal: Montaigne et Descartes ou les paradoxes de la philosophie moderne sur la nature des animaux*. Paris: Vrin, 2000.

Goodridge, John. *Rural Life in Eighteenth-Century English Poetry*. Cambridge, UK: Cambridge University Press, 1995.

Gouhier, Henri. "Ce que le vicaire doit à Descartes." *Annales Jean-Jacques Rousseau*, vol. 35, 1959–1962, pp. 139–157.

Grande, Nathalie. "Une vedette des salons: le caméléon." In *L'animal au XVIIe siècle: Actes de la 1ère journée d'études du Centre de recherches sur le XVIIe siècle européen (1600–1700) (Université Michel de Montaigne-Bordeaux III)*, edited by Charles Mazouer. Tübingen, Germany: Gunter Narr, 2003.

Grant, Teresa. "White Bears in *Mucedorus, The Winter's Tale*, and *Oberon, The Fairy Prince*." *Notes & Queries* 246, n.s., 48, no. 3 (September 2001).

Greenblat, Stephen, ed. *The Norton Anthology of English LIterature*, vol. 1. New York: W.W. Norton, 2005.

Griffith, Eva. "Christopher Beeston, His Property and Properties." In *A Handbook on Early Modern Theatre*, edited by Richard Dutton. Oxford, UK: Oxford University Press, 2007.

Guerber, H. A. *Myths of Northern Lands*. New York: American Book Company, 1895.

Guerrini, Anita. "The Ethics of Animal Experimentation in Seventeenth-Century England." *Journal of the History of Ideas* 50, no. 3 (1989): 391–407.

Guerrini, Anita. *Experimenting with Humans and Animals: From Galen to Animal Rights*. Baltimore: Johns Hopkins University Press, 2003.

Guichet, Jean-Luc. *Rousseau, l'animal et l'homme: L'animalité dans l'horizon anthropologique des Lumières*. Paris: Cerf, 2006.

Guichet, Jean-Luc. *La Traité des animaux de Condillac*. Paris: Ellipsis, 2004. "L'animal dans la peinture de chardin." *Dix-huitième siècle* 36, (2004): 547–555.

Hahn, Daniel. *The Tower Menagerie: The Amazing True Story of the Royal Collection of Wild Beasts*. London: Pocket Books, 2004.

Hall, Thomas Steele, trans. René Descartes, *Treastise on Man*. Cambridge, MA: Harvard University Press, 1972.

von Haller, Albrecht. *A Treatise on the Sensible and Irritable Parts of Animals*. London: J. Nourse, 1755.

Haraway, Donna. *The Companion Species Manifesto: Dogs, People, and Significant Otherness*. Chicago: Prickly Paradigm Press, 2003.

Le Hardy, William, ed. *Middlesex Sessions Records* (New Series), 4 vols. London: Guildhall, 1935–1941.

The HarperCollins Study Bible: New Revised Standard Version. Edited by Wayne Meeks. New York: HarperCollins, 1993.

Harrison, Peter. "Animal Souls, Metempsychosis, and Theodicy in Seventeenth-Century English Thought." *Journal of the History of Philosophy* 31, no. 4 (1993): 519–544.

Harrison, Peter. "Descartes on Animals." *Philosophical Quarterly* 42 (1992): 219–227.

Harrison, Peter. "Reading Vital Signs: Animals and the Experimental Philosophy." In *Renaissance Beasts: Of Animals, Humans, and Other Wonderful Creatures,* edited by Erica Fudge, pp. 186–207. Urbana: University of Illinois Press, 2004.

Harvey, William. *The Anatomical Exercises of William Harvey.* Edited by Geoffrey Keynes. 1928. Reprint, New York: Dover, 1995.

Harvey, William. *Anatomical Lectures.* Edited and translated by Gweneth Whitteridge. Edinburgh: E. and S. Livingstone, 1964.

Harvey, William. *Disputations Touching the Generation of Animals,* Edited and translated by Gweneth Whitteridge. Oxford, UK: Blackwell, 1981.

Heaney, Seamus. *Beowulf: A New Verse Translation.* London: W. W. Norton, 2000.

Heidegger, Martin. *Poetry, Language, Thought.* Edited and translated by Albert Hofstadtler. New York: Harper and Row, 1971.

Heywood, Thomas. *The Dramatic Works of Thomas Heywood now first collected with illustrative notes and a memoir of the author in six volumes.* Edited by Shepherd [?] London: John Pearson, 1874.

Homer. *The Iliad.* Translated by Robert Fagles. New York: Penguin, 1990.

Homer. *The Odyssey.* Translated by E. V. Rieu. New York: Penguin, 1991.

Hoquet, Thierry. *Buffon illustré, les gravures de l'Histoire naturelle (1749–1767).* Paris: Publications scientifiques du Muséum national d'Histoire naturelle, 2007.

Houel, Jean. *Histoire naturelle des deux éléphans, mâle et femelle, du Muséum de Paris, venus de Hollande en France en l'an VI.* Paris: l'auteur, 1803.

The Husbandman's Magazine. London, 1718.

Jeaffreson, John Cordy, ed. *Middlesex County Records* (Old Series), 4 vols. London: Middlesex County Records Society, 1886–1892. Reprint, London: Greater London Council, 1972.

Jones, Philip E. *The Butchers of London: A History of the Worshipful Company of Butchers of the City of London.* London: Secker and Warburg, 1976.

Jonson, Ben. *Bartholomew Fair.* Edited by G. R. Hibbard. London: Ernest Benn, 1977.

Jonson, Ben. *Ben Jonson.* 11 vols. Edited by C. H. Herford, Percy Simpson, and Evelyn Simpson. Oxford, UK: Clarendon, 1925–1963.

Junius [pseudonym]. "The Air-Pump." *Gentleman's Magazine* 10 (April 1740): 194.

Kant, Immanuel. "What Is Enlightenment." *Basic Writings of Kant.* Edited by Allen W. Wood, pp. 135–141. New York: Modern Library, 2001.

Keene, Derek. "Metropolitan Values: Migration, Mobility and Cultural Norms, London 1100–1700." In *The Development of Standard English, 1300–1800,* edited by L. Wright. Cambridge, UK: Cambridge University Press, 2000.

Kete, Kathleen. *The Beast in the Boudoir: Petkeeping in Nineteenth-Century Paris.* Berkeley: University of California Press, 1994.

Lacépède, Bernard Germain-Étienne. "Quelques idées concernant les établissements appelés Ménageries." In *La Décade Philosophique* (20 Frimaire, Year IV), vol. VII, pp. 449–462.

Landry, Donna. "The Bloody-Shouldered Arabian and Early Modern English Culture." *Criticism* 46, no. 1 (2004): 41–69.

Landry, Donna. *The Invention of the Countryside: Hunting, Walking, and Ecology in English Literature 1671–1831*. New York: Palgrave, 2001.

Locke, John. *An Essay Concerning Human Understanding*. Amherst, NY: Prometheus, 1995.

Loisel, Gustave. *Histoire de la Ménagerie de l'antiquité à nos jours*. 3 vols. Paris: Doin et fils, 1912.

Lower, Richard. "The Method Observed in Transfusing the Blood out of One Animal into Another." *Philosophical Transactions* 2 (1666): 353–358.

Lubin, Laurence. "Philip Reinagle's 'Extraordinary Musical Dog.'" *Music in Art International, Journal for Music Iconography* 22 (1998): 157–173.

Lukács, Georg. "Reification." In *Dictionary of Marxist Thought*, edited by Tom Bottomore, pp. 463–465. London: Blackwell, 1983.

Lukács, Georg. "Reification and the Consciousness of the Proletariat." In *History and Class Consciousness*, pp. 87–111. New York: Merlin, 1967.

Mabille, Gérard. "La Ménagerie de Versailles." *Gazette des Beaux-Arts* 116 (1974): 5–36.

MacDonogh, Katherine. *Reigning Cats and Dogs: A History of Pets at Court since the Renaissance*. New York: St. Martin's Press, 1999.

Marie, Alfred, and Jeanne Marie. *Versailles au temps de Louis XIV*. Paris: Imprimerie Nationale, 1976.

Markham, Gervase. *Markham's Faithful Farrier*, 1631.

Marret, Bernard. *Les Singeries dans la peinture. Portraits de l'artiste en singe*. Paris: Somogy, 2001.

Marvin, Garry. "Wild Killing." In *Killing Animals*, Animal Studies Group, p. 25. Urbana: University of Illinois Press, 2006.

Marx, Karl. *Capital, Volume 1*. Translated by Ben Fowkes. New York: Penguin, 1990.

Mascall, Leonard. *The Government of Cattel*, 1662.

Masumi, Iriye. "Le Vau's Ménagerie and the Rise of the Animalier: Enclosing, Dissecting, and Representing the Animal in Early Modern France." PhD diss., University of Michigan, 1994.

Mémoires de l'Académie royale des sciences depuis 1666. Paris: La Compagnie des Libraires, 1734.

Merchant, Carolyn. *The Death of Nature: Women, Ecology and the Scientific Revolution*. San Francisco: HarperCollins, 1983. Reprint, 1989.

Mills, John. *A Treatise on Cattle*, 1795.

Mitchell, W. J. T. "Illusion: Looking at Animals Looking." In *Picture Theory: Essays on Verbal and Visual Representation*, pp. 329–344. Chicago: University of Chicago Press, 1994.

Molière, Jean-Baptiste Poquelin de. *Oeuvres complètes de Molière*. Vol. 2. Edited by Robert Jouanny. Paris: Garnier Frères, 1962.

Monro, primus, Alexander. "The History of Anatomy." 1739. MS 166, Medical Library, University of Otago, Dunedin, New Zealand, ff. I–IV.

Montagu, Jennifer. *The Expression of the Passions: The Origin and Influence of Charles Le Brun's Conference sur l'expression générale et particulière*. New Haven and London: Yale University Press, 1994.

Montaigne, Michel de. *Essais*. Paris: GF Flammarion, 1972.

Mukerji, Chandra. *Territorial Ambitions and the Gardens of Versailles*. Cambridge, UK: Cambridge University Press, 1997.

Les Nopces de Pelée et de Thetis, Comedie Italienne en Musique, entre-meslée d'un Ballet sur le mesme sujet, dansé par sa Majesté. Paris: Robert Ballard, 1654.

Opperman, Hal. *J. B. Oudry.* Paris: Réunion des musées nationaux, 1982.

Opperman, Hal. *J.-B. Oudry 1686–1755,* pp. 183–184. Fort Worth, TX: Kimbell Art Museum, 1983.

Orléans, Charlotte-Elisabeth, duchess of. *Letters from Liselotte.* Translated and edited by Maria Kroll. London: Victor Gollancz, 1970.

Orléans, Charlotte-Elisabeth, duchesse d'. *Fragments of Original Letters, of Madame Charlotte Elizabeth of Bavaria, Duchess of Orleans; Written from the Year 1715 to 1720, to His Serene Highness Anthony Ulric, Duke of B- W-; and to Her Royal Highness Carolina, Princess of Wales. Translated from the French. In two volumes.* London, 1790.

Overton, Mark. *Agricultural Revolution in England: The Transformation of the Agrarian Economy, 1500–1850.* Cambridge, UK: Cambridge University Press, 1996.

Palmer, Clare. "Madness and Animality in Michel Foucault's *Madness and Civilization.*" In *Animal Philosophy: Ethics and Identity,* edited by Peter Atterton and Matthew Calarco, pp. 72–84. New York: Continuum, 2004.

Palmeri, Frank, ed. *Humans and Other Animals in Eighteenth-Century British Culture: Representation, Hybridity, Ethics.* Burlington, VT: Ashgate, 2006.

Paster, Gail Kern. "Melancholy Cats, Lugged Bears, and Early Modern Cosmology: Reading Shakespeare's Psychological Materialism across the Species Barrier." In *Reading the Early Modern Passions: Essays in the Cultural History of Emotion,* edited by Gail Kern Paster, Katherine Rowe, and Mary Floyd-Wilson, pp. 113–129. Philadelphia: University of Pennsylvania Press, 2004.

Patterson, Charles. *Eternal Treblinka: Our Treatment of Animals and the Holocaust.* New York: Lantern Books, 2002.

Paulson, Ronald. *Popular and Polite Art in the Age of Hogarth and Fielding.* Notre Dame, IN: University of Notre Dame Press, 1979.

Perkins, David. "Cowper's Hares." *Eighteenth-Century Life* 20, no. 2 (1996): 57–69.

Perrault, Charles. *Contes.* Paris: GF Flammarion, 1991.

Perrault, Claude. *Description anatomique d'un caméléon, d'un casoar, d'un dromadaire, d'un ours et d'une gazelle.* Paris: F. Léonard, 1669.

Perrault, Charles. "Little Red Riding Hood." *The Classic Fairy Tales.* Edited by Maria Tatar. New York: Norton, 1999.

Perrault, Claude, comp. *Mémoires pour servir à l'histoire naturelle des animaux.* 2 vols. Paris: Imprimerie Royale, 1671–1676.

Peumery, Jean-Jacques. *Les origines de la transfusion sanguine.* Amsterdam: Israel, 1975.

Picon, Antoine. "Vers une histoire naturelle des animaux." *Claude Perrault, 1613–1688 ou la curiosité d'un classique,* pp. 53–74. Paris: Picard, 1988.

Pinault Sørensen, Madeleine, ed. *De la physionomie humaine et animale: dessins de Charles Le Brun gravés pour la Chalcographie du musée Napoléon en 1806.* Paris: Réunion des musées nationaux, 2000.

Pinault Sørensen, Madeleine, ed. "La Physiognomonie." *Musée du Louvre, Département des Arts graphiques, Inventaire général des dessins, École française, Charles Le Brun (1619–1690).* 2 vols. Paris: Réunion des musées nationaux, 2000, vol. 2, pp. 571–650.

Pinault Sørensen, Madeleine. "Les animaux du roi: De Pieter Böel aux dessinateurs de l'Académie royale des Sciences." In *L'animal au XVIIe siècle, Actes de la 1ère journée d'études du Centre de recherches sur le XVIIe siècle*, edited by Charles Mazouer, pp. 159–183. Tübingen, Germany: Gunter Narr, 2003.

Pinault Sørensen, Madeleine. *The Painter as Naturalist: From Dürer to Redouté*. Paris: Flammarion, 1991.

Pinault Sørensen, Madeleine. *Sur le vif: Dessins d'animaux de Pieter Boel (1622–1674)*. Paris: Réunion des musées nationaux, 2001.

Pinks, William J. *The History of Clerkenwell*. 2nd ed. Edited by Edward J. Wood. London: Charles Herbert, 1881.

Plato. *Timaeus and Crito*. Translated by Desmond Lee. London: Penguin, 1977.

Pluvinel, Antoine de. *L'Instruction du Roy en l'exercice de monter à cheval*. Amsterdam: Jean Schipper, 1666.

Podbersceek, Anthony L., Elizabeth S. Paul, and James A. Serpell, eds. *Companion Animals and Us: Exploring the Relationships between People and Pets*. Cambridge, UK: Cambridge University Press, 2000.

Pomian, Krzysztof. "Vision and Cognition." In *Picturing Science, Producing Art*, edited by Caroline Jones and Peter Galison, pp. 211–231. New York: Routledge, 1998.

Pope, Alexander. "Bounce to Fop." *The Poems of Alexander Pope*. Edited by John Butt, pp. 823–826. London: Methuen, 1965.

Pope, Alexander. *Rape of the Lock. The Poems of Alexander Pope*. Edited by John Butt, pp. 281–42. London: Methuen, 1965.

Porta, Giovanni Battista della. *De humana physiognomia*. Frankfurt: Iacobi Fischeri, 1618.

Posner, David. "An Aspect of Watteau: 'Peintre de la réalité.'" In *Études d'art français offertes à Charles Sterling*, edited by Albert Châtelet and Nicole Reynau, pp. 279–286. Paris: Presses Universitaires de France, 1975.

Prockter, Adrian, and Robert Taylor. *The A to Z of Elizabethan London*. Lympne Castle, Kent, UK: Harry Margary in association with the Guildhall Library, 1979.

Raber, Karen L. "'Reasonable Creatures': William Cavendish and the Art of Dressage." In *Renaissance Culture and the Everyday*, edited by Patricia Fumerton and Simon Hunt, pp. 42–66. Philadelphia: University of Pennsylvania Press, 1999.

Raber, Karen, and Treva J. Tucker, eds. *The Culture of the Horse: Status, Discipline, and Identity in the Early Modern World*. New York: Palgrave, 2005.

Ravelhofer, Barbara. "'Beasts of Recreacion': Henslowe's White Bears." *English Literary Renaissance* 32, no. 2 (Spring 2002): 287–323.

Recueil de planches, sur les sciences, les arts libéraux, et les arts méchaniques: avec leur explication. Paris: Briasson, 1762–1772.

Reis, Timothy. "Calculating Humans: Mathematics, War, and the Colonial Calculus." In *Arts of Calculation: Numerical Thought in Early Modern Europe*, edited by David Glimp and Michelle R. Warren, pp. 137–164. New York: Palgrave, 2004.

Remigereau, François. *Jacques du Fouilloux et son traité de "La vénerie'; étude biographique et bibliographique*. Paris: Les Belles Lettres, 1952.

Reynolds, George F. "*Mucedorus*, Most Popular Elizabethan Play?." In *Studies in the English Renaissance Drama*, edited by Josephine W. Bennett, Oscar Cargill, and Vernon Hall Jr. London: Peter Owen and Vision Press, 1959.

Richardson, John. *The Annals of London*. London: Cassell and Co., 2000.

Riskin, Jessica. "The Defecating Duck, or The Ambiguous Origins of Artificial Life." *Critical Inquiry* 29 (Summer 2003): 599–633.

Ritvo, Harriet. *The Animal Estate: The English and Other Creatures in the Victorian Age*. Cambridge, MA: Harvard University Press, 1987.

Robbins, Louise. *Elephant Slaves and Pampered Parrots: Exotic Animals in Eighteenth-Century France.* Baltimore: Johns Hopkins University Press, 2002.

Rohde, Erwin. *Psyche: The Cult of Souls and the Belief in Immortality among the Greeks.* London: Routledge and Keagan Paul, 1950.

Rosenberg, Pierre, and Jacques Thuillier. *Laurent de La Hyre 1606–1656, L'Homme et l'oeuvre.* Geneva and Grenoble: Skira, 1988.

Rosenblum, Robert. *The Dog in Art from Rococco to Post-Modernism.* New York: Abrams, 1988.

Rosenblum, Robert. "'L'emprunt ne saurait guère être traité de plagiat': Reynolds et le contexte international." Exhibition *Sir Joshua Reynolds 1723–1792.* 1985, Galeries nationales du Grand Palais, Paris; 1985–1986, Royal Academy of Arts, London, Paris: Editions de la Réunion des musées nationaux, 1985.

Rosenfield, Leonora Cohen. *From Beast-Machine to Man-Machine: The Theme of Animal Soul in French Letters from Descartes to La Mettrie.* New York: Oxford University Press, 1940. Reprint, New York: Octagon, 1968.

Rousseau, Jean-Jacques. *A Discourse on Inequality.* Translated by Maurice Cranston. New York: Penguin Books, 1984.

Rousseau, Jean-Jacques. *Émile.* Translated by Barbara Foxley. London: Everyman's Library, 1963.

Rousseau, Jean-Jacques. *La Nouvelle Héloise.* Translated by Judith H. McDowell. University Park: Pennsylvania State University Press, 1968.

Rousseau, Jean-Jacques. *Lettres morales. Œuvres complètes.* Vol. IV. Paris: Gallimard, 1964.

Rousseau, Jean-Jacques. *Oeuvres complètes.* Paris: Gallimard, 1959.

Rowse, A. L. *Shakespeare's Southampton, Patron of Virginia.* New York: Harper and Row, 1965.

Rudden, Bernard. *The New River: A Legal History.* Oxford, UK: Clarendon, 1985.

Ruysch, Frederik. *Dilucidatio valvularum in vasis lymphaticis et lacteis,* 1665. Edited by A. M. Luyendijk-Elshout. Nieuwkoop, the Netherlands: B. de Graaf, 1964.

Salkeld, Duncan. "Literary Traces in Bridewell and Bethlem, 1602–1624," *Review of English Studies,* n.s., 56, no. 225 (June 2005): 379–385.

Salvadori, Philippe. *La chasse sous l'Ancien Régime.* Paris: Fayard, 1996.

Saule, Béatrix. *Versailles triomphant: une journée de Louis XIV.* Paris: Flammarion, 1996.

Schaffer, Simon. "Natural Philosophy and Public Spectacle." *History of Science* 21 (1983): 1–46.

Schatborn, Peter. "Bessten nae't level." *De Kroniek van hat Rembrandthuis* 29 (1977): 3–32.

Schupbach, William. "A Select Iconography of Animal Experiment." In *Vivisection in Historical Perspective,* edited by Nicolas Rupke. New York: Routledge, 1989.

Scudéry, Madeleine de. *Nouvelles conversations de morale.* Paris: Veuve de Sébastien Marbe-Cramoisy, 1688.

Senior, Matthew. "The Ménagerie and the Labyrinthe: Animals at Versailles, 1662–1792." In *Renaissance Beasts: Of Animals, Humans, and Other Wonderful Creatures,* edited by Erica Fudge, pp. 208–232. Urbana: University of Illinois Press, 2004.

Senior, Matthew. "Seeing the Versailles Ménagerie." *Papers in French Seventeenth-Century Literature* XXX 59 (2003): 351–363.

Senior, Matthew. "'When the Beasts Spoke': Animal Speech and Classical Reason in Descartes and La Fontaine." In *Animal Acts: Configuring the Human in Western*

History, edited by Jennifer Ham and Matthew Senior, pp. 61–84. New York: Routledge, 1997, pp. 61–84.

Serjeantson, R. W. "The Passions and Animal Language, 1540–1700." *Journal of the History of Ideas* 62, no. 3 (2001): 425–444.

Shakespeare, William. *Cymbeline. The Arden Shakespeare*. Edited by J. M. Nosworthy. London: Methuen, 1955.

Sisson, C. J. "The Red Bull Company and the Importunate Widow." *Shakespeare Survey* 7 (1954): 57–68.

Sloan, Phillip. "Natural History, 1670–1802." In *Companion to the History of Modern Science*, edited by R. C. Olby et al., pp. 295–313. London: Routledge, 1990.

Smith, J. A., and K. M. Boyd, eds. *Lives in the Balance*. Oxford, UK: Oxford University Press, 1991.

Sørensen, Bent. "L'éléphant de Jacques François Joseph Saly." *Gazette des Beaux-Arts* (October 1995): 139–148.

Steggle, Matthew. "'Greene's Baboone': Thomas Greene, Ape Impersonator?". In *Theatre Notebook* 60 (2006): 72–75.

Strong, Roy. *Van Dyck: Charles I on Horseback*. London: Allen Lane for the Penguin Press, 1972.

Stubbs and the Horse. Kimbell Art Museum, Fort Worth, TX, 2004–2005.

Thirsk, Joan, ed. *The Agrarian History of England and Wales,* vol. IV, *1500–1640*. Cambridge, UK: Cambridge University Press, 1967.

Thirsk, Joan, ed. *The Agrarian History of England and Wales,* vol. V, *1640–1750*. Cambridge, UK: Cambridge University Press, 1985.

Thomas, Keith. *Man and the Natural World: Changing Attitudes in England, 1500–1800*. New York: Oxford University Press, 1983.

Tighe, William Joseph. "The Gentlemen Pensioners in Elizabethan Politics and Government." PhD diss., University of Cambridge, 1983.

Tomkis, Thomas. *Albumazar*. London, 1615.

Topsell, Edward. *The Historie of Foure-Footed Beastes*, London, 1607.

Toscan, Georges. *Histoire du lion de la Ménagerie du Muséum national d'Histoire naturelle et de son chien*, pp. 193–199. Paris: Cuchet, 1795.

Trembley, Abraham. *Mémoires pour servir à l'histoire d'un genre de polypes d'eu douce*. Leiden, Holland: J. and H. Verbeek, 1744.

Vessier, Maximilien. *La Pitié-Salpêtrière: quatre siècles d'histoire et d'histoires*. Paris: Hôpital de la Pitié-Salpêtrière, 1999.

Voltaire. *Dictionnaire Philosophique*. Paris: Garnier Flammarion, 1964.

Whitaker, Katie. *Mad Madge: Margaret Cavendish, Duchess of Newcastle, Royalist, Writer and Romantic*. London: Chatto and Windus, 2002.

Wickham, Glynne, Herbert Berry, and William Ingram, eds. *English Professional Theatre, 1530–1660*. Cambridge, UK: Cambridge University Press, 2000.

Williams, Neville. "The Master of the Royal Tents and His Records." In *Prisca Munimenta: Studies in Archival and Administrative History Presented to Dr. A. E. Hollaender*, edited by Felicity Ranger. London: University of London Press, 1973.

Wolloch, Nathaniel. *Subjugated Animals: Animals and Anthropocentrism in Early Modern European Culture*. Amherst, NY: Humanity Books, 2006.

Wright, James. *Historia Histrionica: An Historical Account of the English Stage Shewing the Ancient Use, Improvement and Perfection, of Dramatick Representation in This Nation*. London, 1699.

Wyett, Jodi L. "The Lap of Luxury: Lapdogs, Literature and Social Meaning in the 'Long' Eighteenth Century." *Literature Interpretation Theory* 10 (2001): 275–301.

Yvon, Claude. "L'âme des bêtes." In *L'encyclopédie, ou Dictionnaire raisonné des sciences, des arts et des métiers*. 35 vols. Paris and Neuchâtel, 1751–1780, vol. 1, pp. 343–353.

NOTES ON CONTRIBUTORS

Richard Byrne is lecturer in international history at the University of Liverpool. His area of research is Enlightenment political thought.

Eva Griffith is honorary fellow to the Board of English Studies at the University of Durham. Her publications include work on the Jacobean stage with New Dictionary of National Biography entries on "Susan Baskervile," "Anne Bedingfeild," and "Banks, the exhibitor of Morocco the performing horse." She is currently completing a monograph on the Red Bull playhouse.

Anita Guerrini is professor of history and environmental studies at the University of California, Santa Barbara. Her most recent book is *Experimenting with Humans and Animals: From Galen to Animal Rights* (Johns Hopkins, 2003) and she has published several articles on the uses of animals in early modern natural philosophy.

Jean-Luc Guichet is Directeur de programme at the Collège international de Philosophie, Paris, where he leads a seminar titled "Animality and Anthropology from the Enlightenment to the Present." He is a member of the Centre National de la Recherche Scientifique George Chevrier research group at the Université de Bourgogne. His works include *Rousseau, l'animal et l'homme* (Cerf, 2006); a commentary on the *Traité des animaux de Condillac* (Ellipses, 2004); and *La liberté* et *Le pouvoir* (Quintette, 1988 and 1995).

Madeleine Pinault Sørensen is Chargée d'études in the Département des Arts graphiques at the Musée du Louvre; she is the author of *The Painter as Naturalist: From Dürer to Redouté* (Flammarion, 1991); *La Physiognomonie: Inventaire général des dessins de Charles Le Brun (1619–1690)* (Réunion des musées nationaux, 2000); and *Sur le vif: Dessins d'animaux de Pieter Boel (1622–1674)* (Réunion des musées nationaux and Franco Maria Ricci 2001).

Karen Raber is associate professor of English at the University of Mississippi. She is coeditor, with Treva J. Tucker, of *The Culture of the Horse: Status, Discipline and Identity in the Early Modern World* (Palgrave, 2005) and, with Tom Hallock and Ivo Kamps, of the forthcoming *Early Modern Ecocriticism: From Shakespeare to the Forentine Codex*, as well as author of a monograph and many essays on gender and early modern women writers.

Matthew Senior is associate professor of French at Oberlin College. He is the author of *In the Grip of Minos: Confessional Discourse in Dante, Corneille, and Racine* (Ohio State University Press, 1994) and the coeditor, with Jennifer Ham, of *Animal Acts: Configuring the Human in Western History* (Routledge, 1997). He has published extensively on seventeenth-century French literature, religious history, and philosophy.

Amy Warthesen is completing her Ph.D. in Romance Studies at Cornell University and teaches French at Emory and Henry College. Her dissertation is titled "Architecture of War and Desire: Literature, Political Mythologies, and the Gardens of Versailles."

Janice C. Zinser is Ruberta T. McCandless Professor of French at Oberlin College. She is the author of numerous articles on late medieval French literature, including "The use of exempla in Alain Chartier's Esperance," and entries on Guillaume Alexis, René d'Anjou, Alain Chartier, Le Jardin de Plaisance et Fleur de Rhétorique, Martin Le Franc's Le Champion des dames, Les Quinze Joies de Mariage, Jean Regnier, and Michault (Le Caron) dit Taillevent (*Medieval France: An Encyclopedia*, Garland 1995). Her research centers on debate and dialogue genres of the medieval period, particularly among the works of Alain Chartier.

INDEX